ILLUSTRATED DICTIONARY

OF

MICROELECTRONICS

AND

MICROCOMPUTERS

Other Pergamon titles of interest

DEBENHAM   Microprocessors: Principles & Applications

DUMMER   Electronic Inventions & Discoveries, 3rd edition

ERA   The Engineering of Microprocessor Systems

GUILE & PATERSON   Electrical Power Systems, Volumes 1 and 2, 2nd edition

HINDMARSH   Worked Examples in Electrical Machines & Drives
                     Electrical Machines & their Applications, 4th edition

HOLLAND   Microcomputers for Process Control
                     Microcomputers & Their Interfacing

HOWSON   Mathematics for Electrical Circuit Analysis

RODDY   Introduction to Microelectronics, 2nd edition

YORKE   Electric Circuit Theory

Pergamon related Journals
(*Free specimen copy gladly sent on request*)

Computers and Electrical Engineering

Electric Technology USSR

Microelectronics and Reliability

Solid State Electronics

ILLUSTRATED DICTIONARY

OF

MICROELECTRONICS

AND

MICROCOMPUTERS

R. C. HOLLAND B.Sc., M.Sc.

West Glamorgan Institute of Higher Education, Swansea, Wales

PERGAMON PRESS

OXFORD · NEW YORK · TORONTO · SYDNEY · PARIS · FRANKFURT

U.K.	Pergamon Press Ltd., Headington Hill Hall, Oxford OX3 0BW, England
U.S.A.	Pergamon Press Inc., Maxwell House, Fairview Park, Elmsford, New York 10523, U.S.A.
CANADA	Pergamon Press Canada Ltd., Suite 104, 150 Consumers Road, Willowdale, Ontario M2J 1P9, Canada
AUSTRALIA	Pergamon Press (Aust.) Pty. Ltd., P.O. Box 544, Potts Point, N.S.W. 2011, Australia
FRANCE	Pergamon Press SARL, 24 rue des Ecoles, 75240 Paris, Cedex 05, France
FEDERAL REPUBLIC OF GERMANY	Pergamon Press GmbH, Hammerweg 6, D-6242 Kronberg-Taunus, Federal Republic of Germany

First edition 1985

Library of Congress Cataloging in Publication Data

Holland, R. C.
Illustrated dictionary of microelectronics and microcomputers.
1. Microelectronics — Dictionaries. 2. Microcomputers — Dictionaries.
I. Title.
TK7804.H56   1985   621.381'7'0321   84-10994

British Library Cataloguing in Publication Data

Holland, R. C.
  Illustrated dictionary of microelectronics
  and microcomputers.
  1. Microelectronics — Dictionaries
  I. Title
  621.381'71'0321   TK 7874

ISBN 0–08–031634–4 (Hardcover)
ISBN 0–08–031635–2 (Flexicover)

Printed in Great Britain by A. Wheaton & Co. Ltd., Exeter

Preface

Throughout the 1970s and 1980s the expanding technology of microelectronics has brought with it a new vocabulary. The introduction of new electronic devices and systems, particularly the microcomputer, has been so rapid that a large number of new names, definitions and expressions have evolved into common use by workers in the field. This book is an attempt to present a coherent explanation of this new technology. Terms are presented alphabetically, with cross-referencing where necessary, and illustrations are included when a diagrammatic approach assists the definition. In this way the book is more than simply a glossary of terms — it presents detailed explanations of this new technology.

The book should prove to be a useful source of definitions and descriptions to enable a reader with a rudimentary knowledge of electronic or computer principles to understand this new vocabulary. All recent circuits, systems and applications are described. Although primarily aimed at the electronics engineer and student, the book should act as a useful reference guide for the computer hobbyist, computer science student and even the business computer user.

The author wishes to thank his family and colleagues for their support during the preparation of this book.

A

Abort Discontinue operation of the program which is currently being executed within the *computer*. Control is returned to the master program (*operating system* or *monitor*).

Absolute addressing This is an *addressing mode* which is used with *jump instructions*, i.e. *program* instructions which transfer control to a different part of the program. The absolute *memory* address is specified as follows:

JMP 1000H   ;Jump to the memory
             address hexadecimal 1000

or

JZ 0400H   ;Jump, if zero, to memory
            address hexadecimal 0400

The full address is included in the instruction, e.g.

First word | JMP |
Second word | 1000 |

This addressing mode must be distinguished from the alternative mode which can be used with jump instructions — *relative addressing*. This specifies the relative position, compared with the jump instruction, of the instruction to which program control is to be transferred.

Access time The time interval between a *memory* device (*semiconductor memory* or *backing store*) receiving the address of an item of information and presenting that item in a usable form.

Accumulator A specialised *register* within a *microprocessor* which receives the result of *ALU* operations. Microprocessors possess one or more accumulators which can be used when arithmet-

ical, logical and *shift* operations are required in an *instruction*.

Accuracy A measure of the validity of a measurement. The accuracy of *binary* numbers should not be confused with the resolution of such numbers. For example, a 10-*bit* binary representation of a plant measurement offers more resolution (1 in 1024) than an 8-bit representation (1 in 256), but less accuracy if it is incorrectly generated or processed.

Acoustic coupler A device that allows a *computer* to connect through the telephone network to a remote *peripheral* or another computer. The telephone handset is placed in the acoustic coupler, which is connected to the computer. The coupler contains a *modem*, which converts the *digital* signals into audio acoustic signals.

Acquire See *Capture*.

A/D See *Analogue to digital converter*.

ADC See *Analogue to digital converter*.

Add To generate the sum of two or more numbers. The addition of two single-*bit* numbers is described as follows:

Augend	Addend	Carry	Sum
0 +	0	0	0
0 +	1	0	1
1 +	0	0	1
1 +	1	1	0

Truth table

The addition of two multi-bit numbers is demonstrated as follows:

Carry	00001110	
Augend	00101110	46 +
Addend	10001011	139
Sum	10111001	185

Decimal equivalent

If the final carry bit of this 8-bit addition process is 1, then the 8-bit sum is not the complete answer — a ninth bit, which represents arithmetic overflow, is required. For this reason, when single *byte* addition is carried out in an 8-bit *microprocessor* the ninth bit is held in the *carry bit*, which forms part of the *status register*. A *program* that performs addition should therefore check this bit if an overflow condition can be predicted.

In addition to a straightforward byte addition instruction, most 8-bit microprocessors offer an *instruction* which adds bytes and also adds the value of the carry from a previous operation, i.e. adds with carry.

Care must be taken when adding *two's complement* numbers, i.e. numbers in which the left-hand bit is reserved as a sign bit. For example:

$$\begin{array}{r} 1010\ 1101 \\ 1011\ 1000 \\ \hline 1\ 0110\ 0101 \\ \uparrow \end{array} + \qquad \begin{array}{r} -83 \\ -72 \\ \hline +101 \end{array} +$$

Carry ignored

A positive answer (+101) is erroneously achieved unless the carry bit is checked.

See *Arithmetic and logic unit*.

Adder A circuit that performs 1-*bit* addition, as shown in Fig. 1.

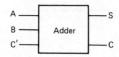

FIG. 1. 1-bit adder.

The C′ signal represents the carry from a previous circuit. The adder circuit is in fact constructed using two *half-adders*, and is sometimes referred to as a *full-adder*. The *truth table* for the circuit is shown under *Add*.

A multi-bit adder is available in *integrated circuit* form, e.g. the SN7483, which is shown in Fig. 2.

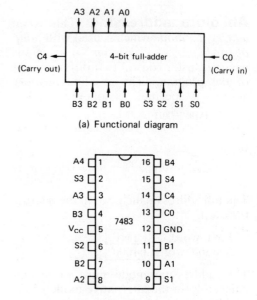

(a) Functional diagram

(b) IC pin layout

FIG. 2. The SN7483 4-bit full-adder.

The *arithmetic and logic unit* within a *microprocessor* contains an adder circuit.

Address A number that indicates a specific location in *memory* (*semiconductor* or *backing store*) or *input/output*. Normally addresses are 16 *bits* and therefore have a range of 0 to 64K.

Address bus A set of *parallel* connections (normally 16) which are generated by the *CPU* (or *microprocessor*) and pass to *memory* and *input/output* circuits.

Each memory and input/output device connects to as many of the address bus lines as are necessary to select every address on that device. For example, the circuit of Fig. 3 shows the address bus connections to a memory *IC* (1K locations) and to an input/output *IC* (4 locations or addresses).

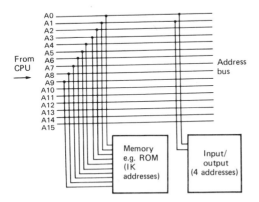

(*Data bus* connections are not shown)

FIG. 3. Address bus connections to memory and input/output.

The 1K (1024) memory IC requires 10 address lines ($2^{10} = 1024$ combinations) in order to select each location. The input/output IC requires 2 address lines to select each of its 4 addresses.

Address decoding
The technique of selecting a specific *memory* location or *input/output* device. Decoding circuits in *microcomputers* use the *address bus* to select a specific memory or input/output device; the device itself then performs any further address decoding, e.g. to select a specific memory location.

The principal element in an address decoding circuit is a *decoder*, which normally performs 2 to 4 or 3 to 8 decoding. The circuit shown in Fig. 4 demonstrates address decoding to select one of two *ROMs*.

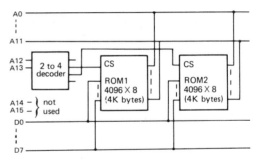

FIG. 4. Address decoding circuit (for 2 memory chips).

Address lines A0 to A11 are required to select each of the 4K addresses on each *chip*, i.e. the chips perform internal address decoding to select the required *byte*. The higher-order address lines A12 and A13 are connected to a 2 to 4 decoder, which generates four *chip select* signals. Each of these signals can be used to select one discrete ROM chip; only two such memory devices are shown connected here. Thus the decoded start address which selects the first byte in ROM1 is:

A15 A14	A13 A12	A11 A10 A9 A8
Not used	0 1	0 0 0 0

2 to 4
decoder

A7 A6 A5 A4 A3 A2 A1 A0
0   0   0   0   0   0   0   0

This is *hexadecimal* 1000.

Refer to *decoder* to confirm the operation of a 2 to 4 decoder as summarised in its *truth table*.

The decoded start address of ROM2 is:

A15 A14	A13 A12	A11 A10 A9 A8
Not used	1 0	0 0 0 0

2 to 4
decoder

A7 A6 A5 A4 A3 A2 A1 A0
0   0   0   0   0   0   0   0

This is hexadecimal 2000.

The same address decoding techniques are used to select input/output chips.

Address format
The arrangement of the parts of an *address* for a *floppy* or *hard disk*, e.g. drive number, *track* and *sector*.

Addressing modes
Different methods of specifying the location of a *data* item which is to be accessed in an *instruction*. For example, a data item may be held:

(a)   in a *register*;
(b)   in a *memory* location;
(c)   in the second *word*/words of the instruction; etc.

See *Direct addressing, Absolute addressing, Immediate addressing, Indexed addressing, Relative addressing, Paged addressing* and *Autodecrement/ autoincrement*.

Algorithm
A set of procedures which are required to achieve a desired result. The term is applied to programming, and it is the name given to a description of the steps which a *program* must perform, e.g.

(a)   Read a set of switches.
(b)   Display a number if any switch is pressed.
(c)   Sound an alarm if a particular switch is pressed.
(d)   Call a program which reads and processes an instrumentation signal.

Allophone
A sound that is generated by a *speech synthesiser* system. Words can be constructed using several allophones. The alternative method of speech synthesiser generates individual complete words. The allophonic technique enables a wider range of words to be generated,

but quality of word reproduction is often poor.

Alphanumeric
The normal range of numbers (0 to 9) and letters (A to Z). An alphanumeric code sometimes includes additional special control codes. An example of the use of alphanumeric characters is in the use of an alphanumeric display, which may display *characters* in the form of a *dot matrix* or a *segment display* pattern.

ALU
See *Arithmetic and logic unit.*

Analogue
A signal which is continuous, i.e. it can take any value over its range. For instance, an analogue voltage may take any value over a range of 0 to 10 V, and may represent a plant measurement, e.g. temperature. An analogue signal cannot be handled by a *computer*, and it must be converted to a *digital* form before processing can occur.

Analogue to digital converter
Converts an *analogue* voltage into a *digital* representation for use by a *computer* system. A typical system of connection for an analogue to digital converter (or A/D or ADC) is shown in Fig. 5.

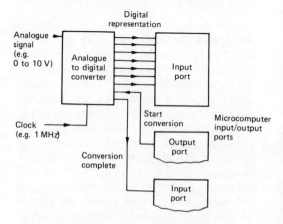

Fig. 5. Connection of A/D to microcomputer.

4

The A/D converter is a single IC (*integrated circuit*). The digital representation may be 8, 10, 12 or (rarely) 14 *bits* — an 8-bit device is shown in the diagram. Typical analogue voltage ranges are 0 to 2.5 V, 0 to 5 V and 0 to 10 V. The conversion process is initiated by the setting of the Start Conversion signal, and it is timed by the fast Clock pulses. The A/D generates a Conversion Complete signal, which should be checked by the *microcomputer*. The microcomputer *program* should only read the digital representation of the analogue signal when conversion is complete.

The Start Conversion and Conversion Complete signals perform a *handshake* function between microcomputer and A/D.

There are two common techniques employed in the A/D conversion process — see *Successive approximation* and *Integrating A/D*.

AND The *logic* AND function operates on two *bits* as shown in Table 1.

A	B	A.B
0	0	0
1	0	0
0	1	0
1	1	1

Table 1. Truth table for AND function.

The function "A and B" is represented by A.B, where the dot (called "period") represents the logic AND operation. Therefore the result of an AND operation is only set to 1 if both source bits are set to 1. The *truth table* is a convenient method of representing every possible bit combination.

The AND function can be performed by *hardware* (electronic circuitry) or *software* (*computer program*). The hardware

AND *gate* can be represented by the circuit symbols shown in Fig. 6.

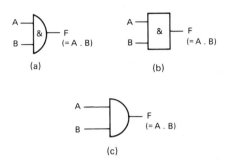

FIG. 6. Circuit symbols for AND gate.

A useful *TTL integrated circuit* which offers three AND gates is the SN7411, which is illustrated in Fig. 7.

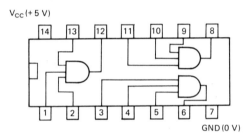

FIG. 7. Triple 3-input AND gate (SN7411).

Notice that these gates have three inputs. Clearly each input must be set to 1 to cause the gate output to be set to 1. Two- and four input gates are also commonly available.

The software version of the AND function operates as follows. The *instruction set* of every *microprocessor* contains an instruction which performs the AND operation. For example, the AND instruction for an 8-bit microprocessor may be:

ANA B;AND the contents of registers
A and B

The effect of this instruction is, for example:

5

A register = 0101 0101
B register = 0000 1111

Result = 0000 0101

Therefore, the instruction sets a 1 in each bit of the 8-bit result only if both corresponding bits in the source data items are 1. This function is of value when it is required to *mask* (i.e. set to zero) certain bits in a data item, e.g. the top 4 bits in the A register in the example above.

ANSI (American National Standards Institute)
An organisation responsible for setting standards, e.g. for *computer* systems.

Application package/software
A *program* or set of programs that performs a particular function, e.g. *stock control* or *payroll*, and which may have to be tailored to satisfy the requirements of a particular user.

Architecture
The name given to the generalised *hardware* configuration of a *microcomputer*.

Argument
The name given to a number which is passed from one part of a *program* to another. For example, a section of *high-level language* program may call a *subroutine* and wish to pass a number to that subroutine. Alternatively it may wish to enter a section of *machine code* program and require to pass a *data* item.

Arithmetic and logic unit
The heart of a *microprocessor* which performs arithmetic, *logic* and other functions. It is commonly called the ALU. Refer to *Microprocessor* to see its overall role within the microprocessor.

The functions which are performed by

the ALU are summarised in Fig. 8 for an 8-*bit* microprocessor.

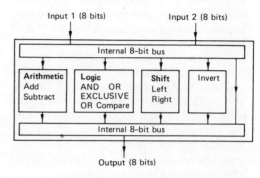

FIG. 8. Internal organisation of the ALU.

There are two input channels, which are normally fed from microprocessor *registers*, and one output channel, which normally feeds the *accumulator*.

Arithmetic operations are normal add and subtract. Multiply and divide are only available in 16-bit microprocessors.

Logic functions are *AND*, *OR* and *EXCLUSIVE OR*. Additionally two numbers can be compared, i.e. checked if they are identical or if one is greater than the other.

Shift left and shift right functions can be performed using one 8-bit input. These operations are useful if it is required to remove bits in a *data* value (e.g. shift a number one place to the left so that the most significant bit is lost), or to multiply or divide numbers by powers of 2 (e.g. shift left one place multiplies the number by 2, shift left one more place multiplies it by 4, etc.).

The invert, or "complement", function changes each bit in a single 8-bit data value. Thus each 0 is changed to a 1, and each 1 is changed to 0.

Additionally a direct path through the ALU exists, i.e. no processing is performed on an input data value or number. Thus an input from one of the microprocessor's registers can be passed directly through the ALU to transfer into another register.

Arithmetic shift A shift that retains the setting of the sign *bit*. Additionally it is a shift operation which effectively multiplies or divides a signed number by powers of 2. For example:

$$+3_{10} = 0000\ 0011$$

$$\uparrow$$

sign bit (0 = positive
1 = negative)

Shifting left 1 place gives $0000\ 0110 = +6_{10}$.

Therefore multiplication by 2 has occurred.

Similarly:

$$-6_{10} = 1111\ 1010$$ (see *Two's complement*
for negative
$$\uparrow$$ number representation)
sign bit

Shifting right 1 place gives:

$$1111\ 1101 = -3_{10}$$

$$\uparrow$$
1 shifted in

Therefore division by 2 has occurred.

Thus arithmetic right shift *instructions* ensure that a 0 (for positive number) and a 1 (for negative number) is shifted into the sign bit.

Notice that errors can occur if the penultimate bit (the bit after the sign bit) is different from the sign bit for a shift left instruction. For example:

$$+64_{10} = 0100\ 0000$$

Shifting left 1 place gives $1000\ 000 = -128_{10}$ not the correct $+128_{10}$.

Therefore the programmer should take great care with this particular instruction.

Array A list of numbers or *variables* which is accessed in a *high-level language program* using a two-dimensional reference (occasionally three-dimensional). For example, if six numbers are stored by the program, and it is required to reference them using two-dimensional co-ordinates as follows:

TOM(1,1)=100   TOM(1,2)=150   TOM(1,3)=360
TOM(2,1)=400   TOM(2,2)=135   TOM(2,3)=270

then any number from this list of 100, 150, 360, 400, 135 and 270 can be accessed and used within the program, e.g.

50 CHARLIE=TOM(2,1)+500

So CHARLIE takes the value 900.

ASCII (American (National) Standard Code for Information Interchange) This is a world-wide standard code for 7-bit coded *characters* (plus 1 bit for *parity* check) which is used for information interchange between *computers* and external *peripherals* (*VDUs*, *printers*), or other computers. The full *alphanumeric* set of numerals, letters, punctuation symbols and special control characters is included, as shown in Table 2.

See *RS 232-C*.

Assembler A program that translates *assembly language* statements (in *mnemonic* form) into *machine code*.

There are two types of assembler:

(a) Full assembler, which waits until the complete program is entered, and then generates the machine code version — comments, which describe program operation, can normally be entered and memorised with this type (see also *Macroassembler* and *Two-pass assembler*).

(b) Line-by-line assembler, which converts each assembly language *instruction* into machine code as each instruction is entered.

Assembly language A programming *language* that is line-for-line convertible to *machine code*, but which uses *mnemonics* (that help to describe *instruction* action) and *labels* (words in place of absolute memory addresses).

7

Character	Hex.
NUL	00
SOH	01
STX	02
ETX	03
EOT	04
ENQ	05
ACK	06
BEL	07
BS	08
HT	09
LF	0A
VT	0B
FF	0C
CR	0D
S0	0E
S1	0F
DLE	10
DC1	11
DC2	12
DC3	13
DC4	14
NAK	15
SYN	16
ETB	17
CAN	18
EM	19
SUB	1A
ESC	1B
FS	1C
GS	1D
RS	1E
US	1F
SP	20
!	21
"	22
#	23
$	24
%	25
&	26
`	27
(	28
)	29
*	2A
+	2B
,	2C
-	2D
.	2E
/	2F

Character	Hex.
0	30
1	31
2	32
3	33
4	34
5	35
6	36
7	37
8	38
9	39
:	3A
;	3B
<	3C
=	3D
>	3E
?	3F
@	40
A	41
B	42
C	43
D	44
E	45
F	46
G	47
H	48
I	49
J	4A
K	4B
L	4C
M	4D
N	4E
O	4F
P	50
Q	51
R	52
S	53
T	54
U	55
V	56
W	57
X	58
Y	59
Z	5A
[	5B
\	5C
]	5D
∧	5E
–	5F

Character	Hex.
	60
a	61
b	62
c	63
d	64
e	65
f	66
g	67
h	68
i	69
j	6A
k	6B
l	6C
m	6D
n	6E
o	6F
p	70
q	71
r	72
s	73
t	74
u	75
v	76
w	77
x	78
y	79
z	7A
{	7B
		7C
}	7D
~	7E
DEL	7F

Note Characters hex. 00 to 1F are control characters. Character hex. 7F is delete, or rub-out.

Table 2. ASCII Code

Therefore the programmer must understand machine operation, but he does not need to generate the *bit* pattern (or *hexadecimal* equivalent) of each instruction. He calls an *assembler* to perform the conversion for him. The assembly language version of the program is often called the "source code", and the generated machine code version is called the "object code".

An example of an assembly language program is:

```
        MVI A,9      ;Move 9 into A register
LOOP:   OUT 40H      ;Output A to port address 40
        DCR A        ;Decrement A
        JNZ LOOP     ;Jump, if A is not zero, to
                      LOOP
```

Notice that MVI, OUT, DCR and JNZ are mnemonics which are chosen to meaningfully represent the instruction required. LOOP is a label, which allows the programmer to write the program without having to worry about the memory location of the OUT instruction when he refers to it in the JNZ instruction. See also *Pseudo-instruction* and *Macro-assembler*.

Assign

To allocate a name to a *variable* in a *program*.

Astable multivibrator

A circuit which generates *pulses*. Strictly it is a multivibrator, or two-state circuit, which has no stable state, i.e. it oscillates from one state to the other continuously. It is used as a pulse generator circuit for applications such as *CPU clock*, *A/D converter clock*, etc.

It can be constructed using two inverting *gates* as in Fig. 9:

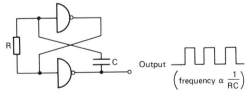

FIG. 9. Astable multivibrator using two inverters.

An alternative circuit which uses a 555 timer chip (effectively two inverting gates connected *back-to-back*) which gives greater control of pulse waveform is shown in Fig. 10.

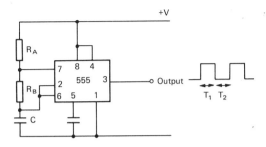

FIG. 10. Astable multivibrator using 555 timer.

$$T_1 = 0.7(R_A + R_B)C$$
$$T_2 = 0.7R_B C$$

Thus the pulse frequency, as well as the *mark/space ratio*, can be selected by suitable choice of R_A, R_B and C.

Asynchronous

A circuit or a system that is not synchronised by a common *clock*.

In a synchronous *counter* circuit, each stage of the counter is triggered at each occurrence of the common clock pulse. In an asynchronous counter circuit, the stages do not share a common clock pulse signal but trigger one after the other.

In *serial* data transmission systems (see *RS 232-C*) an asynchronous link does not use a clock pulse which is common between, and therefore connected between, transmitting and receiving circuitry. In place of this an identifying start pulse is generated by the transmitting circuit before the *character* code, so that the receiving circuit is primed to receive the character.

ATE (Automatic Test Equipment)

Computer based equipment is commonly used to test manufactured electronic components and systems. The advantages of this technique are speed and detail of test procedures, as well as reprogrammable nature of test equipment.

Attribute A property or characteristic assigned to a *data* value in a *program*, e.g. *real* or *integer*, single length or double length number.

Audio cassette A domestic audio cassette recorder can be used to store *programs* and *data* from *microcomputers*. Such recorders are cheap and readily available. See Fig. 11.

Press PLAY and REC to write program
Press PLAY to read program

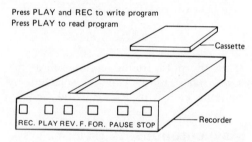

FIG. 11. Audio cassette recorder.

Autodecrement/Autoincrement

A variation of *indirect addressing* in which the *memory* address, which is used to reference a *data* item, is automatically decremented (1 subtracted) or automatically incremented (1 added) when the *instruction* is completed. Few *microprocessors* possess this feature, and the autoincrement is the more common of the two.

For example,

MOV Register 1, Indirect Register 3+

is an instruction *mnemonic* (for demonstration purposes only) which moves the contents of Register 1 to the memory address which is held in Register 3 (indirect addressing), and adds 1 to the contents of Register 3. Therefore, when the instruction is completed Register 3 holds the address of the memory location which follows that used in the instruction.

B

Backing store A *data* storage medium that "backs up" the *main memory* within a *computer*. Normally a backing store is an electromechanical system which provides a large amount of memory (100 *Kbytes* up to several *Mbytes*) but with an *access time* that is far slower than main memory.

See *Floppy disk*, *Hard disk*, *Audio cassette*, *Cartridge disk* and *Bubble memory*.

Backplane A circuit board that supports other boards in an electronic system. Therefore, other boards plug into a backplane, which carries interconnections between boards, in the following manner:

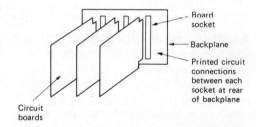

FIG. 12. Backplane supporting circuit boards.

Whilst the boards which plug into the backplane support components, the backplane itself normally supports only interconnections. Invariably these interconnections are *printed circuit*, but they could be wire connections. If the backplane supports circuitry, it is commonly referred to as the *motherboard*.

Back-to-back A circuit in which the output is connected to the input. An example of a back-to-back connection is shown in Fig. 13 and applies to a *microcomputer serial input/output* channel.

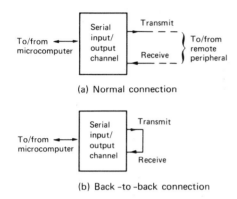

(a) Normal connection

(b) Back-to-back connection

Fig. 13. Serial link in normal and back-to-back connection.

In the normal mode of connection a separate transmit and receive signal connect the microcomputer to the remote *peripheral*, e.g. a *VDU*. If the input/output channel is connected "back-to-back", then the link to the remote peripheral is isolated, and the signal that is transmitted from the channel on the output connection is received simultaneously on the input connection. Such an arrangement assists fault tracing if a failure in the overall microcomputer drive to the peripheral exists because it allows testing of the input/output channel in isolation from the interconnecting cables and the remote peripheral itself.

Back-up A standby facility which can be activated in the event of failure, e.g.

(a) Back-up of *hardware* — spare modules of electronic circuitry (or electromechanical *peripherals*) which can replace faulty modules either by manually changing the module or even by automatic changeover to the standby unit, e.g.

dual *floppy disk* drives on a large *microcomputer* system.

(b) Back-up of *software* — second copy of a computer *program* or *data* file which can be used to overwrite corrupted software.

(c) Back-up of technical service — advisory service by a source of hardware or software expertise.

Base The total number of distinct symbols in a numbering system; sometimes called *radix*. The normal *decimal* (or "denary") system uses a base of 10, e.g.

Decimal 6 can be represented as 6_{10} (6 to the base of 10), and also as 6×10^0 (10 to the power 0).

Thus a larger number is:

$$\text{Decimal } 527 = 5 \times 10^2 + 2 \times 10^1 + 7 \times 10^0$$
$$= 500 + 20 + 7 = 527_{10}$$

Computers use *binary* numbers (base 2), but we normally refer to these numbers using the *hexadecimal* (base 16) numbering system because it makes the numbers shorter and more manageable.

BASIC BASIC is by far the most common *high-level language* that is used with *microcomputers*. The word BASIC stands for Beginners All-purpose Symbolic Instruction Code.

BASIC was designed to be an easy-to-use language which programmers can apply to write and test *programs* rapidly with a minimum knowledge of microcomputer operation. The extent of standardisation of this language throughout the microcomputer industry is such that a BASIC program which is written for one machine can be transferred normally with a minimum of amendment to another machine.

An example of a simple BASIC program is:

```
10  REM  TEST  PROGRAM  TO
    DEMONSTRATE SIMPLE
    ARITHMETIC
20  FIRST=999
30  SECOND=123
40  REM DISPLAY SUM
50  PRINT FIRST+SECOND
60  REM DISPLAY PRODUCT
70  PRINT FIRST*SECOND
80  END
```

Each line, or "statement", is numbered. It is normal to increment line numbers by 10 so that additional statements can be inserted later if the program is amended. The statements at lines 10, 40 and 60 are REM (or remark) statements, and are not implemented when the program is run — they simply allow a method of program documentation to be built into the program listing. The two numbers are given the names of *variables*, e.g. FIRST and SECOND, which can be virtually any collection of letters, but are normally chosen by the programmer to be as meaningful as possible. The PRINT commands cause the value of the variable, or a combination (sum and product in the example above) of variables, to be displayed on the computer's *CRT* screen.

After a BASIC program is entered into a microcomputer, it is run at a later time by an *interpreter* or *compiler* which converts it into *machine code* before execution.

Different versions of variable complexity and ease of application, of BASIC are available, e.g. basic BASIC, extended BASIC, structured BASIC, and versions which are tailored to a specific microcomputer (perhaps to include commands which activate colour *graphics*).

An example of a more complicated BASIC program which demonstrates more of the standard commands is:

```
10  REM THIS PROGRAM
    DISPLAYS THE SQUARE
    ROOTS OF SEVERAL
    NUMBERS
20  DATA 49,184,26,403,72
30  FOR I=1 TO 5
40  READ CHARLIE
50  PRINT "SQUARE  ROOT  OF";
    CHARLIE;  "IS";  SQR(CHAR
    LIE)
60  NEXT
70  END
```

In this example the DATA and READ commands are used in conjunction with each other. The DATA command specifies a list of data items, and whenever the READ command is implemented in the program each succeeding data item is extracted and given the variable name CHARLIE. The FOR and NEXT commands similarly work together, because the section of program which is enclosed by these commands (lines 40 and 50 in this example) is executed the number of times specified in the FOR statement (5 times in this example). Notice that the PRINT command demonstrates the use of two print options — text, in inverted commas, and variables, e.g. SQR(CHARLIE). Thus when the program is executed, by typing in RUN, the following is displayed:

```
SQUARE ROOT OF  49 IS  7.0000
SQUARE ROOT OF 184 IS 13.564
SQUARE ROOT OF  26 IS  5.0090
SQUARE ROOT OF 403 IS 20.075
SQUARE ROOT OF  72 IS  8.4853
```

Baud rate The speed of *data* transmission, expressed in signal elements per second. Normally the term is applied to *serial* data transmission systems in which one signal element is one *bit*, so that baud rate = bits per second.

Examples of application of the term are:

(a) Serial transmission using the *RS 232-C* interface between *computers* and *peripherals* (or other computers). In this case normally 8 data bits are transmitted one after the other (together with a start bit and a stop bit) along a single conductor, so that one *character* requires 10 bits, as follows:

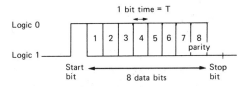

FIG. 14. Serial data transmission waveform.

If $T = 0.001667$ sec (1.667 msec) then baud rate =

$$\frac{1}{1.667 \times 10^{-3}} = 600$$

Thus a baud rate of 600 gives 60 characters per second. This is a typical transmission speed between computer and *printer*. Faster speeds are typical for *VDUs* and inter-computer links. The standard range of baud rates which can be generated by *UARTs* (generators of this serial waveform) are:

110, 300, 600, 1200, 2400, 4800 and 9600

(b)   Serial transmission to and from *floppy disk* (or *hard disk*) read/write *head* and controlling circuit, again expressed in bits per second.

(c)   *Bus* transfer speeds, e.g. the speed of *byte* transfer from a microcomputer master board (containing *microprocessor* and *bus drivers*) along a *backplane* to supporting boards using the *address bus* and *data bus*.

BCD (Binary Coded Decimal)

This code uses 4 *bits* to represent the 10 *decimal* numbers 0 to 9, as shown in Table 3.

Decimal number	BCD code
0	0000
1	0001
2	0010
3	0011
4	0100
5	0101
6	0110
7	0111
8	1000
9	1001

Table 3. BCD (Binary Coded Decimal)

Notice that the last 6 of the possible 16 codes are not used. Normally two BCD *digits* are packed into one *byte*. For example, the BCD number 8413 can be held in two bytes as follows:

0001 0011	13
1000 0100	84

Normally it is inconvenient to handle BCD numbers within a *microcomputer program* because conversion to pure *binary* numbers may be required.

Benchmark

Benchmark   A parameter for comparison between two systems. Benchmarks are commonly applied to compare *microprocessors* as follows:

(a)   Time to perform 8-*bit* addition.

(b)   Time to perform a more complicated and extensive test exercise, e.g. a *program* which transfers a block of *data*, with manipulation (perhaps shifting and logical modification), from one area of *memory* to another.

Bidirectional

Bidirectional   Signal flow can pass in either direction. Bidirectional signal flow along the same conductor (or conductors) is uncommon in most electronic systems, but the most familiar example is the bidirectional *data bus* within a *microcomputer*.

Binary

Binary A number system which uses a *base* of 2; the normal *decimal* number system uses a base of 10. Only two symbols are used in the binary system — 0 and 1. It is far easier to design electronic circuits which handle only two signal levels, e.g. a voltage and no voltage, and it is for this reason that *computers* handle numbers in binary form.

A "bit" (binary digit) can take the value of 0 or 1, and forms one part of a binary number, as follows:

Binary $1101 = 1101_2 = 1 \times 2^3 + 1 \times 2^2 + 0 \times 2^1 + 1 \times 2^0$
$$= 8 + 4 + 0 + 1 = 13_{10}$$

Thus 1101 is the binary representation of decimal 13. Each bit therefore represents a component, in "powers of two", of the overall number. 8-bit *microprocessors* represent numbers using 8 bits, e.g.

Binary 0100 1100 =

128	64	32	16		8	4	2	1	(powers of 2)
0	1	0	0		1	1	0	0	= 76_{10}

Therefore the largest number that can be represented using 8 bits is 255.

A method for performing conversion in the opposite direction, i.e. from decimal to binary, is as follows:
Convert 12_{10} to binary.

			1	1 (third remainder)
Continually →	2	⌐3	0 (second remainder)	
divide by 2	2	⌐6	0 (first remainder)	
	2	⌐12		

Answer = 1100_2

Binary dump

Binary dump A transfer of the contents of *memory* to a storage medium, e.g. *magnetic tape* or *printer*, in *binary* (or *hexadecimal*) form.

Bipolar

Bipolar Possessing two poles, i.e. containing electric charges of opposite polarity. The *TTL* family of *integrated circuits* uses bipolar *transistors*, in which both positive and negative charge carriers exist. The recent *MOS* and *CMOS* families use *unipolar* transistors, in which only one type (positive or negative) of charge carrier occurs — these transistors are often called *FETs* (Field Effect Transistors).

Bipolar integrated circuits (*ICs*) are classified by circuit type:

(a) *TTL* (Transistor Transistor Logic);
(b) *ECL* (Emitter Coupled Logic);
(c) *I²L* (Integrated Injection Logic).

The conventional circuit symbol for a bipolar transistor is shown in Fig. 15.

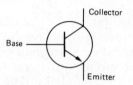

FIG. 15. Bipolar transistor circuit symbol (NPN transistor).

The *planar* construction of a bipolar transistor is illustrated in Fig. 16 for a TTL IC (integrated circuit).

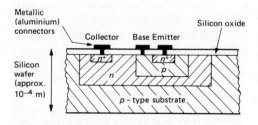

FIG. 16. Bipolar "silicon planar epitaxial" transistor.

The manufacture of this device involves oxidation of the surface of the silicon wafer, followed by a sequence of photomask and diffusion processes in order to transform areas of the silicon into p (majority carriers are positive) and n (majority carriers are negative) type. Metallic interconnections, which are applied by masking and evaporation, to other transistors and to other components (resistors and diodes which are diffused into the same substrate in a similar manner to transistors) are effected along the wafer to form an "integrated circuit".

Bistable multivibrator
A circuit element that has two stable states. Thus its output can be either at the 0 or 1 state. It is often known by its alternative name of "flip-flop". Figure 17 shows how a simple bistable latch circuit can be constructed using two *NAND* gates.

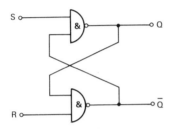

FIG. 17. Bistable multivibrator (using cross-coupled NAND gates).

The *truth table* for this circuit is shown in Table 4.

S	R	Q	Q̄
0	0	No change	
1	0	1	0
0	1	0	1
1	1	Indeterminate	

Table 4. Truth table for NAND gate bistable

Lines 2 and 3 of this table show that the outputs Q and Q̄ (*NOT* Q) change in response to changes in the level of the inputs S (Set) and R (Reset). The circuit is normally used in these two modes only.

This particular flip-flop circuit is *"asynchronous"*, i.e. the output changes at the same time as the input. In a *"synchronous"* flip-flop the output changes in accordance with the input at a time determined by a separate *clock* input.

Bistables can be triggered in two ways:

(a) Edge triggered, or dc level triggered. The change in dc level triggers the bistable — this change can be either a positive or negative transition.

(b) Master-slave. This technique requires both a positive and a negative transition on a clock pulse before the output is set.

Refer to the following types of bistable:

(1) *SR bistable;*
(2) *D-type bistable;*
(3) *J-K bistable;*
(4) *Master-slave bistable.*

The applications of bistables are in *counters, registers* and in circuits which require that a single *bit* (or signal level) should be latched.

Bit
A contraction of *"binary digit"*. Therefore a bit can take one of two states — 0 and 1.

Bit slice microprocessor
A *microprocessor* that is constructed using several *ICs* and can be designed to operate any tailored *instruction set* and any *bit* length, e.g. 8, 12, 16, 32 or even more. Bit slice microprocessors are uncommon, but they are used occasionally when a special function or high-performance system is required.

Each *chip* in a bit slice microprocessor performs a single function within the overall range of functions (*ALU, registers*, etc.) which apply to a conventional single-chip microprocessor. The advantage of this approach is that:

(a) extremely fast performance is possible, since *bipolar* (*TTL* or *ECL*) logic can be used for the circuit building blocks;

15

(b)   a specially-selected set of *instructions* can be designed.

This latter feature is obtained by suitable design of the *control unit* with an associated *ROM* which contains the *microinstructions* for each instruction. Therefore the instruction set can be customised for a particular application.

The word "slice" is used in the name for this type of microprocessor since a single chip, which is used to construct part of the ALU or support part of a register, may only handle 2 or 4 bits of the typical 12- or 16-bit words which are processed by the system.

Blast   Program   an   *EPROM*.   The process of writing *bits* into an EPROM is called "programming" or "blasting" the device.

Block   A set of items. The term is often applied with *microcomputers* to describe a set of *data* items (normally *bytes*) which are:

(a)   held in memory (*semiconductor memory* — *ROM* or *RAM* — or *backing store*);
(b)   transferred between microcomputer and *peripheral* (e.g. *printer*) as a contiguous group of *characters*.

Block diagram   A diagram which represents a system, with all the principal parts represented by functional blocks. A block diagram is a useful technique to describe the modular actions within an electronic system, e.g. a *microcomputer* based system as shown in Fig. 18 for a microcomputer based cash register.

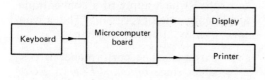

FIG. 18. Block diagram of microcomputer based cash register.

The principal modules within the system are defined within blocks.

A similar technique can be used to describe *software*, and a common method of indicating the modular structure and flow of a *program* is called a *flow chart*.

Blocking   diode   A   conventional diode that is used to block current flow. A particular application with microcomputers is one in which a large number of contact closure signals is connected to *input/output ports* in a *matrixing* arrangement, as shown in Fig. 19.

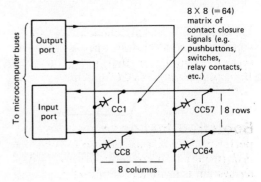

FIG. 19. Use of blocking diodes in matrix digital input system.

A large number (64) of *digital input* signals is connected to the microcomputer using a matrix of intersecting output and input lines. This arrangement uses only 2 ports (1 output and 1 input) and is in contrast to using 8 input ports in non-matrixing arrangement. However, a blocking diode must be placed in series with each contact closure to prevent current paths from one row of contact closures to another. This occurs if diodes are not used and several contacts are closed together, e.g. if CC1, CC8 and CC57 are closed with CC64 open, then when the right-hand column is read in, a current path exists from the top output line through CC57, CC1 and CC8 to incorrectly set a 1 on the bottom input line. This path is prevented by the blocking diodes.

16

Board tester An item of equipment which can be used to test a manufactured circuit board. Typically the equipment is *microcomputer* based, and it exercises the circuit board under test by injecting signals and examining the response. See *ATE*.

Boolean logic A series of symbolic operations which operate on *binary* numbers — named after George Boole. The operations are *AND, OR, NOT* and *EXCLUSIVE OR* and can be performed by *hardware* (using *gates*) or *computer software*.

Bootstrap To load the main *program* (*operating system*) into the *computer's* memory and enter that program. See *Bootstrap loader, Cold boot* and *Warm boot*.

Bootstrap loader A *program* that performs a *bootstrap* function. When a *disk* (floppy or hard) based *microcomputer* system is switched on initially, or if it is required to restart the system, a bootstrap loader program is run to perform the following:

(a)   set up *input/output* circuits (e.g. if *programmable* devices are used);
(b)   load the *operating system* from a reserved area on disk (usually *floppy disk*) into memory;
(c)   enter the operating system.

Normally the bootstrap loader is *ROM* based and it is entered automatically on machine switch-on, or it can be activated by operation of a special key or push-button.

See *Cold boot* and *Warm boot*.

Bounce The unwanted repeated operation of a mechanical contact which provides a contact signal to a *computer*. See *Contact bounce*.

Branch The transfer of *program* control from the normal sequential execution of the program to a different part of the program. Normally this is implemented in a *machine code* program in the form of a *conditional jump instruction*.

Breakpoint A stop that is inserted into a *program* under test so that operation of the program can be checked. A *debugger* or *trace* program possesses the facility to insert a "breakpoint" into a program under test; normally the breakpoint is specified as the *memory* address of a specific instruction. For example, if the command

E1040

is entered into a debugger program, then the test program is executed up to the instruction which is loaded at memory address 1040. The debugging program is then re-entered so that the contents of *registers* and memory locations can be examined to confirm correct operation.

Bridge A conventional electrical circuit which has application when a *transducer* signal is connected to a *microcomputer*. Most transducers, which measure temperature, weight, level, etc., are of the variable-resistance type. Such a transducer is connected across one arm of a Wheatstone bridge, as shown in Fig. 20.

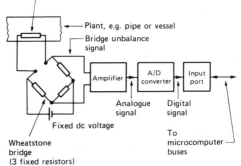

FIG. 20. Bridge circuit — for transducer input signal to microcomputer.

The transducer may be a resistance thermometer (or "thermistor"), which measures temperature. As the transducer resistance varies with temperature, it causes a variable unbalance signal in the bridge. This signal is amplified and converted into a *digital* form, using an *A/D converter*, before entering an *input port*.

Bubble memory A non-volatile solid-state *memory* that uses microscopic magnetic domains in an aluminium garnet substrate. Figure 21 shows the main features on a *92K bit* single *integrated circuit* (IC) in the conventional *dual-in-line* (DIL) package.

Total memory capacity = 144 (usable loops) × 641 (bubbles per loop) = 92 304 bits.

Additional control and timing circuitry is required externally to the device to facilitate connection to a *microprocessor's bus* systems. The following signal descriptions apply to the signals which are handled within this circuitry:

(a) Generate. Bits are written into memory in serial form using the current pulses in the generate loop — a magnetic bubble is created by a current pulse for a logic 1, and no bubble is created by the absence of a current pulse for a logic 0.

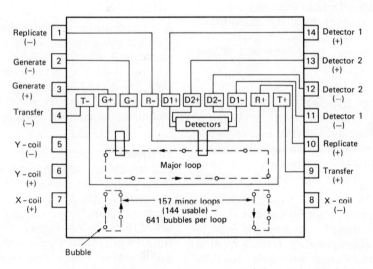

Fɪɢ. 21. Bubble memory dual-in-line chip (Texas Instruments TBM 0101 – 92K bits).

A single *bit* (0 or 1) is stored in one of the "minor" loops as a magnetic bubble (for 1) or no magnetic bubble (for 0). Internal coils are pulsed from external drive circuits so that a rotating magnetic field causes the minor loops within the garnet substrate to rotate continuously. No bits are stored on the major loop, which acts merely as a transfer medium for loading bits into the memory, i.e. within the minor loops, or out of memory.

Bubbles are transferred from the major loop to the required minor loop.

(b) Transfer. A pulse on this signal causes transfer (for both read and write operations) between the major loop and the required minor loop. Thus it is effectively a minor loop addressing signal, and is activated when the shifted bubble position in the major loop is adjacent to the top of the required minor loop.

(c) Detect. Bits are read from the major loop (after transfer from the minor loop) on the Detector 1 and Detector 2 signal connections. Two detect signals are used so that a differential output (difference between the two) can be generated to offset the effect of noise on the detect bits. Notice that the Replicate signal is pulsed when each bit is read from the major loop if it is required to reinstate bubbles back into the minor loop. In this way bubbles are recreated in the major loop downstream of the detect position so that they can be written back into the minor loop.

Clearly bubble memory transfers bits in and out serially. This means that data transfer is slow compared with *semiconductor memory* (*ROM* and *RAM*). For example, average access time = 4 msec (4 milliseconds), which is far slower than a typical access time for RAM of 300 nsec (300 nanoseconds). Hence bubble memory is quite unsuitable for the *main memory* within a *microcomputer* — program execution times would be approximately 10,000 times slower with bubble. However, bubble memory is a challenger to the *floppy disk* for slow back-up memory. Although bubble devices possess smaller storage capacity (maximum of 128K *bytes* compared with 800K bytes for floppy disk), they possess similar access times. They are not as conveniently removable as floppy disks, however, and they tend to be used only for storing a back-up of the main program (*operating system*) for reloading into RAM.

Buffer 1. In *software* a buffer is a section of *memory* which is used to hold a list of *data* items. Often one *program* loads a buffer, whilst another program removes the data items for processing

2 In *hardware* a buffer is a temporary

storage *register* which is used to staticise a series of *bits*. Alternatively it is a circuit that is used to restore the logic level of bits.

Bug A *software* error. A fault in a *program* which causes incorrect processing, e.g.

(a) numbers are processed incorrectly;
(b) program sequence follows an incorrect path;
(c) program "*crashes*" completely — perhaps control of the computer is lost to an uncontrolled *loop* within the program.

Burn-in The process of running a new electronic circuit or system for a regulated period to allow for early failure of marginal components.

Bus A set of conductors which carry a group of signals that share a common function. A *microcomputer* possesses three buses — the *address bus*, *data bus* and *control bus*. These buses are generated by the *microprocessor* (or *CPU*) as shown in Fig. 22.

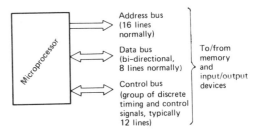

Fig. 22. The three buses of a microprocessor.

See also *Common buses*, which connect from main microcomputer boards to supporting boards.

Bus conflict The situation which occurs if more than one device attempts to use a *bus* at any time. Unwanted bus conflict can occur if, for example, two *memory ICs* attempt to feed data onto the *tri-state data bus* within a *microcomputer*. This is prevented by correct design of an *address decoding* circuit which ensures that only one memory device is selected at any time.

Bus controller A circuit that generates signals which coordinate transfers along a *bus*. This is not required normally for a *microprocessor*'s three buses, but may be required for alternative buses (see *Common buses*).

Bus driver A circuit that is inserted into a *bus* so that the bus signals are provided with sufficient electrical drive capacity to activate correctly devices that are connected to the bus. When *microcomputer* buses are connected over some distance (perhaps greater than 0.5 m) to *memory* and *input/output* circuits, the capacitative loading on the buses can cause timing problems and *bit* transfers can be detected erroneously. This applies particularly when the overall microcomputer circuit is distributed over several boards. In this case bus driver *ICs* are inserted at each end, i.e. on each board, of the bus connections.

A typical 8-bit driver IC is shown in Fig. 23.

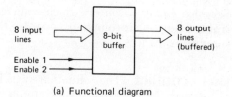

(a) Functional diagram

ENABLE 1 — 1	20 — V_{CC}
IN1 — 2	19 — ENABLE 2
OUT8 — 3	18 — OUT1
IN2 — 4	17 — IN8
OUT7 — 5	16 — OUT2
IN3 — 6	15 — IN7
OUT6 — 7	14 — OUT3
IN4 — 8	13 — IN6
OUT5 — 9	12 — OUT4
GND — 10	11 — IN5

SN74244

(b) Pin connections

FIG. 23. 8-bit buffer (the SN74244).

The entire 8-bit *data bus*, or one-half of a 16-bit *address bus*, could be buffered using this IC. An alternative *tri-state* buffer is the SN74373.

Business computer A *computer* that is used for commercial or business applications. The *microcomputer* offers the traditional range of functions of a *mainframe computer* within a small, cheap, single-user machine. Such functions, or "packages", are:

(a) *payroll*;
(b) *mailing list*;
(c) *ledger* (sales, invoice, general);
(d) *word processor*; etc.

Refer to *Desktop computer*.

Bus terminator A simple circuit that prevents reflections at the end of a *bus*. It is not normally required for a *microcomputer*'s buses.

Byte Group of 8 *bits*. This is the most common grouping of bits in *microcomputers*, and can be used:

(a) to represent numbers in an 8-bit *microprocessor* (2 bytes are required in a 16-bit microprocessor);

(b) to represent *program instructions* in a microprocessor (1-, 2- or 3-byte instructions are used in an 8-bit microprocessor);

(c) to represent *characters* (using the *ASCII* code).

C

C A *high-level language.* C is used in *minicomputers* and *microcomputers.* It was developed by Bell Laboratories and used in the writing of the *Unix operating system.* C is noted for its powerful *low-level language* capability, i.e. detailed *bit* and *byte* processing is possible within a high-level language *program* written in C.

CAD (Computer Aided Design)

The technique of employing *computers* to assist in the design of electronic circuits, mechanical systems and even civil engineering structures. One of the most widespread applications of CAD *software packages* is for electronic design as follows:

(a) design of a multi-*chip* circuit, e.g. to perform a complicated gating function;
(b) layout of *ICs* and other components on the circuit board, including design of *printed circuit* layout;
(c) design of actual IC, i.e. preparation of photomasks involved in fabrication process for an IC using the silicon *planar* process.

Such design packages are available on either *mainframe computers* or *microcomputers.*

CADMAT (Computer Aided Design, Manufacture and Test)

The overall technology of *CAD*, *CAM* and other *computer* based *ATE* (automatic test equipment).

CAE (Computer Assisted Education) See *CAL.*

CAL (Computer Assisted Learning)

The use of *computers* to provide educational learning procedures. A typical CAL system is a *software package* that generates a sequence of *CRT* displays which provide information in a progressive sequence. The *program* is "*interactive*" with the student, i.e. the student is required to answer questions (via a keyboard) correctly before the next graded page of information is offered.

Call Jump to a *subroutine.* All *microprocessors* possess an *instruction* (normally with a *mnemonic* of CALL) which causes *program* control to transfer to a subroutine at a specified *memory* address. The contents of the *program counter* are automatically stored (normally on the *stack*) so that the calling program can be re-entered at the correct point, when the subroutine is finished, using the *return* instruction.

CAM (Computer Aided Manufacturing)

The technique of employing *computers* to assist in the manufacture of a wide range of items. *Minicomputers* and *microcomputers* can be applied in a diverse range of industrial applications to assist the manufacturing process, e.g.

(a) *PCB* manufacture;
(b) machining processes;
(c) *robots* for product positioning,

21

automatic welding, etc., in assembly line processes;

(d) mathematical modelling for both batch and continuous processes;

(e) automatic inspection and test (*ATE*).

CAM (Content Addressable Memory)

A *memory* system that possesses the ability to make a comparison between *data* already stored and data which is presented at the input. Typically a CAM *integrated circuit* can store four words of two *bits*. Several such devices are connected together in an array, and the whole system could be used to detect a dangerous sequence of signals in a process control application.

Capture

The act of staticising a series of signal levels within a *logic analyser*. A logic analyser is an item of test equipment and it can be set to respond to a predetermined combination of stimuli in order to "*trap*" or "capture" the levels of signals within an electronic system (frequently a *microcomputer*).

Carry flag

A *flag* which is set in a *microprocessor*'s *status register* when the result of an arithmetic operation (in the *ALU*) causes an overflow. Consider the following addition in an 8-bit microprocessor:

$$\begin{array}{r} 0110\ 0101 \\ 1100\ 1100\ ^{+} \\ \hline 1\ 0011\ 0001 \\ \uparrow \end{array}$$

Carry bit (sets carry flag)

Cartridge disk

A magnetic disk storage medium for *binary data*. Removable cartridge disk systems represent the most common bulk storage (*backing store*) technique for *mainframe computers* and *minicomputers*, but are rarely ap-

plied with *microcomputers*. The construction of a cartridge disk is illustrated in Fig. 24.

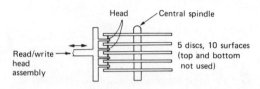

FIG 24. Cartridge disk construction.

8 of the 10 surfaces are used for data storage. As the disk unit rotates the read/write head assembly traverses horizontally to locate the required position ("track" or "cylinder") on the appropriate surface.

The cartridge is removable. It is held permanently in a plastic container to provide protection. Memory capacities range from 5M *bytes* to 50M bytes.

Cartridge tape

A magnetic storage medium for *binary data*. There are two versions of magnetic tape which are used for providing a *backing store* for *microcomputers* — *audio cassette* and *digital cassette*/cartridge. The former is applied with *home computers*. *Digital cassettes* are similar to audio cassettes but offer greater storage capacity. *Digital cartridges* provide higher operating speeds and greater storage than digital cassettes, and are packaged in plastic containers of the following sizes:

(a) 6 × 4 × 0.27 in, 300 ft — gives 2.87M *bytes* storage.

(b) 3.2 × 2.4 × 0.4 in, 140 ft — gives 772K bytes storage.

Typical access time in both cases is 20 sec, which means that such devices are only suitable for slow reload of the *system* (the main program) into *main memory*. For this reason digital cartridge systems are rarely applied with microcomputers.

The most popular method for *bit* storage is *phase encoding*. At the *byte* level *data* are stored in blocks, called "records", according to the *ANSI* standard shown in Fig. 25.

This operating system is an updated version of the more familiar *CP/M*.

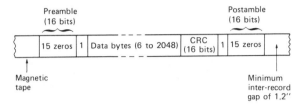

FIG. 25. Digital cartridge data format (ANSI standard).

Note that CRC is a *cyclic redundancy* check character, which is used for error detection.

Cascade connection
The connection of different parts of an electronic system in tandem, i.e. the output of one part is the input of another. Figure 26 shows a cascade connection from *microcomputer output port* through a digital to analogue (*D/A*) converter and an amplifier to a servo (mechanical position control system).

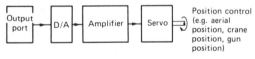

FIG. 26. Example of cascade system (microcomputer-driven servo).

Cassette
A magnetic medium in tape form that is used for *data* storage. There are two types: *audio cassette* and *digital cassette*.

CCD
See *Charge coupled device*.

CDOS (Cromemco Disk Operating System)
The *operating system* that is applied with *disk* based *microcomputers* manufactured by Cromemco.

Central processor unit
See *CPU*.

Centronics interface
A standard interface between a *computer* and a *parallel*-driven *printer*. The 11-wire connection is named after the manufacturer (Centronics) of the dominant printer, with its associated interfacing signals, which was connected originally to *microcomputers*. Other manufacturers of parallel printers generally apply the same interface.

Figure 27 shows the interface with its signal identities.

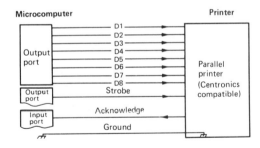

FIG. 27. Centronics interface (computer to printer).

The Strobe and Acknowledge signals perform a *handshaking* function. The computer sets the Strobe signal when it has placed an 8-bit code (in *ASCII*) on the D1 to D8 lines. The printer replies with Acknowledge.

Contrast with the standard *serial* interface — the *RS 232-C*.

Channel A *data* path. Examples of the use of the term in *computer* applications are:

(a)   one of several *analogue* input signals;

(b)   one of several communication channels in an *FDM* (frequency division multiplexing) *telemetry* system.

Character A letter, number (0 to 9) or other symbol that can be displayed on a *CRT* or printed on a *printer* by a *computer*. Characters are invariably stored within a computer's *memory* and transferred between computer and *peripheral* (e.g. *VDU* or printer) using the standard *ASCII* 8-*bit* code.

Character generator A circuit that generates *characters* on a *CRT* screen or *printer*. More specifically the term is applied to describe the *ROM memory chip* that stores the *bit* patterns that are used to construct the characters in a *dot matrix* form.

The action of a character generator ROM in a printer is demonstrated in Fig. 28.

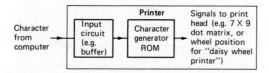

FIG. 28. Character generation in a printer.

Changing the character generator ROM alters the printer character set in a dot matrix printer; this may be useful if an unconventional character set, e.g. foreign language, is applied.

Character graphics The simplest form of *graphics* that is applied with *microcomputers*. Character graphics consist of the construction of lines and crude shapes by placing suitable text

characters, e.g. exclamation mark or letter O, in adjacent positions on the *CRT* screen. Strictly the technique should be defined as "semi-graphics".

Character printer A printer that prints using fully formed *characters*, in contrast to a *matrix printer*, which constructs characters in a *dot matrix* form. There are two principal types:

(a)   *daisy wheel printer*;
(b)   *golfball printer*.

Contrast with a *matrix printer*, which is faster but produces poorer quality printed characters.

Character recognition A machine based process of detecting written *characters*.

Character set The set of *characters* that can be processed by an *input* or *output peripheral*, e.g. *printer*. See *ASCII*.

Charge Coupled Device (CCD) A *serial* access *semiconductor memory* device. *Bits* are held within the device as a series of packets of electric charge within a silicon substrate. An example of the internal organisation of such an *IC* is shown in Fig. 29.

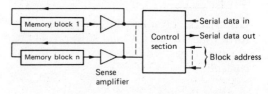

FIG. 29. Internal organisation of charge coupled device.

Data bits are stored in each memory block in consecutive positions, so that when data are read out from a chosen memory block the charge packets are shifted sequentially from left to right. A sense amplifier detects the presence or absence of an electric charge, and passes the data through the control section and out of the device.

CCDs are unsuitable for *main memory* because data transfer is *serial* and not *parallel*. This causes slow transfer speeds, e.g. access time can be as high as 1 msec. However, CCDs, like *bubble memory*, offer an alternative to electromechanical *backing stores* (e.g. *floppy disk*) for back-up storage.

Check bit
A binary digit (*bit*) that is used to mark a particular condition, e.g. *parity* bit, *status* bit.

Check digit
An extra *digit* in a *data* item that can be used to detect errors.

Checkerboard
A test pattern of 1s and 0s which is stored in successive *memory* locations in order to check a memory device.

Checksum
A number that is used to confirm successful loading of *data* in to a *computer*. For example, consider the following data list which may be loaded into a computer on *paper tape*.

Data bytes (e.g. total of 128)	Checksum

FIG. 30. Use of checksum for data list.

The *program* which reads in the data adds up all the data *bytes* (ignoring *carry*). This total is then added to the checksum, and the result should be zero if no read errors have occurred.

Chip
An alternative name for an *IC* and used as an abbreviation for "*silicon chip*".

Chip Enable (CE)
An alternative name for *Chip Select* (CS).

Chip Select (CS)
A signal that enables a *three-state* device. Each *IC* that is wired to a *microprocessor*'s *data bus* possesses a discrete chip select signal, so that only one device can use the bus at any time. Therefore a separate chip select signal must be generated for each *ROM*, *RAM* and *input/output* IC in a *micro-computer*. This is performed in an *address decoding* circuit.

Clear
Set a *memory* location or a circuit, e.g. a *counter*, to zero.

Clock
A timing reference for an electronic system. A clock is a regular stream of *pulses* that synchronise and trigger events. See *CPU clock*.

CMOS (Complementary Metal Oxide Semiconductor)
Integrated circuits made from *field effect transistors* ("*unipolar*" transistors) of both P- and N-type connected in a "complementary" manner. CMOS technology is a development of *MOS* technology, and its particular advantage is extremely low power dissipation.

CMOS ICs offer the same circuit functions as the more familiar *TTL* and MOS versions. Examples are:

(a) Standard gating ICs, e.g. *AND*, *OR*, *counters*, *decoders*. The name of this range is the "4000B" series of ICs. An alternative range is the 74C00 series, which is designed to be pin-compatible with the normal TTL range.
(b) *Memory* ICs.
(c) *Microprocessors*.
(d) *Op-amps*, i.e. *linear* circuits.

The particular advantages of CMOS devices over TTL and MOS equivalents are low power consumption, wide supply voltage range and high *noise immunity*.

Care must be taken when handling and storing CMOS devices in order to avoid static electric charge, which can damage the devices.

Figure 31 shows a CMOS *NOR* gate.

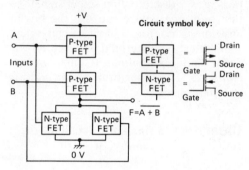

FIG. 31. CMOS NOR gate.

The complementary nature of the circuit is indicated by the presence of both P- and N-type *FET*s (field effect transistors), which for simplicity are indicated by boxes. If either A or B is logic 1 (+V), one N-type FET conducts and one P-type FET becomes non-conducting. This causes the output F to go low (0 V). This produces the NOR logic function.

Typical gate characteristics are: speed 35 nsec, power dissipation 10 nW/gate, noise immunity 2V, fan-out 50 plus.

CMOS memory devices offer extremely high packing density, e.g. 4K bits RAM, and the circuit for a single-*bit* storage cell for a *static RAM* device is indicated in Fig. 32.

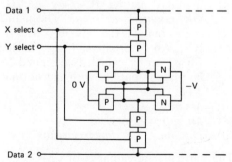

FIG. 32. CMOS static RAM flip-flop (1-bit storage).

This *flip-flop* is selected when both X and Y select lines are set to −V. A 1 or 0 is written into the flip-flop by setting either Data 1 or Data 2. Access time is typically 150 nsec.

CMRR (Common Mode Rejection Ratio)
A measure of the ability of a circuit to reject *common mode* electrical *noise*. It is expressed for an *analogue* amplifier as:

$$CMRR = 20\log_{10} \frac{\text{Differential voltage gain (normal gain)}}{\text{Common mode voltage gain}}.$$

It is a parameter that is frequently quoted for an *op-amp*, which possesses a high common mode rejection characteristic.

COBOL
A *high-level language*. Cobol (Common Business Oriented Language) is applied with many *mainframe computers* and some *minicomputers*, but is not common with *microcomputers*. It is principally designed for commercial applications.

Code
A method of representing *data*. The most common code that is applied with computers is the *ASCII* code, which is used to represent *characters* (letters and numbers). See also *BCD* and *EBDIC*.

Alternatively the term is applied occasionally as an abbreviation for *machine code*.

Coding
The list of *program instructions* in *machine code*.

Coding sheet
A formatted sheet that allows a programmer to lay out his *program* in an orderly manner. It is particularly useful for an *assembly language* program.

Cold boot The operation of loading the main *program* ("*operating system*") from backing store into *main memory*. Contrast with *Warm boot*. A cold boot is performed by running a *bootstrap loader* program and is required at machine switch-on or if the operating system is corrupted in main memory.

Colour graphics The facility of a *microcomputer* to generate colour *CRT* (television monitor) displays which use shapes and lines. Typically a *personal computer* has the ability to generate 8 colours and to draw lines and shapes using a point-matrix on the screen of 256 × 176 points.

Combinational logic A non-programmable gating system, which employs only simple *gates* and *logic* elements, e.g. *AND, OR*. In a combinational logic system all signals, at each point in the system, change (or are liable to change) together. Contrast with a *sequential logic* system (e.g. a *shift register*), in which signals in the system change at different times.

Consider the example in Fig. 33.

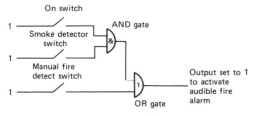

FIG. 33. Combinational logic system — fire alarm.

In this arrangement the output may change immediately in response to a change in an input. Signals do not pass through the system in a series of timing stages. Therefore the output is set to 1 (to sound an audible alarm) if:

(a)   the manual fire detect switch is set;

or

(b)   the on switch is set **and** the smoke detector switch is set.

See *AND* gate and *OR* gate.

Command A statement in a *high-level language program*. Each line in the program is a command.

Command driven A *software* facility that is controlled by special command words which are keyed in by the user. An example is a *debugger program* that performs different functions, as selected by a command entered by the operator, on a test program. An easier way for a non-programmer to "drive" a software package, e.g. a business accounts program, is to use a "*menu*" driven approach.

Command organiser The part of an *operating system* (the main program in a *disk*-based *microcomputer*) that interprets commands which are entered by the operator. Typical commands are:

(a)   run a *program*;
(b)   list all programs in the system;
(c)   erase a program;
(d)   print a program *listing* on a *printer*.

Comment A written statement within a *program instruction* which describes the operation of that instruction. The comment is ignored when the program is run, and serves only to make the program listing more understandable when displayed or printed.

A comment can be inserted in both *assembly language* and *high-level language* programs, as follows:

(a)   Assembly language

MOVI C,6   ;   Set loop count of 6
                 in register C

Instruction   Comment
mnemonic

(b) High-level language
160 LUCY=HELEN*SUE
170 REM NOW DISPLAY THE
SQUARE ROOT
180 PRINT SQR(LUCY)

Line 170 is a comment statement. See *BASIC*.

Common area
An area of *memory* that is accessed by more than one *program*.

Common bus
A set of interfacing connections that enable circuit boards to be interconnected. Several common bus standards have been designed to enable *microprocessor* boards to be interconnected with *input/output* and *memory* boards. The most common examples are:

(a) *S-100 bus* } both require a multi-way
(b) *IEEE 488 bus* } connection along a back-
       } plane;
(c) *RS 232-C*, which is a *serial* interface.

Common mode
An electrical *noise* signal that is present on both input connections to an electrical circuit (normally an amplifier).

Consider the instrumentation signal connection in Fig. 34.

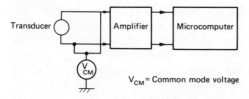

V_{CM} = Common mode voltage

FIG. 34. Common mode noise signal in instrumentation system.

The unwanted common mode voltage is often caused because the transducer circuit and the amplifier operate at different dc voltage levels with respect to earth; also it can be an ac voltage. It is overcome by using an *op-amp* (operational amplifier), which amplifies the difference between the two input voltages. See *CMRR*.

Communications link
A *data* transmission system. The term is often applied to *computer* links, via *serial* interface, to remote *peripherals* (e.g. *VDU* and *printer*) and other computers.

Comparator
A circuit that compares two signals (*analogue* or *digital*) and indicates the result of the comparison as one of two levels — expressed as a *binary digit* (*bit*) 0 or 1. The most common comparator operation is one which compares two analogue voltage levels and sets an output of +V (to indicate 1) or 0 V (to indicate 0) as follows:

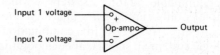

FIG. 35. Comparator circuit using an op-amp.

If input 1 voltage exceeds input 2 voltage by even a small amount, the op-amp amplifies the difference using an extremely high gain to set the output to full-scale (+V). If input 2 voltage is the larger voltage, then the output is at the opposite logic level (0 V). One of the comparison voltages could be at 0 V, so that the circuit effectively tests the input against 0 V. In this mode the circuit can perform a sinewave to squarewave conversion.

Gating circuits can be applied to compare two multi-bit digital signals.

Note that additionally a *software* compare operation can be implemented by the use of a compare *instruction*.

Compatibility
The ability of one *computer* to process *software* from another computer. Alternatively the ability of an item of *hardware* to interconnect with another.

Compiler A *program* that converts a *high-level language* program into a *machine code* program. After a compilation process has been implemented on a program, two versions of that program exist — the source program, in high-level language, and the object program, in machine code. Contrast with an *interpreter*, which converts a *high-level language* into machine code at program run-time; no machine code version is stored within the software system.

A compiled version of a high-level language program runs much faster than a high-level language version which runs in an interpretive mode. However, more programmer operation is required prior to run-time in order to generate the machine code version of the program.

Complement To change each 1 to 0 and each 0 to 1. This function is performed in *hardware* by the use of an *inverter*, and in *software* by the use of a complement *instruction*, e.g. an 8-*bit* number, held within a *microprocessor register*, can be complemented — all bits inverted.

Computer The general name for a programmable *data* processing system. Every computer can be described by the generalised representation of Fig. 36.

Computers are *digital* in operation, i.e. they obey a *program* of *instructions* that are represented in *binary digit* (*bit*) form as a series of 1s and 0s. Similarly, *data* values which are processed are held as a series of 1s and 0s. The *CPU* (Central Processor Unit) obeys the program and processes data items, both of which are held in *memory*. The *input/output* section is used when data are transferred in or out of the machine, e.g. to *printer*, *terminal* (*VDU*) or *disk*.

There are three general categories of digital computer:

(a) *Mainframe computer*, which is applied in multi-user large filing applications.

(b) *Minicomputer*, which has less powerful data processing capabilities and is widely applied in process monitoring and control applications and smaller filing systems.

(c) *Microcomputer*, which is the latest and smallest version, and has heralded the widespread application of computers in consumer products (toys, calculators, etc.) and single-user computing systems.

Computer numerical control (CNC) Automatic control by *computer* of drilling, cutting, boring and milling machines. The normal arrangement is shown in Fig. 37.

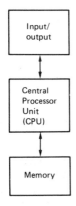

FIG. 36. Generalised representation of a computer.

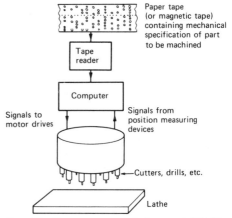

FIG. 37. Computer numerical control (CNC).

The mechanical specification of the part that is to be machined, e.g. hole diameters at specific positions, etc., is prepared on paper tape or magnetic tape off-line on a separate tape preparation device. The tape is read in to the computer (*minicomputer* or *microcomputer*) in sections — one machine operation is completed before the next section of tape is read. The computer performs full automatic control of machine operations and uses feedback signals indicating position of the machine tools.

Clearly "numerical" control of this type offers considerable benefits of more accurate and faster machining operations over manually operated machine tools. Several such CNC systems can be linked to a central factory computer, which can in turn supervise separate computer-driven *robots*, to perform overall factory automation.

Conditional jump A *program instruction* that causes a *jump* operation only if a specified condition is satisfied. When the *CPU* obeys a conditional jump instruction, it checks the value of one or more *status bits* within the *status register*; these bits are set by the previous instruction. If the bit, or bits, are set then the jump is obeyed; if not the program continues to the following instruction.

Consider the following section of program, which is written in *assembly language*:

```
        MVI C,20    ;Load C register with
                    loop count of 20
REPEAT:DCR C,       ;Decrement C register
        JNZ REPEAT  ;Jump if C is not zero
        OUT 2       ;Output A register to
                    input/output address 2
```

The JNZ instruction is a conditional jump instruction. The jump (back to the instruction labelled REPEAT) is implemented repeatedly when it is encountered during program execution until the contents of the C register have been decremented to zero. The JNZ instruc-

tion checks the value of the zero status bit that is set by the DCR instruction which precedes it. Thus the jump is implemented 20 times before program operation continues through to the OUT instruction.

Configuration The arrangement of *hardware* units within a *computer* system.

Console An operator desk that supports manual controls and displays. A *computer* console of the type that was employed on early *mainframe computers* is replaced on the *microcomputer* by a *VDU* or by a *keyboard* and *CRT*.

Constant A fixed value which is used in a *program*.

Contact bounce The phenomenon of repeated operation that occurs when a mechanical contact is opened or closed in order to provide an electrical signal. Unwanted rebounds occur for all types of contact closure, e.g. pushbutton, switch, relay contact, limit switch, etc. The effect is demonstrated in Fig. 38.

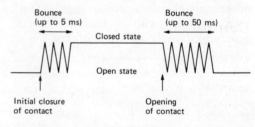

FIG. 38. Contact bounce.

When a contact is connected to a *computer* as a *digital* input signal, the bounce effect can cause the computer to incorrectly record additional operations of the contact. This can be prevented by inserting additional *hardware*, e.g. smoothing capacitor or a *monostable multivibrator*, between contact and *input port*. However, it is simpler and cheaper to apply a *software* solution. Suitable choice of speed at which scanning software reads the contacts can overcome the problem. For example, if a keyboard of push-buttons is scanned by software once every 100 msec, or slower, then no more than one rebound can be detected. However, if the program scan is too slow, e.g. once every ½ sec, then the legitimate operation of a key may be missed.

Continuous The description given to a signal that can take any value over its range. An alternative and more familiar word is "*analogue*".

Control block An area of *memory* that contains information which is required to perform a *software* operation. An example of the use of a control block is when one *program* in a system requires a *disk* transfer operation, e.g. *read* a *data* file into memory. The identifying information, e.g. source address on disk and destination address in memory, is placed in a control block so that a separate disk control program can access this block and implement the required disk transfer.

Control bus One of the three *buses* in a *microcomputer*. The signals on the control bus synchronise and control transfers along the other two buses — the *address bus* and the *data bus*. It is generated by the *CPU* (the central *chip* in the machine). See *Microcomputer* for a description of the overall role of the control bus.

Whilst the address bus and the data bus consist of signal lines that have the same function, e.g. each line in the address bus carries one *bit* of a multi-bit number that specifies an address in *memory* or *input/output*, signal lines in the control bus can have quite dissimilar roles. There are normally 8 to 12 lines in the control bus

and they have the following typical functions:

(a) CPU clock in;
(b) clock out (for use by any input/output chip that may require a clock);
(c) *interrupt* lines (perhaps 2 to 5);
(d) *DMA* (direct memory access) demand and accept signals;
(e) read/write (to select direction of data transfer to or from the CPU);
(f) input/output selected (to distinguish between data transfers to/from memory or input/output);
plus one or two miscellaneous signals.

The specific component within the CPU that handles the control bus signals is the *control unit*.

Control character A *character* in the *ASCII* character set that does not represent a normal letter or number, but instead activates a control action. Examples are carriage return (for a printer) and delete.

Controller An electronic circuit that activates *data* transfers between a *CPU* and a sub-system of a *microcomputer*. Examples are:

(a) *floppy disk controller* (controls a floppy disk drive unit);
(b) *interrupt* controller (coordinates the processing of several interrupt lines);
(c) *DMA* controller (administers data transfers by Direct Memory Access);
(d) *PLC*, or Programmable Logic Controller (the name given to a complete microcomputer that exercises sequence control of an industrial process).

Control register The addressable *register* on a programmable *input/output chip* that is used to "program" or "initialise" the device. Consider the two common input/output chips shown in Fig. 39.

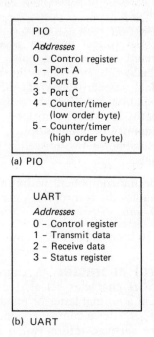

```
PIO

Addresses
0 - Control register
1 - Port A
2 - Port B
3 - Port C
4 - Counter/timer
    (low order byte)
5 - Counter/timer
    (high order byte)
```

(a) PIO

```
UART

Addresses
0 - Control register
1 - Transmit data
2 - Receive data
3 - Status register
```

(b) UART

FIG. 39. Control register for PIO and UART.

In the case of the PIO (*parallel* input/output), *data bytes* can be sent by *software* to the control register to select the directions of the *ports* (in or out) and the timing of the *counter/timer*. The control register within the UART (*serial* input/output) is used to select the transmission speed (*baud rate*), number of data bits, etc. — see *RS 232-C* for the signal specification.

Control unit The part of the *CPU* that examines and implements an *instruction*. See *CPU* for a description of the overall role of the control unit. Figure 40 describes the operation of the control unit in more detail.

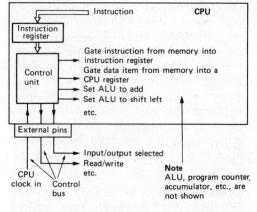

FIG. 40. Operation of control unit.

Each operation of the control unit is triggered by the *CPU clock* signal. Firstly the control unit fetches from *memory* the instruction which is to be obeyed next. Secondly it examines this instruction in the *instruction register* and sends out a sequence of control signals around the CPU and beyond the CPU (on the *control bus*) in order to execute it. For example, this may involve setting the *ALU* to perform a subtract operation on a number which is held within one of the CPU's registers. Alternatively a *data* value may be gated out of the CPU to an *input/output chip*, e.g. to transmit a *character* to a *printer*.

Conversational mode A method of operator/*computer* information transfer in which the computer produces a message (on a *CRT* normally) to request operator entry at various stages in the execution of a *program*.

Conversion The transformation of one signal type to another. Examples of converter circuits are:

(a) *analogue to digital converter*, and vice versa;

(b) *parallel* to *serial* converter, and vice versa (see *UART*, which is the most common application of such a converter; also *Shift register*);

(c) *binary* to *BCD* converter, and vice versa (this conversion can also be performed by *software*);

(d) sine-wave to square-wave converter (e.g. using a *Schmitt trigger* or a *comparator*).

Core A magnetic storage device that employs a small ferrite toroid to store one *bit* (0 or 1). Core stores dominated *computer main memory* systems until the advent of *semiconductor* stores (*ROM* and *RAM*). It can be read from and written to (like RAM) but possesses the advantage that it is non-volatile, i.e. it retains its *bit* pattern even when power is removed.

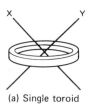

(a) Single toroid

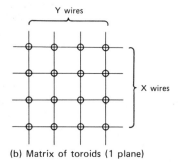

(b) Matrix of toroids (1 plane)

FIG. 41. Core store.

A ferrite core can be magnetised in one direction or the other by passing one-half of the full magnetising current through each of the X and Y wires. The direction of current flow determines the direction of magnetisation. In Fig. 41(b) a "plane" of toroids is arranged in a matrix arrange-

ment — in practice a plane may be 128 × 128 (= 16 384 total) toroids. Each plane stores 1 bit of a multi-bit number. Therefore, 16 planes are required in one assembly if the core store is to support a 16-bit computer. Two additional wires, which are not shown in the diagram for simplicity, run through every toroid in a plane, as follows:

(a) the "sense" wire reads out the 1 or 0 from the addressed toroid during a read operation;

(b) the "inhibit" wire is used during write operations when a 0 is required to be stored.

Notice that core store is "destructive read-out", i.e. all addressed bits are set to 0 whenever a read operation is implemented. Therefore, a read-write cycle is required, so that whenever a 1 is read out, it is immediately reinstated.

Corrupt To destroy *program instructions* or *data* items. Corruption can occur in *main memory* or *backing store* by *hardware* failure or by *software* malfunction.

Counter An electronic circuit that implements a count (normally in *binary*) of incoming *pulses*. A counter consists of a series of *flip-flops*, as shown in Fig. 42.

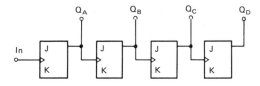

FIG. 42. Counter circuit (4-bit).

This circuit consists of four *master-slave JK bistables* (each J and K are held to 1). Each stage in the counter divides by 2, e.g. Q_A changes after every incoming pulse, Q_B changes after 2 pulses, Q_C changes after 4 pulses and Q_D changes

33

after 8 pulses. Thus after 9 pulses the outputs are:

Q_A	Q_B	Q_C	Q_D
1	0	0	1

(binary for 9 — in reverse order)

A practical counter chip is the SN7493, as shown in Fig. 43.

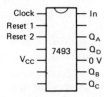

FIG. 43. SN7493 4-bit binary counter.

The circuit within the chip is basically that of Fig. 42. A separate clock is not required if Q_A is connected back to the clock pin. The counter can be reset to all 0s if Reset 1 and Reset 2 are set to logic 1. If Q_B and Q_D are connected to these reset signals then the counter resets itself to zero automatically after 10 input pulses, i.e. it is a decade counter.

Counter/timer A *microcomputer input/output* circuit that can:

(a) count external pulses;
(b) generate a time delay.

It is sometimes known as a "programmable timer" or an "interval timer".

The circuit possesses the two quite separate (a) and (b) facilities because it uses a *counter* that can be used to increment (count up) or decrement (count down), as shown in Fig. 44.

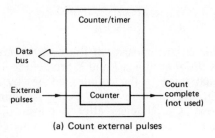

(a) Count external pulses

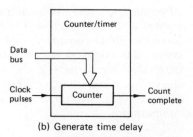

(b) Generate time delay

FIG. 44. Counter/timer circuit applications.

In (a) an external *pulse* stream is connected at the input of the counter and the counter is set to increment (count up). The microcomputer can read the count attained at any time by reading in the counter contents along the *data bus*. Similarly it can reset the count to zero at any time to initiate a new count.

In (b) the counter is used in the decrement (count down) mode. It is initially loaded with a number by *software*, and then this number is counted down to zero using fixed interval clock pulses. When the count reaches zero, the count complete signal is set. If this signal is connected into the microcomputer in some way (e.g. *polled* as a single-*bit* input, or connected as an *interrupt*), a *program* can detect the count complete state. In this way a precise time delay (determined by the initial count which is set into the counter and by the speed of the clock pulses) can be obtained.

If the counter is "initialised" to reset itself when it reaches a count of zero, then a continuous stream of pulses is generated. If this signal is connected as a timer interrupt, then a *real time clock* can be updated in *memory*.

CP/M (Control Program for Microprocessors) The most common *operating system* (main *program* in a multi-programming system) that is applied with *microcomputers*. CP/M is a registered trademark of Digital Research. Several other operating systems are merely variations of CP/M.

CP/M is applied within a wide range of microcomputer systems which are based on *Intel* 8080, 8085 and *Zilog* Z80 *microprocessors*. Several versions are available, e.g. CP/M 1.3, 1.4 and 2.2. A 16-bit version (CP/M 86) can be applied on systems based on the Intel 8086 microprocessors.

A CP/M system requires bulk storage, e.g. *floppy disk*, and a large *main memory*, e.g. 48*K RAM*. CP/M itself occupies typically between 8K and 10K, and comprises three parts (or modules) as follows:

(a) CCP (Console Command Processor), which interprets operator commands entered at the *VDU* keyboard.
(b) BDOS (Basic Disk Operating System), which organises file (program) transfers between memory and disk (floppy or hard).
(c) BIOS (Basic Input/Output system), which services the *keyboard*, VDU display and *printer*.

The free area of memory, which is not used by CP/M, is called the TPA (Transient Program Area).

CP/M "built-in" commands, which the operator can specify, are:

(1) DIR — display the names of all the programs held on disk (called the "directory").
(2) TYPE — print a listing of a program on the VDU or printer.
(3) ERA — erase a program.
(4) REN — rename a program.
(5) SAVE — store a memory area on disk.

The method by which specific programs can be called off disk to run in place of CP/M is by means of the following "transient" commands:

(1) CHARLIE — run the application program called CHARLIE.
(2) ED — call the Editor program in order to create a new program or modify an existing program.

(3) ASM — call the Assembler to convert an *assembly language* program into a *machine code* version.
(4) LOAD — to load the machine code program into memory.
(5) PIP — to copy programs from one floppy disk to another.
(6) DDT — to test and *debug* an executable machine code program.

CPS *Characters* per second. This is a measurement of *data* transmission rates of characters between *computers* and *peripherals* such as *printers* and *VDUs*.

CPU (Central Processor Unit)

The *computer* module that handles the fetching, decoding and implementation of *program instructions*. The CPU in a *microcomputer* is normally a single *integrated circuit* (or "chip") called the microprocessor, and its internal organisation is summarised in Fig. 45 for an 8-*bit* device.

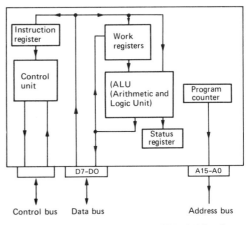

Fig. 45. Internal organisation of CPU (8-bit microprocessor).

The roles of the specific modules are:

(a) *Program counter* — indicates the *memory* address (*ROM* or *RAM*) of the next instruction to be obeyed; the contents are incremented automatically by the CPU when each instruction is completed.

(b) *Instruction register* — holds the instruction currently being obeyed within the CPU.

(c) *Control unit* — examines the instruction in the instruction register and sends out control signals, e.g. to the *ALU*, to implement that instruction.

(d) *Work registers* (frequently called A, B, C etc.) — provide temporary storage of *data* items which are being processed within the program; one register is often called the *accumulator* and is used to receive the results of most ALU operations.

(e) *ALU* (Arithmetic and Logic Unit) — performs any processing, e.g. arithmetic or logical operations, that is required on data items.

(f) *Status register* — indicates the "status" of the ALU as data values are processed within the ALU, e.g. one bit in the status register (called "zero status bit") indicates if a zero result is passed out of the ALU.

The CPU continually performs a *fetch/ execute cycle* on each instruction in a list of instructions which is held in memory. Each instruction is transferred into the CPU, and then implemented. The program counter is incremented to address the following instruction in memory.

Instructions and data items are processed within the CPU in 8-bit modules for this 8-bit microprocessor. The same diagram applies to a 16-bit microprocessor, but registers and data paths within the CPU are all 16-bit wide.

Notice that the three buses (address, data and control) emanate from the CPU.

See *Microprocessor*.

CPU clock The *pulse* source that triggers each activity within a *CPU* (Cen-

tral Processor Unit). The pulse generator circuit for a *microprocessor* is either:

(a) within the microprocessor *chip* itself, so that only a synchronising crystal must be connected to the chip;

or

(b) external to the chip, e.g. an *astable multivibrator* which is crystal controlled.

CPU clock speeds vary from 1 MHz to 16 MHz. Normally several CPU clock pulses are required to operate each *instruction*.

Crash A catastrophic malfunction of a *computer*, e.g. when the operator cannot gain access to its facilities. Normally a crash is caused by faulty *software*. Typically a *program* loops uncontrollably. Faulty *hardware*, e.g. corruption of the program in *RAM*, can also cause a crash.

A crash can be overcome normally by operator action, e.g. restart the computer or reload the main program (*operating system*) from *disk* into *memory*. See *Bootstrap*.

CRC See *Cyclic Redundancy Check*.

Cross-assembler An *assembler* that generates *machine code* for a *CPU* which is a different type to that used for the assembly process.

Often cross-assemblers are available on *mainframe computers* or *minicomputers* in order to assemble (generate machine code) *programs* for a microprocessor. Alternatively a *microcomputer* that is used for program development may offer cross-assemblers for one or more assembly languages for different microprocessors.

Cross-compiler A *compiler* that generates *machine code* for a *CPU* that is a different type to that used in the compilation process.

See *Cross-assembler*.

Cross-talk Electrical noise that is generated in a signal from an adjacent conductor that carries a different signal. Cross-talk can occur in *data* transmission cables.

CRT (Cathode Ray Tube) A display device that is commonly used with *computers* to present information to an operator. The well-established CRT, which for generations has performed the display role in domestic television receivers, is the most flexible display device for computer applications also.

A common method of driving a CRT directly from a *microcomputer memory* (*RAM*) is shown in Fig. 46.

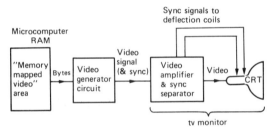

FIG. 46. CRT driven by microcomputer.

The picture information is held as a series of *bytes* (typically a total of 8K) in the microcomputer memory. A *video generator* circuit extracts bytes from memory (under *DMA* control) and generates a video waveform. This is passed to the tv (television) monitor, where it is amplified and passed to the CRT cathode, which modulates the intensity of the electron beam as it scans across the phosphor screen. The X and Y coil deflection signals are generated from the sync signals which are separated from the video waveform.

The same basic arrangement is applied

when a television receiver is driven from a microcomputer, e.g. in a home computer application. The only difference is that the video signal is modulated onto a UHF carrier before it is connected to the aerial socket of the television receiver. The television tuner provides demodulation to pass the video signal to the video amplifier before application to the CRT. A wide range of monochrome and colour, text and *graphics* displays are possible with CRTs.

See also *Memory mapped video, Raster scan, Video signal* and *Video generator*.

CRT controller A circuit that generates a *video signal* for a *CRT*. Display information is extracted from *microcomputer memory* by a CRT controller and converted into a conventional television video waveform. Several manufacturers offer a single *chip* that can perform this function.

For a full description of the circuit operation see ·*Video generation*. Refer also to *Memory mapped video*.

Crystal A quartz crystal that resonates at a specific frequency. The main application of a crystal is as a device which controls the frequency of an oscillator, particularly a *CPU clock* generator circuit. A typical crystal-controlled *CPU* clock circuit is shown in Fig. 47.

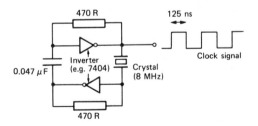

FIG. 47. Crystal-controlled clock generator circuit.

The crystal locks the frequency to a precise value to give accurate and repeatable timing within the CPU.

CTC (Counter/Timer Chip) See *Counter/timer*.

Current tracer
A hand-held fault-finding tool that is applied with *printed circuit boards*. The diagram in Fig. 48 illustrates its application.

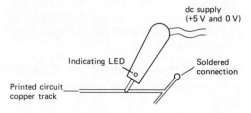

FIG. 48. Current tracer.

The device has an inductive tip which is placed against a copper track on the board under test. *Pulses* are detected and are slowed down before passing to the indicating *LED*. Thus fast pulses can be indicated visually.

This tool has application in any *digital* circuit, e.g. a *microcomputer* or *gate* circuit. Pulses can be injected (see *Logic pulser*) at any point and traced through interconnecting copper tracks through different parts of the succeeding circuit. The device is particularly useful for locating short-circuits across copper tracks, and for identifying *chips* which develop faulty open-circuit or short-circuit inputs.

Cursor
A small area of light that indicates the *CRT* screen position at which *characters* which are entered by the operator will appear. Normally the cursor is a flashing square of light and has the same size as a character which is displayed.

CUTS (Computer Users Tape System)
The standard specification for *data* storage on *audio cassette* recorders. *Logic* 1 and logic 0 are stored as short bursts of different frequency sinewaves.

For a full description of the signal specification see *Kansas standard*; this is the more common name for the specification.

Cycle stealing
The process by which *computer input/output* circuits use part of the "*machine cycle*" (i.e. time for the execution of a *program instruction*) to perform *data* transfers directly between input/output and *memory*. These *DMA* (direct memory access) transfers occur when the *CPU* is not using the three *buses*, i.e. during "*dead time*" on the buses.

Cycle time
The time for a *memory* device to complete a *read* or *write* function; an alternative name is "*access time*".

Figure 49 demonstrates the timing for a *ROM chip*.

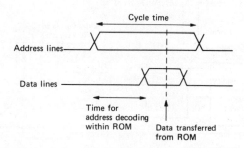

FIG. 49. Cycle time for memory read from ROM.

The CPU sets the selected memory address on the *address bus*. A short time (typically 300 nsec) is required for the ROM chip to decode the address and select the required location. Data is then presented onto the *data bus*. The total cycle time is typically 500 nsec. *RAM* possesses lower access time, whilst *floppy disk* is far higher (e.g. 50 msec).

Cyclic redundancy check (CRC)
A method of error detection with blocks of transmitted *data*. It serves the same purpose as a *checksum*, but is more

difficult to generate and more reliable in detecting errors.

A CRC data value is generated at the transmission end by dividing the data pattern of *bits* by a *binary* polynomial; the remainder is the CRC *character*. At the receiving end, the complete message (data plus CRC character) is divided by the same binary polynomial. A result of zero indicates error-free transmission.

See *Cartridge tape*.

D

D/A   See *Digital to analogue converter*.

DAC   See *Digital to analogue converter*.

Daisy chain   A connection system in which signal conductors are linked from one electronic module to another. Figure 50 demonstrates this arrangement for a *bus* system that is linked to several *memory* or *input/output* boards.

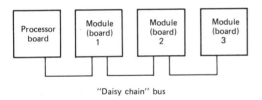

"Daisy chain" bus

FIG. 50. Example of daisy chain connection system.

Daisy wheel printer   A *printer* that employs a printing head which consists of a wheel of preformed *characters* supported on spokes. A daisy wheel printer gives high-quality printing, but is relatively slow in operation, e.g. 50 characters per second (cf. 100 characters per second or more for a *matrix printer*).

Darlington driver   A circuit that provides a high current drive capability in order to switch electrical devices such as a solenoid, relay, motor (small) or lamp. The circuit is an *open collector driver*, i.e. an external load must be supplied. A typical application of a Darlington driver is to interpose a *microcomputer output port* and a remote high-

current device (up to 500 mA drive current).

Typically seven or eight driver stages are supported on the same *integrated circuit*.

Data   A generalised term that can describe numbers, characters or facts in a manner that is suitable for processing by humans or machines. Normally data are numerical representations for items of information.

In *computer* applications the term is often used to describe *binary* numbers or character lists (usually in *ASCII*) and to distinguish them from *programs*. Thus areas of *memory* and *disk files* are defined as holding either programs or data.

Data acquisition   The collection of *data* from external equipment, normally *analogue* sensors. Commonly a data acquisition system consists of a multi-channel analogue input system, which connects to a *computer*, as shown in Fig. 51.

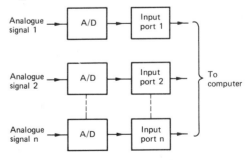

FIG. 51. Analogue input data acquisition system.

In this arrangement each analogue transducer signal (representing temperature, level, weight, etc.) passes through a separate *A/D* (analogue to digital converter) and *input port*. Refer to *Multiplexing* for a description of an alternative arrangement which shares an A/D and input port amongst several analogue signals.

Effectively it "points to" the memory location that is to be accessed, and *indirect addressing* is applied as follows:

```
LXI H,2000H      ;Load HL register-pair with
                  memory address hex. 2000
MVI A,M          ;Move from memory
                  (indicated by contents of HL)
                  into A register — indirect
                  addressing
```

Data base The main collection of *data files* that is used by *programs* within a *computer* system. A data base may be as small as a simple *data table* which is held in *memory* or it may be as large as a series of data files which are *disk* based.

Data bus A set of signal lines that carry *data*. The most common application of a data bus is within a *microcomputer*, where it forms one of the three system buses — *address bus, control bus* and data bus. The latter, which is *bidirectional* and *tri-state*, is used to carry data (*program instructions* or data values, which are normally numbers or *characters*) in *binary* form between *CPU* and *memory* or *input/output*.

The data bus consists of 8 lines for an *8-bit microprocessor*, and normally 16 lines for a 16-bit microprocessor. However, in some 16-bit devices only 8 lines are used and 16-bit data values are transferred in two halves.

See *Microcomputer* and *CPU* for a description of the overall role of the data bus.

Data counter A term that is applied occasionally to describe a *CPU register* that is used to access *data* items in *memory*. This register is normally 16 *bits* wide in order to address 64K of memory.

An example of a data counter register is the HL register-pair (total of 16 bits) that is applied with the *Intel* 8080, Intel 8085 and *Zilog* Z80 *microprocessors*.

Data domain A method of examining the *digital* values of electronic signals only — their precise voltage levels and timing are ignored. The expression is often applied with a *logic analyser*, which is an item of test equipment that displays information in the "data domain".

Data encryption A technique of converting *data* items into a special code for security reasons. A special *input/output chip* is offered by several manufacturers, and this device fits into the *microcomputer address bus* and *data bus* in the normal manner for input/output chips (see *PIO* and *UART*). The device generates an 8-*bit* code for connection to a communication link, e.g. an *RS 232-C serial* link, or to a *backing store* (*hard disk* or *floppy disk*). The device is bidirectional, i.e. it performs encryption and decryption. An alternative name for this device is "data ciphering processor" or DES (Data Encryption System).

Data management The method of organisation of *data files* within a *business computer*. The term describes the method of access by the operator of *data files* of numbers, text (e.g. mailing lists, reports), etc.

Data processing The general name given to the process of manipulating information and *data* within a *computer*.

Data sheet The name given to the document that supports an electronic component, e.g. an *integrated circuit*, and describes its full technical specification. Typical operating parameters which are listed are:

(a) supply voltage range;
(b) operating temperature range;
(c) circuit family, e.g. *TTL*, *MOS* or *CMOS*;
(d) package type and pin identities;
(e) current levels;
(f) timing characteristics;
(g) applications.

Data table A list of *data* values held in *memory*. Many *programs* operate on a series of numbers or *characters*, and these are conveniently held in consecutive locations in memory.

DC regulator A device that generates a fixed dc voltage, normally for use as a power source for an electronic circuit. Typically the device is constructed in *integrated circuit* form, and it normally requires a heat sink to dissipate the heat energy which is generated.

A common circuit arrangement is shown in Fig. 52.

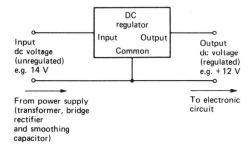

Fɪɢ. 52. DC regulator.

Dead-time The time during which conductors are not utilised for signal transfer. Specifically the "dead-time" on the three *buses* within a *microcomputer* is when the *CPU* is not utilising the buses for *data* transfer, i.e. when an *instruction* is applying only internal processing within the CPU.

Debouncing See *Contact bounce*.

Debug To locate and eliminate errors in a *computer program*. The word can also be applied to the process of fault-finding in a *hardware* circuit.

Debugger A *program* that is applied to debug a new and untested program. Invariably a program under development requires to be run and tested in sections. A debugger program, which is normally located in *ROM* or on *disk*, offers the following test facilities:

(a) execute to completion;
(b) execute to a *breakpoint*, i.e. run to a specific *instruction*;
(c) *single-step*, i.e. obey one instruction at a time;
(d) examine and alter *CPU registers*;
(e) examine and alter *memory* locations;
(f) *trace* a section of program, i.e. display the contents of all CPU registers after each instruction is implemented.

Decimal Pertaining to a *base* of 10. The normal human numbering system applies decimal numbers. *Computers* use *binary* numbers. An alternative name for decimal is "denary".

Declaration A statement that is applied in some *high-level languages* to establish *data* items and give attributes to them.

Decoder A conversion circuit that activates a single output for a particular coded input.

The operation of a "2 to 4" decoder is shown in Fig. 53.

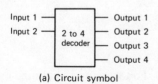

(a) Circuit symbol

Input 2	Input 1	Ouput 4	Output 3	Output 2	Output 1
0	0	0	0	0	1
0	1	0	0	1	0
1	0	0	1	0	0
1	1	1	0	0	0

(b) Truth table

FIG. 53. 2 to 4 decoder.

Only one of the four outputs can be set to 1 at any time; the particular output selected is determined by the *binary* code on the two input signals. This device is available as an SN74139 *chip*.

Another common decoder *integrated circuit* is a 3 to 8 decoder, which is available as an SN74138 chip — refer to *Truth table* for a description of its operation. The next stage in the decoding hierarchy is a 4 to 16 decoder, but a 4 to 10 decoder (e.g. the SN74145), which does not use the final six codes, is more common.

The most frequent application of a decoder is to generate *chip select* signals for a range of *memory* chips or *input/output* chips that may be connected into a *microcomputer* — see *Address decoding*.

Decrement To subtract 1 from a number. Virtually every *microprocessor* possesses a decrement *instruction*, which operates on the contents of a *CPU register*. Frequently the contents of a *memory* location can also be decremented. A decrement instruction is used frequently at the bottom of a *program*

loop, in which a loop count within a register is decremented to zero.

Dedicate To reserve an item of equipment for a single purpose.

Default To assign a predefined *data* value to a *variable* in a *program* in the absence of an action or statement to the contrary.

Delimiter A special *character* that is used to signify the boundary of a particular section of an operator command to a *computer*. Operation of the space key on a *keyboard* often acts as a delimiter, e.g. the command:

TYPE CRUNCH . ASM

Delimiter (space)   Delimiter (period)

causes the program named CRUNCH. ASM to be displayed. The first delimiter ("space") marks the end of the *software* function (TYPE, or display a *program* listing) that is required. The second delimiter ("period", or the full-stop character) marks a subdivision within the overall program name CRUNCH.ASM; it indicates the end of the program name (CRUNCH) and the start of the program file version (ASM, or *assembly language* version).

De Morgan's rules Two standard rules of *boolean logic* which specify relationships between the *AND* and *OR* functions, as follows:

(a) $\overline{A.B} = \overline{A} + \overline{B}$

Expressed in written form, this rule states that NOT(A AND B) is equivalent to (NOT A) OR (NOT B).

(b) $\overline{A+B} = \overline{A}.\overline{B}$

Similarly, this rule states that NOT(A OR B) is equivalent to (NOT A) AND (NOT B).

In each case A and B can both have either *binary* values 0 or 1. *NOT* is simply an inversion function.

These rules can be verified by the use of *truth tables*. The particular value of the rules is that entire logic or gating systems can be built using only one type of *gate* — a NAND (inverting AND) or a NOR (inverting OR). If only NOR gates are used, the AND and NAND functions can be generated using rule (a), whilst if only NAND gates are used, the OR and NOR functions can be generated using rule (b). Consider the gating system of Fig. 54 as an example.

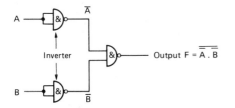

FIG. 54. Gating system applying de Morgan's rule (b).

de Morgan's rule (b) states: $\overline{A+B} = \overline{A}.\overline{B}$
Inverting both sides gives: $A+B = \overline{\overline{A}.\overline{B}}$

which is the function of the circuit, thus producing an OR operation.

Denary An alternative name for *decimal*.

Desktop computer A single-user microcomputer that is conveniently mounted on a table or desk. The name is not normally applied to describe a *home computer*, which uses a domestic television receiver for operator display purposes. Rather it is used to describe a *business computer* or a computer that is used for scientific applications. A *floppy disk* or *hard disk* is used as a *backing store*. Typical business microcomputers are listed in Table 5.

This list is for example purposes only and it is by no means exhaustive; a much larger range of machines is offered by a large number of manufacturers. Prices range from £500 to several thousand pounds. More expensive machines include *printer*, good quality terminal (*VDU*) and perhaps even a hard disk replacing the standard floppy disk.

Development system See *Microprocessor development system* (MDS).

Device The name often given to a *peripheral*.

Model	Manufacturer	CPU	Memory	Disk(floppy)
Apple	Apple	6502	64K–128K	140K
CBM 8000	Commodore	6502	32K–96K	150K
TRS80 model 100	Tandy	Z80	64K	–
CBM 700	Commodore	6509	128K–896K	340K
Cromemco C10	Comart	Z80	64K	380K
Sharp MZ80B	Sharp	Z80	64K	280K
RML 380Z	Research Machines	Z80	32K–56K	144K
Superbrain	Icarus	Z80	64K	160K
IBM	IBM	8088	64K–512K	640K
Sirius	ACT	8088	48K–896K	2400K
Rainbow	DEC	8088	64K–256K	800K

Table 5. Typical business (desktop) microcomputers.

Diagnostic A facility that aids the detection of a fault or malfunction. Normally the term describes a *program* that tests part of the *hardware* of a *computer* system, e.g.

(a) *RAM* test — writes all 1s and 0s into all RAM *memory* locations and confirms by a read operation;
(b) exercise a *printer* by generating a test message;
(c) test a write and read cycle for a block of test *data* to *floppy disk* or *hard disk*.

Difference/Differential amplifier See *Transistor differential amplifier*.

Digit Each individual symbol within a number system. In the *decimal* (*base* 10) system there are 10 digits — 0 to 9. In the *binary* (base 2) system there are only two digits — 0 and 1. The base of a number must be specified (or understood) if that number is expressed in digits.

Digital Possessing discrete states. Electronic digital systems, e.g. *computers*, operate using only two states, i.e. in *binary*. The most common electrical signals that represent these states are:

1 = +5 V
0 = 0 V

but other voltage levels are possible — see *Positive logic* and *Negative logic*.

Digital cassette A magnetic storage medium for use with *computers*. Digital cassettes are descended from *audio cassettes* and are offered in two sizes:

(a) 720K *bytes* (282 feet, 0.15 inch tape);
(b) 200K bytes (100 feet, 0.15 inch tape) — called "mini-cassettes".

Whilst audio cassettes store *bits* as bursts of different frequency sinewaves, digital cassettes employ the *phase encoding* method of bit storage. Digital cassettes can store far more information than audio cassettes and are faster and more reliable. However, they are more expensive.

Both types of cassettes are "sequential access", i.e. after rewind the whole of the early part of a tape must be driven past the read/write head if the required *program* or *data file* is stored partway through the tape (e.g. if several programs are stored on the tape). For this reason cassettes are quite unsuitable for quick-access bulk storage with a computer — the *floppy disk* and *hard disk* give fast "random access" (access time typically 20 msec compared with 20 sec for cassette). Application of digital cassettes is therefore limited, e.g. for system program reload with a *minicomputer*.

See also *Cartridge tape*.

Digital to analogue converter (D/A) Converts a *digital* representation of a signal, as used in a *computer*, into an *analogue* signal. The analogue signal may be used to feed into an industrial control system (e.g. a *servo*), to a *plotter* or pen recorder. A typical circuit arrangement is shown in Fig. 55.

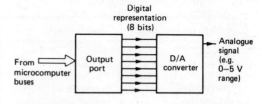

FIG. 55. Connection of D/A converter to microcomputer.

The single-chip D/A converter (normally a *resistor ladder D/A*) is connected to an *output port*, and it continually updates the analogue signal in response to changes in the digital *bit* pattern. 10-bit and even 12-bit D/A devices are available if greater resolution is required.

Digital voltmeter (DVM) A
multi-function item of test equipment which is *digital* in operation. Recent DVMs are *microprocessor*-based, and are usually battery-driven portable devices. The following electrical characteristics can be measured:

(a)   voltage (dc and ac);
(b)   current (dc and ac);
(c)   resistance;
(d)   transistor characteristics (occasionally).

In more powerful versions, averaging of several readings and self-calibration may be available.

Digitise To generate a *digital* representation of an *analogue* quantity. See *Analogue to digital converter*.

DIL (Dual-in-line) package The
standard *integrated circuit* package. Figure 56 illustrates the physical appearance and pin numbering arrangement.

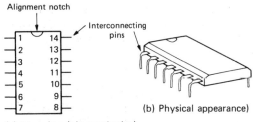

(a) Plan view (pin numbering)

Fɪɢ. 56. DIL (Dual-in-line) package.

Direct access A *memory* device or
storage system in which access is immediate and independent of the previous location accessed. It is synonymous with *random access*. *ROM*, *RAM* and disk (*floppy disk* and *hard disk*) are all direct

access; *magnetic tape* (audio and digital) is not.

Direct addressing The most common *addressing mode* that is applied
within a *program instruction*. In direct addressing a *data* item is accessed directly in a *CPU register* or in any *memory* location, as follows (using *Intel 8085 assembly language mnemonics*):

(a)   Direct register addressing, e.g.
MOV A,D
moves the contents of the D register to the A register. Both source and destination addressing modes are "direct register".
(b)   Direct memory addressing, e.g.
STA 4020H
moves (stores) the contents of the A register into memory location *hexadecimal* 4020. The destination (memory location hexadecimal 4020) is referenced by "direct memory" addressing; the source (A register) is direct register addressing.

Notice that some manufacturers use the term "direct addressing" when the instruction contains the memory address where the data value is located. This addressing mode is better known by the name *"absolute addressing"*.

Direct memory access (DMA)
Data transfer between *memory* and *input/ output* without intervention by the *CPU*. Figure 57 shows the action of DMA using the three-block diagram of a *microcomputer*.

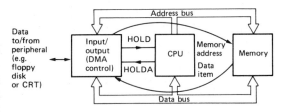

Fɪɢ. 57. DMA transfer within a microcomputer.

The transfer of a block of data items, e.g. 128 *bytes*, from memory to a peripheral device is as follows:

(a) the DMA input/output circuit (often a single *chip*) generates the HOLD signal to the CPU;
(b) the CPU responds with the HOLDA (HOLD acknowledge) when it does not require to use the buses (*address bus, data bus* and *control bus* — the latter is not shown for simplicity);
(c) the DMA input/output circuit assumes control of the buses, and sets the memory address of the first data item (byte) to be transferred on the address bus;
(d) the data item is passed out of memory along the data bus and directly into the input/output circuit, i.e. the CPU is by-passed.

The sequence is repeated as necessary in order to transfer the entire block of data items.

In some microcomputers *program* operation is delayed whilst DMA transfers occur. In other microcomputers data transfers occur during *dead-time* on the buses, and normal CPU execution is not affected and no delays occur. This method of performing DMA transfers is sometimes referred to as *cycle stealing*, and is in contrast to "burst DMA" in which the CPU is suspended continuously until the complete block transfer under DMA is completed.

Typical peripheral devices that operate under DMA control are *floppy disk* and *hard disk* and *video generation* to a *CRT*.

Directory The list of all *programs* or *files* within a *computer* system. Most *operating systems* (the main program in a *disk*-based computer) contain a facility which the operator can call in order to display the system directory on his *CRT* or *VDU*.

Disable Inhibit the function of a *hardware* module, e.g. an *interrupt* signal.

Dis-assembler A program that generates *assembly language instructions* from *machine code*. This is the reverse of the far more common process of converting an assembly language *program* into machine code using an *assembler* in preparation for running the program within the *computer*. However a dis-assembler operation may be useful if a machine code program requires debugging; it is far easier for a programmer to follow the operation of a program which is listed in assembly language rather than in machine code.

Disk A bulk storage device that acts as a *backing store* for a *computer*. A disk store is either *floppy disk* or *hard disk*.

Diskette A name that is given occasionally to a small 5¼-inch *floppy disk*. The alternative larger size (8 inch) is termed simply a "disk".

The construction of a diskette, which is loaded into a floppy disk drive unit when it is required for use within a *computer* system, is shown in Fig. 58.

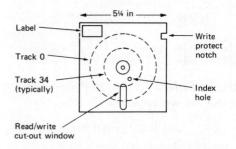

FIG. 58. Construction of 5¼-inch diskette.

Information is stored in concentric circles called "tracks". Each track contains several "*sectors*" (1 sector = 128 *bytes* normally). The write protect notch must be covered to prevent write operations,

e.g. if important *programs* or *data files* held on the diskette must not be overwritten.

Typically 128K bytes are held on a single-sided *single-density* diskette. Data are recorded with a density of 2581 *bits* per inch.

An alternative name for a 5¼-inch floppy disk is a "mini-disk".

Displacement The number of *words* that must be skipped in a *program* when a *conditional jump instruction* is obeyed if *relative addressing* is used. The number of words can be negative or positive. Refer to *Relative addressing* for a full description.

Display A device that conveys information in a transitory form to an operator. The most common display systems applied with *computers* are optoelectronic in operation, as follows:

(a) *LED* (Light Emitting Diode) — conveys one *bit* of information, e.g. ON/OFF.

(b) *CRT* — can display several thousand *characters* or a graphical representation of information to an operator.

(c) *Segment display* — can display a multi-digit number or, if a large number of segments are used, letters also.

Distributed processing A multi-*computer* system in which each computer performs a separate and dedicated task. Such a system has several advantages over a single-computer system, e.g. faster response, greater throughput, improved security/reliability (if one computer fails the main functions in the overall system can still be used).

The principle of operation of a distributed processing system is shown in Fig. 59.

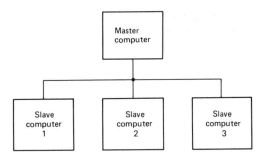

FIG. 59. Distributed processing system.

Normally one computer (the master computer) controls the system. Each slave computer performs an autonomous and dedicated function, but a communication channel, which may be a *serial* link or a *common bus*, links each slave to the master. Information can flow, therefore, from slave to slave under control of the master.

Typical systems which conform to this hierarchy arrangement may be:

(a) *Minicomputer* for master, *microcomputers* for slaves. For example, an industrial control application may use a minicomputer to operate a centralised factory data collection and display system, perhaps using several *VDUs* and *printers*, and microcomputers for data collection and control on individual processes.

(b) Microcomputers for each module in the system. The master machine may be *disk* based, whilst the slaves could be single-*chip* (*CPU, ROM, RAM, input/output* on a single *IC*) devices and could control single external control systems or even single *peripherals* (e.g. *plotter*). See *Local area network*.

Divide The normal arithmetic process of numerical division, as applied in *computers* using *binary* numbers. 8-*bit microprocessors* do not possess a divide *instruction* whilst 16-bit devices do. If a divide instruction is not available, division can be implemented by *software* as repeated subtraction of the divisor from the dividend.

Division of binary numbers by hand is demonstrated as follows:

$$\begin{array}{r} 11 \\ 0100\overline{)1101} \\ 100 \\ \hline 101 \\ 100 \\ \hline 1 \end{array}$$

Divisor→ 0100, ← Quotient (11), ← Dividend (1101), ← Remainder (1)

Thus $1101 \div 0100 = 11$ remainder 1 (in binary).

Expressed in *decimal:*

$$13 \div 4 = 3 \text{ remainder } 1$$

DMA See *Direct memory access.*

DOS (Disk Operating System)

The master *program* in a *disk* based *computer*. See *Operating system.*

Dot matrix A method of constructing *characters* using an array of dots. Character generation on a *CRT* and on a *matrix printer* is achieved using this technique. Consider the construction of the letter R in Fig. 60.

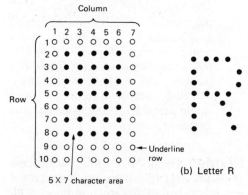

5 X 7 character area

(a) 5 X 7 matrix (in 7 X 10 frame)

(b) Letter R

FIG. 60. Dot matrix character construction.

Apart from the underline row, a spare column and row around the character area allows spacing between characters on the CRT or printer.

Double density (disk) A measure of the packing density of *bits* stored on a *floppy disk*. Either single or double density is used. Double density recording has the following specification:

(a) 8 inch disk —packing density = 6400 bits per inch
data transfer rate = 500K bits per second

(b) 5¼-inch diskette — packing density = 5162 bits per inch
data transfer rate = 250K bits per second

Double density recording for the diskette is rarely used.

See *Single density (disk).*

Double precision arithmetic

The use of two *words* to represent a number. Some *8-bit microprocessors*, e.g. the *Zilog* Z80, possess a facility to perform arithmetic using double-length (uses two *CPU registers* for each number) numbers.

See also *Floating point* arithmetic.

Download Transfer a *program* or *data file* from one *computer* to another. An example of a download operation is the transfer of a program that has been written and tested on a *development system* into a second microcomputer for execution. The second microcomputer may perform a simple *EPROM* programming function. The method of connection between machines is normally a *serial* link (*RS 232-C*).

Drive The electric motor that causes rotation in a *backing store* device, e.g. *floppy disk, hard disk* or *cassette* recorder. However, the term is often used to describe the entire peripheral device.

Driver A circuit that enables a signal to pass to succeeding circuits or long interconnections with reduced electrical deterioration. Drivers are often required to generate sufficient electrical power (e.g. high current) or to avoid timing problems.

Line driver *ICs* are frequently required with transmission lines in order to eliminate *data* errors caused by electrical noise and timing problems.

See *Bus driver* and *Open collector driver*.

Dry joint Faulty soldered connection. A common fault with *printed circuit boards* is that a soldered connection, e.g. a component wire connection to a copper track, fractures due to substandard soldering when the board is manufactured.

D-type bistable A single-input clocked *bistable multivibrator* or *flip-flop*. Figure 61 demonstrates the operation.

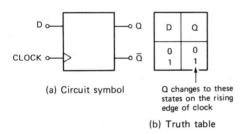

(a) Circuit symbol

D	Q
0	0
1	1

Q changes to these states on the rising edge of clock

(b) Truth table

FIG. 61. D-type bistable.

The data *bit* (0 or 1) present on the input is transferred to the output on the rising edge of the CLOCK signal. A typical D-type *IC* is the SN7474, which consists of two such circuits on the same *chip*.

D-type bistables are employed in storage *registers* and *shift registers*.

Dual-in-line package See *DIL package*.

Dual slope A/D See *Integrating A/D*.

Dump To transfer the contents of a block of *memory* locations to a *peripheral*. Frequently it is required to dump a *program* or *data* area in *computer memory* to a *backing store* or to a *printer*.

Duplex Bidirectional *data* flow along a *serial* communication link. The method of serial connection (*RS 232-C*) between two *computers* can be:

(a) *full duplex*, i.e. data can pass in both directions simultaneously;

(b) half duplex, i.e. data can only pass in one direction at a time — in this arrangement one computer acts as the master and the other as the slave.

Contrast with *Simplex*.

DVM See *Digital voltmeter*.

Dynamic memory A memory device in which stored *bits* must be regularly refreshed to prevent corruption. The only device that exhibits this characteristic is one of the two basic types of *RAM*. Refer to *RAM* for a full description.

E

EAROM (Electrically Alterable Read Only Memory)

A *ROM* that can be modified electrically whilst connected in-circuit. Effectively, therefore, it acts like a *RAM* with long write times, e.g. 10 msec erase time plus 1 msec write time.

EAROMs are used in applications which require a non-volatile *memory* and which also require that modifications to the contents of memory locations may be required occasionally. However, EAROMs require several different dc voltage supplies and also supporting circuitry. For these reasons RAM (probably low-power *CMOS*), with battery back-up, is a more common arrangement for non-volatile read/write memory applications.

EBDIC (Extended Binary Coded Decimal Interchange Code)

An 8-*bit* code (gives 256 *characters*) that can be applied to transmit *binary data*. It is not as popular as the *ASCII* code.

Echo

The action by *computer software* of returning a *character* that is entered on a keyboard back to the *CRT* display.

ECL (Emitter Coupled Logic)

A *bipolar family* of *logic* and gating circuits. The other two principal bipolar families are *TTL* and I^2L. ECL offers the advantage of being the fastest technology of all, e.g. switching speed of 2 nsec. Unfortunately circuit packing density is low and power consumption is high, and therefore the *MOS* and *CMOS unipolar* families dominate for complex circuitry. However, ECL is used in *mainframe computers* and *minicomputers* when speed is a prime requirement.

In most other logic families *transistors* are held in either a fully-saturated ON or a fully-saturated OFF state. ECL attains higher switching speeds because the transistors are never fully saturated.

Figure 62 demonstrates the circuit operation of an ECL *OR* (and *NOR*) gate.

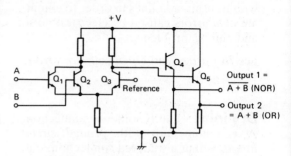

Fig. 62. ECL OR and NOR gate.

If either A or B (or both) goes high, then transistor Q_1 or Q_2 (or both) switches on, i.e. it conducts and its output goes low. This sends Q_4 off and Q_5 on. When both A and B are low, Q_4 and Q_5 are in the opposite state.

This ECL circuit is manufactured in *IC* form.

Edge triggering

The activation of a circuit at the edge (positive-going or negative-going) of a triggering *pulse*. *Bistables* (or *flip-flops*) are commonly edge-triggered circuits, as shown in Fig. 63.

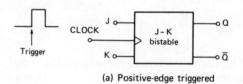

(a) Positive-edge triggered

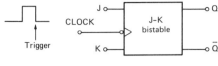

(b) Negative-edge triggered

FIG. 63. Edge-triggered bistable.

In (a) the bistable outputs change (as dictated by the states of the J and K inputs) only on the positive edge of the CLOCK pulse. In (b) triggering occurs when the CLOCK pulse is negative-going. Alternative names for these level transitions are *rising edge* and *falling edge*. Refer to *J-K bistable*.

Some bistables are level-triggered, i.e. they are activated at any time whilst the trigger signal is at the required level (1 or 0).

Edit To modify a *program* or *data file*. Much of a programmer's time is spent using an *editor* program in a *disk*-based *computer* in order to enter and amend his new or incorrect program.

Editor A *program* that allows a *computer* operator to enter a new program and to modify an existing program. Whilst an editor is designed to process any generalised text *file*, it is commonly used within a *development system* to process an *assembly language* program.

The main facilities within an editor are:

(a) commence entry of a new file;
       or
       read an existing file from *disk*, and display that file on a *CRT*;
(b) delete lines;
(c) insert lines;
(d) correct part of a line (program instruction);
(e) write the file to disk;
(f) merge (concatenate) two files.

A *word processor* program, whose main function is to create and edit text files such as letters and reports, can also be used with many *disk*-based computers in the same way as an editor in order to enter and modify programs.

Effective address The *memory* address that is derived in an *instruction* as a result of employing an *addressing mode* such as *indirect addressing* or *indexed addressing*.

Eight-bit microprocessor The most common type of *microprocessor* that processes *data* and *program instructions* in 8-*bit* form.

The most popular 8-bit devices are:

(a) *Intel* 8080;
(b) *Intel* 8085;
(c) *Zilog* Z80;
(d) *MOS Technology* 6502;
(e) *Motorola* 6800 (and the 6809).

Elapsed time The total time taken for a *program* to complete its function. This may be longer than the actual execution time of the program.

Electromagnetic interference Unwanted electrical signals that can be generated in circuits from external sources. Such electrical noise signals can be one of two types:

(a) *series mode;*
(b) *common mode.*

Electronic mail The passing of messages between *computers*. The British Telecom Gold system allows computer *terminals* to consult personal mailboxes over the telephone network.

Electrostatic storage A storage device that stores *data bits* as electrostatically charged areas on a dielectric surface.

Emitter coupled logic See *ECL*.

Emulator A system that simulates the operation of another system. Typically one *microcomputer* imitates the action of another using the same *program*, the same *data* and as far as possible the same *hardware*, e.g. *input/output* circuits.

A common application of an emulation process is when the operation of a small prototype microcomputer (e.g. a single board) is emulated on a *microprocessor development system* — see *In-circuit emulator*.

Enable An input signal that activates the function of a particular device or circuit. See *Chip select*.

Encoder A conversion circuit that generates a code that is determined by the setting of one of several input lines. The SN74148 is a 16-pin *IC* which encodes 8 input *bits*, i.e. it is an 8 to 3 encoder. Whichever input line is set causes a 3-bit *binary* code to be generated.

Encoders are not as frequently applied as *decoders*, which are used for *address decoding* and chip selection within *microcomputers*. One application for an encoder is the generation of a 3-bit *interrupt* code when 1 of 8 discrete interrupt lines is set within a microcomputer; the 3-bit code feeds directly to the *microprocessor*.

Encryption See *Data encryption*.

End-Around carry The arrangement within a *computer's ALU* when a carry generated in the most significant *bit* position in a *CPU register* is passed back into the least significant position. This is not commonly applied.

Enhancement An improved feature that is added to a *program*.

Entry point The point in a *program* or a *routine* (part of a program) to which program control can be passed. Some programs possess several entry points, and a calling program must perform various checks before transferring to the correct entry point.

Epitaxial Part of the circuit fabrication technique that is employed to make *planar* epitaxial circuits. Virtually all *integrated circuits*, e.g. *TTL*, *MOS* and *CMOS*, are constructed using the planar technology.

A high resistivity n epitaxial layer is deposited on top of a thick substrate of n^+ silicon in the manufacture of TTL circuits, as shown in Fig. 64.

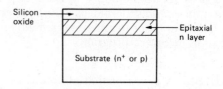

FIG. 64. Epitaxial layer in a planar epitaxial circuit.

The different regions of n and p silicon which are required to construct circuit components, e.g. *transistors*, are then diffused into the epitaxial area using a process of masking and diffusion. See *Planar* and *Bipolar transistor*.

EPROM (Erasable Programmable Read Only Memory) A *PROM* that can be reprogrammed. An EPROM *IC* has a distinctive physical appearance because it contains an erasing window, such that UV (ultraviolet) light can shine through directly onto the silicon *chip* during erasure. An EPROM is used in place of a *ROM* or PROM chip when it is anticipated that it may be required to alter the *program* (and/or *data*) which it contains.

Each storage *bit* in a *MOS* EPROM is based on the use of a floating avalanche gate *FET* (field effect transistor), as shown in Fig. 65.

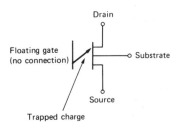

FIG. 65. EPROM — bit storage in a floating avalanche gate FET.

An electric charge can be trapped in the gate, between the drain and source. When UV light is applied during erasure, the initial uncharged state of the gate is restored.

The most popular EPROM is the 2716; the pin layout is shown in Fig. 66.

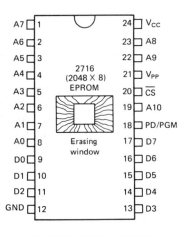

FIG. 66. 2716 EPROM (2K bytes).

The device offers *2K bytes* (i.e. it has a "memory organisation" of 2048 × 8). Thus 11 *address bus* lines and 8 *data bus* lines are connected, as well as a *chip select* line (CS). Apart from two dc supply lines (V_{CC} and GND), two additional signals are required:

(a) V_{PP} — a high voltage (+24 V) is connected to this pin when the device is "programmed" initially; a logic 1 (+5 V) is connected to this pin when the chip is placed in the final circuit.

(b) PD/PGM — this pin is pulsed to logic 1 for 50 msec when a *byte* is programmed (PGM = "programming"); it is set to logic 1 when the chip is placed in its final circuit so that the device operates in the power-down mode (PD = "power-down").

A pin-compatible ROM, e.g. a 2316, can be used in place of a 2716 EPROM in mass-produced applications to save cost — typically 4:1 price difference.

See *PROM programmer* and *EPROM eraser*.

EPROM eraser
A device that erases *EPROMs* by means of an UV (ultraviolet) light source. Figure 67 demonstrates the main features of an eraser.

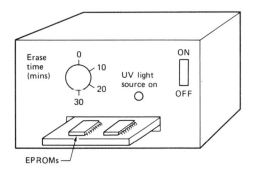

FIG. 67. EPROM Eraser.

When the tray is inserted and the UV light source switched on, erasure commences. 20 minutes is required typically to erase an EPROM. Great care must be taken to avoid contact of the UV light with the human eye, which can be damaged.

The UV light source wavelength is 2537 angstroms. It should be noted that direct sunlight can also cause erasure — approximately 1 week continuous exposure is required. Similarly fluorescent lighting over a period of 3 years has the same effect. Therefore it is important to cover the erasing window on an EPROM after programming with an opaque label or tape.

Equivalence A *Boolean logic* function that generates a 1 if corresponding *bits* in the two compared *data* values are 1s.

Erase To obliterate information in a storage device. See *EPROM eraser*.

Error correcting code A *data* code that employs additional *bits* in order to identify errors. See *ASCII* (parity bit).

EXCLUSIVE OR A logic function that generates a 1 only if the two operands are different, as shown in Table 6.

A	B	A $\oplus$ B
0	0	0
1	0	1
0	1	1
1	1	0

$\oplus$ means EXCLUSIVE OR

Table 6. Truth table for EXCLUSIVE OR function.

This function can be generated on two input *bits* using a *half-adder*. Most *microprocessors* possess an *instruction* that performs an EXCLUSIVE OR function on the contents of a *CPU register* and another multi-bit number, e.g.

XRI AAH ;EXCLUSIVE OR contents of A
register and *hexadecimal* AA

If A contains: 0000 1111
Hex. AA is: 1010 1010
Result is: 1010 0101

Notice that when a *data* item is EXCLUSIVE ORed with itself, the result is zero.

This instruction can be useful when it is required to monitor the state of an *input port*, and to check if any bit changes. A copy of the previous state of the port must be held in *memory*, and this can be compared with the present state by performing an input instruction followed by an EXCLUSIVE OR instruction.

Executable machine code The final version of a *program* before it is run in a *processor*. A program that is written in *assembly language* must be converted into *machine code* before it can be run within a *computer*. Often it also requires a *load* operation to transfer the machine code from *backing store* into the final area of *memory* where it is to reside before it is run. This final version in memory is described as the "executable machine code".

Execute To run a *program* within a *computer*.

The term is also applied to refer to the second half of the *fetch-execute cycle*, when a program *instruction* is implemented.

Execution time The time to implement a *program instruction*.

Executive The name given to the master *program* that runs all other programs in a *multi-programming computer*. This name is traditional with *minicomputers*. "Operating system" is the counterpart in *microcomputers*.

Exponent The power to which a number is to be raised in *floating point* representation. For example:

$$63{,}294 = 0.63294 \times 10^5$$

possesses an exponent of 5 — the power of the *base* 10 to which the *"mantissa"* (0.63294) is to be raised.

Extender card A component-less board that allows a circuit board to be mounted proud of its containing box so that test measurements can be made. Fig. 68 shows the arrangement.

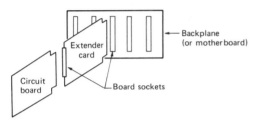

FIG. 68. Use of extender card.

Access to a circuit board for test probes, e.g. from a CRO or *DVM*, is often hampered by adjacent circuit boards. An extender card can be placed between the circuit board and its socket, so that test measurements can be made conveniently at any point on the board. The extender card simply consists of direct printed circuit connections from each input edge connector connection to the corresponding point on its board socket.

Care must be taken with the use of extender cards in *microcomputer* systems, because timing problems can be introduced, e.g. if a *CPU* board is placed on an extender card.

F

Falling edge The transition of a *logic* level from 1 to 0. The term is normally applied to *pulse* signals — the pulse possesses a *rising edge* and a falling edge. See *Edge triggering*.

Family A group of devices with a common function. Examples are:

(a) *integrated circuits* — the most common families are *TTL* and *MOS*;

(b) *microprocessors* — a manufacturer may well make more than one 8-*bit* device, and each device comprises one of a "family".

Fan-out The number of similar circuits that can be driven by a circuit. If a *gate* output signal can drive up to 10 equivalent gate inputs before overloading

occurs, then the fan-out is 10. Fan-outs for the most common *logic* circuit families are:

(a) *TTL* — 10;
(b) *MOS* — 50 or more;
(c) *CMOS* — 50 or more.

For this reason MOS and CMOS *integrated circuits* are more suitable for *microcomputer* construction because one MOS or CMOS *chip* can drive a large number of succeeding chips, e.g. a *microprocessor* can drive its *address bus* to a large number of *memory* and *input/output* chips.

FDM See *Frequency division multiplexing*.

Feedback

A system in which part of the output is connected back to the input. Feedback is applied in electronic amplifiers and control systems.

Ferranti Argus minicomputers

The most common British-made *minicomputer*. Two ranges have been produced — the Argus 500 and the Argus 700. The latter is a 16-*bit* machine with *core* or *semiconductor memory*, and offers a wide range of *peripherals*. Multiuser applications are principally in the process control field, e.g. petrochemical, steel, electricity generation.

Ferranti microprocessors

The only *microprocessors* offered by a British manufacturer. The F100L is a 16-*bit* device and is restricted to military application.

FET (Field effect transistor)

A *transistor* that uses the effect of an electric field applied transversely to a *silicon* wafer to vary the "conductance" (electrical conductivity) through the wafer. A FET is a *unipolar* (i.e. its operation depends on charge carriers of one polarity only) device compared with the conventional transistor which is *bipolar*, and it is the basic component in *MOS* and *CMOS* circuits.

The operation of the simple "junction gate FET", which is produced in a single-component package and can replace the conventional bipolar transistor in certain applications, is shown in Fig. 69.

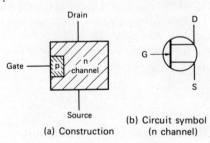

(a) Construction
(b) Circuit symbol (n channel)

FIG. 69. Junction gate FET.

Majority charge carriers flow from the source to the drain, and applying an increasing negative voltage to the gate causes the p area to effectively expand (creating a "depletion" layer) into the n region. This reduces the flow of current between source and drain.

A p channel device can be constructed in a similar manner.

The more common application of an FET is within a MOS or CMOS circuit. In this case the "insulated gate FET" (IGFET) is used, as shown in Fig. 70.

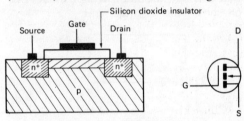

(a) Construction
(b) Circuit symbol

FIG. 70. Insulated gate FET (IGFET).

In this circuit the gate is electrically insulated from the n channel by a layer of silicon dioxide — this gives it its alternative name of MOS (Metal Oxide Silicon) transistor. Normally the device is operated in the "enhancement" mode, such that as the gate voltage goes more positive, the channel conductivity increases, i.e. the channel current is "enhanced".

For descriptions of the applications of FETs in MOS and CMOS circuits refer to *MOS, CMOS, ROM, RAM* and *EPROM*.

Fetch

Reading the next *instruction* from *memory*. The fetch operation is the first half of the *fetch/execute cycle*.

Fetch/Execute cycle

The two-stage process by which every *program instruction* is implemented within a *computer*, as follows:

(a) fetch — the instruction is fetched from *memory* and placed in the *CPU instruction register*;

(b) execute — the instruction *bit* pattern is examined and the instruction is implemented, e.g. memory transfer, *input/output* operations or *ALU* operations may be required.

The fetch process is identical for every instruction. The execute process is different for every different type of instruction.

Consider the following sample instruction:

SUI 4 ;Subtract (immediate) 4 from the A register (accumulator)

Assume that this is a two-*byte* instruction (D6 and 04) for an 8-*bit microprocessor* (e.g. the *Intel* 8085) and that it is held in memory at location *hexadecimal* 3000. The fetch/execute cycle for this instruction is illustrated in Fig. 71 — refer to *CPU* for a description of the main modules within the CPU.

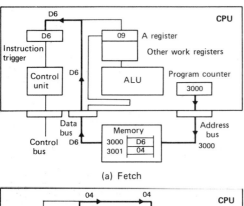

(a) Fetch

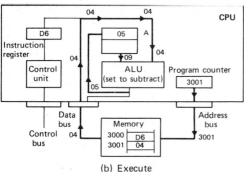

(b) Execute

FIG. 71. Fetch/execute cycle for SUI 4 (subtract 4 from A register).

The implementation of the instruction is as follows:

(a) The contents of the *program counter* are gated out of the *CPU* on the *address bus*. The first byte of the two-byte instruction is read from memory onto the *data bus* and passes into the CPU's *instruction register*.

(b) The *control unit* examines the instruction, and sends out control signals to implement it. Firstly the second byte of the instruction (the data value 04) is read from memory, and secondly the contents of the A register (assume 09) are gated to the *ALU*. The ALU is set to perform a subtraction process, such that the result (09 − 04 = 05) is passed back from the ALU to the A register.

At the conclusion of the instruction the program counter is incremented to 3002 to point to the next instruction in memory. The *CPU clock*, which feeds the control unit, triggers each stage in the fetch/execute cycle such that the CPU steps through memory implementing instruction after instruction.

Fibre optics A major branch of optoelectronics in which polymer and glass fibres are used to transfer information using the medium of light. The principle is demonstrated in Fig. 72.

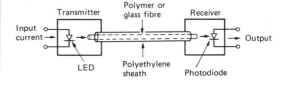

FIG. 72. Fibre optic data link.

When current passes through the transmitting *LED*, light is passed through the optic "cable" fibre (glass or polymer). A photodiode or phototransistor can be used to detect the light at the receiver. Total internal reflection prevents light loss, and the optic cable can therefore be curved.

Both *analogue* and *digital* signals can be transmitted. The former may be instrument signals, and a fibre optic transmission system offers the advantage over an electrical system of elimination of sparking fire hazards. The most important application, however, is for the transmission of telephone conversations in digital form. A major investment programme is planned by British Telecom to convert all telephone trunk traffic to fibre optic links. The particular advantages offered are:

(a)   increased bandwidth — thousands of conversations can be carried on a single fibre;
(b)   freedom from cross-talk and electromagnetic interference;
(c)   minimal losses;
(d)   low cable weight.

Field   Part of a *data* record. Examples are:

(a)   a few *bits* in a data *byte* may represent a particular item of information;
(b)   several bytes in a multi-byte *file* may represent summarising information, e.g. file length, file address;
(c)   specific parts of an *assembly language program instruction* may represent different functions within that instruction, e.g.

Label field	Mnemonic field	Operand field	Comment field
LOOP	MOV	A,C	;Transfer contents of C register to A register

Field effect transistor   See *FET*.

FIFO (First-in First-out) buffer

A *hardware* device that can store several *data* items, with data retrieval from it operating on a first-in, first-out basis. A FIFO is occasionally applied between an *input/output* device and a *microprocessor* to store data *bytes* which are transferred in *asynchronous* form. Figure 73 shows the use of a FIFO between a *UART*, which is used to receive data items in *serial* form and convert them to *parallel* form, and a microprocessor.

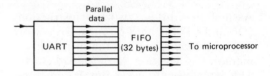

Fig. 73. Use of FIFO between UART and microprocessor.

A burst of serial data items (up to 32 8-bit *characters*) can be received and staticised in the FIFO *buffer*. The microprocessor can read these characters, at some later time, in the same order as they were placed into the buffer.

File   The generalised name for a block of information (a *program* or list of *data* items) which is memorised within a *computer*. *Disk*-based computers store a number of programs (in *machine code* and *high-level* and *assembly language* versions) as well as data lists, and each is referred to as a separate "file".

Firmware   A *program* based in *ROM*.

Fixed point number   A number representation in which the decimal (or *binary*) point has an assumed fixed position. Invariably this position is to the right of the least-significant digit. Consider the normal 8-*bit* binary representation in a *microcomputer*:

8-bit number | 0001 0010 | .

↑
Assumed binary point

Therefore this number is 18_{10} (*decimal* 18).

Fractional numbers can be represented in fixed point form as follows:

| 0000 0011 | . | 1010 0000 |

↑
Assumed binary point

This number is 3.625 in decimal. *Software* that operates on numbers which occupy two *bytes* in this way must be aware of the type of representation that is used.

Flag A *bit* that indicates a specific event or condition. Typical applications are:

(a) *Status register* within a *CPU* — this is a collection of *bistables*, each of which is a flag. These flags indicate the status, e.g. overflow, carry, zero, of the *ALU*.
(b) Indicator flag within a *UART* (*serial input/output* device) to show that a *character* has been received and can be read into the CPU.

Flip-flop The familiar name for a *bistable multivibrator*.

Floating The state when a circuit output is electrically isolated from the input to the succeeding circuit, even though it is physically connected to it. Many *microcomputer* circuits are *three-state*, i.e. each output signal can be 0, 1 or floating. The floating state is such that the output is at a very high impedance.

The *data bus* within a *microcomputer* is three-state, i.e. every device (*microprocessor, memory* or *input/output*) has three-state outputs. When no device is using the data bus, it is in the "floating" state.

Refer to *three-state* for a description of the selection of the floating state.

Floating gate The method of circuit construction that is applied with *FETs* that are used within an *EPROM*. Refer to *EPROM*.

Floating point number A method of representing large numbers using two components — the basic number and the power to which it must be raised. For example:

13,824 can be written as 0.13824×10^5

0.13824 is called the *mantissa*, and 5 is called the *exponent* (power of 10).

A typical floating point number representation within a *computer* is:

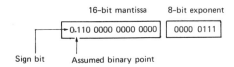

16-bit mantissa · 8-bit exponent

0.110 0000 0000 0000 | 0000 0111

Sign bit · Assumed binary point

This number is $0.625 \times 10^7 = 6,250,000$.

A wide range of variations to this three-*byte* representation are possible, e.g. a single-byte mantissa or an exponent with a *base* of 64 (e.g. 0100 0000 represents 10^0). In every case the floating point number is normalised to avoid multiple representations of the same number.

The type of representation used for a number held within a computer must be known before it is possible to decipher that number. The *software* that operates on it must know if it is double-byte floating point, triple-byte floating point, double-length *fixed point*, etc.

Floppy disk A *computer* bulk storage system that stores *data* on removable magnetic disks. A floppy disk system represents the most common *backing store* for *microcomputers*, and is illustrated in Fig. 74.

Floppy disk controller

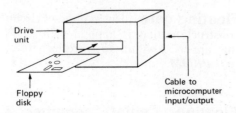

FIG. 74. Floppy disk.

The floppy disk is permanently contained within a protective paper envelope. The complete envelope is inserted into the drive unit, whose spindle grips the centre annulus of the disk and rotates it inside the paper envelope.

There are two standard floppy disk sizes — 8 inch and 5¼ inch (the latter is often called a "diskette"; refer to *Diskette* for a full description). The construction of an 8-inch disk is shown in Fig. 75.

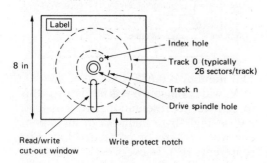

FIG. 75. 8-inch floppy disk.

Data are stored on concentric tracks. Each track is divided into several "*sectors*" — each sector is normally 128 *bytes*. The read/write *head* (or heads if both surfaces are used) comes into contact with the disk surface through the read/write cut-out window when the data transfer operations commence. The write protect notch must be uncovered to prevent write operations if it is required to prevent important *programs* and *data files* from being overwritten. The index hole is sensed optically in order to generate a synchronising signal.

Data are recorded with a density of 3200 *bits* per inch for single density recording and 6400 bits per inch for double density recording. A single-sided double-density disk can record typically 400K bytes. The method of bit storage for single-density recording is shown in Fig. 76, and is termed "frequency modulation" recording.

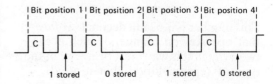

FIG. 76. Bit storage on floppy disk using frequency modulation recording.

A clock pulse C marks the start of each bit position. The presence or absence of a second pulse indicates a 1 or 0 bit stored respectively. For double-density recording no clock pulse is used, so that the number of magnetic flux reversals per inch is unaltered.

Floppy disk access time is governed by the following typical time components:

(a)   track-to-track access time = 8 msec;
(b)   head loading time = 35 msec;
(c)   one disk revolution time = 200 msec.

Therefore overall access times can vary from 35 msec to over 300 msec. Data transfer rates are typically 200K bits per second.

See *Floppy disk controller* and *IBM 3740*.

Floppy disk controller   A circuit that provides timing and sequence control signals for a *floppy disk* drive unit. A single *integrated circuit* is frequently applied to perform this function, as shown in Fig. 77.

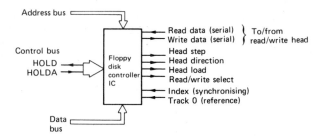

FIG. 77. Floppy disk controller.

The *chip* connects directly onto the *microcomputer's CPU buses* in the same manner as other *input/output* chips, e.g. *port, PIO, UART*. A control *program* sends the chip the required *track* and *sector* address as well as a marker *flag* indicating read or write operation. The chip then uses the Head step and Head direction signals to pulse a *stepper motor* which drives the read/write *head* to the required track. When the disk has rotated to the required sector, the Head load signal is set and the read/write head is placed in contact with the disk surface. Read or write operations can then occur — notice that *bits* are transferred in *serial* form as the disk rotates past the read/write head.

The Index pulse (one pulse per revolution) is used to synchronise the angular position indication (sector counter). Similarly, the Track 0 signal is used as a reference signal.

Normally *data* transfers between *CPU* and floppy disk are performed under DMA (*Direct Memory Access*) control, i.e. once a transfer is requested by *software* the complete transfer sequence is carried out by the floppy disk controller chip.

Refer to *Floppy disk, Direct memory access* and *Diskette*.

Flowchart A diagrammatic representation of the operation of a *computer program*. The flowchart for a program that flashes a *LED* for a fixed number of times is shown in Fig. 78.

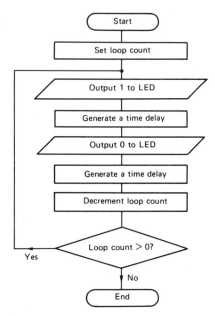

FIG. 78. Program flowchart (flash a LED).

A flowchart can be drawn for programs written in both *low-level languages* and *high-level languages*. The standard symbol shapes applied are:

(a) Oval — for start and end of program;

(b) Rectangle — for normal processing stages;

(c) Rectangle with sloping sides — for *input/output* operations;

(d) Diamond — for a "decision" process, i.e. there are two output paths;

(e) Circle — to indicate a continuation

61

of the flow chart, e.g. to another page (not used in Fig. 78).

It is often useful to draw a flowchart before a program is written in order to clarify program sequence and to highlight any obvious program structure errors.

Format The order in which information is presented. This could apply to a *data* list (series of data values) or to a *program instruction* (order in which different components of the instruction are presented).

Formatting The process of *initialising* a blank *floppy disk*. This involves writing a series of *track* and *sector* addresses over the disk surface prior to using the disk for information storage.

Refer to *IBM 3740* for a description of the formatting *data*.

Forth A *high-level language*. Forth is quite different from other high-level languages, e.g. *BASIC, FORTRAN* or *PASCAL*, because the programmer can build user-defined words which are added to a "dictionary" of commands.

FORTRAN (FORmula TRANslating system) A *high-level language*. Originally FORTRAN was applied in *mainframe computers* and *minicomputers* for scientific and mathematical applications, but it is also applied with *microcomputers*.

Fractional numbers Numbers that include parts of whole numbers. They can be represented in *binary* form in *computers* using *fixed point* and *floating point* numbers.

Free field format The application of any number of blank or space *charac-*

ters in the writing of a *program instruction. Assemblers* are normally free field format, e.g.

CHECK   :MOV D,A   ;Transfer contents of A
                            register to D register

Any number of spaces or blanks

Each field is separated by a *delimiter*, e.g. the : separates the *label* CHECK from the *mnemonic* MOV and the ; separates the *operand* D,A from the *comment* Transfer contents, etc. Any number of spaces is acceptable within these fields.

Free run To allow part of a *microcomputer* to run in a test mode. Typically this involves isolating much of the overall circuit and causing the *microprocessor* to continually obey the same *instruction*. This can be activated by disconnecting the *data bus* and wiring the *bit* pattern for a particular test instruction to the microprocessor's data lines.

Frequency division multiplexing (FDM) A method of *telemetry* transmission. Telemetry is used to transmit *data* over long distances, and FDM is a version that uses several different frequency carriers. For example, for the following carrier frequencies:

1000, 1100, 1200, ... 2900 Hz
(total of 20 carriers)

a *bit* (0 or 1) can be transmitted for each of the 20 channels by a frequency that is slightly lower (say 20 Hz lower) than the carrier for *logic* 0 and slightly higher for logic 1.

See also Time division multiplexing.

Frequency modulation recording See *Floppy disk*.

Frequency shift keying (FSK) The technique of converting a sinewave signal of a particular frequency to a *logic* level, and vice versa. FSK is employed in the storage of *data* on an *audio cassette* recorder, in which a burst of 2400 Hz sinewaves represents logic 1 and a burst of 1200 Hz sinewaves represents logic 0. The full signal specification is described under *Kansas standard*. Refer also to *Phase locked loop detector* for a description of a frequency to logic level converter.

Front end processor A *computer* that operates as a communications controller for another computer. This arrangement releases the main computer to perform more specialised work.

FSK See *Frequency shift keying.*

Full-adder A *logic* circuit that performs an *add* function with a provision for a carry-in from a preceding addition.

A full-adder is constructed from two *half-adders* and is described in *Adder.*

Full duplex A *serial data* communication system in which data can be transferred in both directions simultaneously. See *Half duplex, Duplex* and *Simplex.* A full duplex link is normally used between a *microcomputer* and a *VDU.*

Function The specific purpose or operation of a circuit or a *program*. When the term is applied to the *keyboard* of a *terminal* (e.g. a *VDU*), it describes the application of a key which does not represent a normal character which is displayed or printed, e.g. A, B, C, but instead represents a machine action, e.g. carriage return, line feed.

Fusible-link PROM See *PROM.*

G

Gate An electronic circuit with only one output but more than one input. A gate operates on *digital binary* signals, i.e. *logic* levels 1 and 0. Input signals are combined within the gate to provide one of the following logic functions:

(a) *AND*;
(b) *OR*;
(c) *NAND*;
(d) *NOR*.

General purpose computer A *computer* system that is designed to perform a wide variety of functions.

Generation The level of technical attainment used in the construction of a *computer*. Nominally the four generations are: valves (generation 1), *transis-*

tors (generation 2), *integrated circuits* (generation 3), *VVLSI* elements (generation 4).

GIGO (Garbage In, Garbage Out) A flippancy that describes the quality of information produced by a *computer* if the operator provides it with inaccurate *data* or incorrect commands.

Glitch An unwanted *pulse* or burst of electrical noise.

Golfball printer A *character printer* that produces characters from a spherical printing head. The fully formed characters are positioned on horizontal rings around the head. Tilt and rotate mechanical movement of the head is required for each new character that is printed.

GPIB (General Purpose Interface Bus)
An alternative name for the *IEEE 488 microcomputer common bus* system.

Graphics
The generation of lines and shapes on a *CRT* display. *Microcomputer graphics* are invariably offered in colour, and have application for business and scientific displays, e.g. histograms, graphs, *CAD* (Computer Aided Design), etc., as well as for video games in *home computers*. See *Character graphics, Pixel graphics* and *Vector graphics*.

Graph plotter
See *Plotter*.

H

Half-adder
A *logic* circuit that performs *binary* addition with no provision for carry-in from a preceding circuit. The circuit symbol and *truth table* are shown in Fig. 79 for a 1-*bit* half-adder.

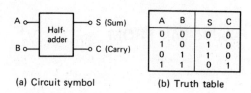

A	B	S	C
0	0	0	0
1	0	1	0
0	1	1	0
1	1	0	1

(a) Circuit symbol   (b) Truth table

FIG. 79. Half-adder.

The circuit can be constructed using only *NAND* gates as shown in Fig. 80.

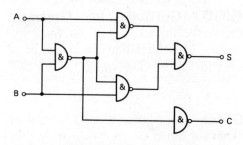

FIG. 80. Half-adder using only NAND gates.

Normally two half-adders are combined to produce a *full-adder*. Refer to *Add* and *Adder*.

Half duplex
A *serial* communication link which is bidirectional but in which *data* can only be transferred in one direction at a time. Refer to *Duplex, Full duplex* and *RS 232-C*.

Half-splitting
The process of fault-finding a circuit, e.g. a *microcomputer*, by considering the overall circuit split at some mid-way point. Tests can then be made to determine if the fault is before or after this mid-way position. The process can then be repeated at other points in the circuit to locate the fault precisely.

Halt
To stop a *computer program* running. Most *microprocessors* possess an *instruction* that initiates a halt condition and prevents the program from progressing any further.

Hand assemble
To convert an *assembly language program* into *machine code* manually. Normally an *assembler* is used to perform this function, and assembly by hand is a long, tedious and error-prone procedure.

Handshake
The process of exchanging control signals when *data* are transferred. Consider the case of transferring a *character* from a *microcomputer* to a *printer*:

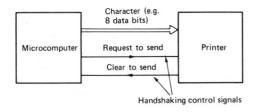

FIG. 81. Handshaking between microcomputer and printer.

A considerable processing speed difference exists between microcomputer and printer, and one method of resolving this difference is for the microcomputer to "ask" the printer (Request to send) if it is ready to receive a character, i.e. to confirm that the printer has finished processing the previous character. The printer generates a "reply" signal (Clear to send) when character transfer can occur. The microcomputer can either *"poll"* the Clear to send signal, i.e. scan it continuously until it is set, or it can use it as an *interrupt* signal, i.e. the microcomputer *program* is interrupted when the signal is set.

An alternative and less efficient method, which does not use handshaking, of data transfer to a printer is to generate program delays between each character transfer.

Hard disk A *backing store* device that is based on a rotating magnetic disk that is rigid and non-removable; contrast with *Floppy disk*. A hard disk is applied with *microcomputers* if more storage capacity (typically 10*M bytes*), faster access and more reliability than floppy disk is required. However, it is typically five times more expensive.

A typical storage specification is:

(a) storage density = 6400 *bits* per inch (bpi);
(b) transfer speed = 1200K *bytes* per second;
(c) rotational speed = 3000 revs per minute;
(d) access time = 25 to 60 msec.

A hard disk is better known by workers in the field as a *"Winchester"* disk after the name of the dominant manufacturer.

Hard sectored disk A *floppy disk* that identifies the divisions between *sectors* (typically 1 sector = 128 *data bytes*) by means of holes in the disk. A hard sectored disk consists, therefore, of a concentric ring of holes around the disk periphery. Contrast with the far more popular *Soft sectored disk*, in which sector addresses are written onto the disk surface between sectors.

Hardware Physical equipment (rather than *programs*) in a *computer*. The name hardware is applied to describe the electronic circuitry, containing box/cubicle and supporting *peripherals*.

Hard-wired logic An interconnected system of *gates* that performs a fixed *logic* function. The overall function is fixed by the interconnection system that is used and not by a *program*. In this way a clear distinction is drawn between:

(a) a hard-wired logic system of *AND*, *OR*, *NAND* or *NOR* gates (plus other circuit elements as necessary, e.g. *flip-flops*) that performs an unalterable circuit function;
(b) a *computer* system with discrete *input/output* signals that can be programmed (by *software*) to perform the same function.

See also *Combinational logic*.

Head The electromagnetic device that transfers *data* on and off the surface of magnetic storage systems, e.g. *floppy disk, hard disk, audio cassette* and *digital cassette*.

The typical arrangement with a floppy disk or hard disk read/write head is shown in Fig. 82.

Disk rotates

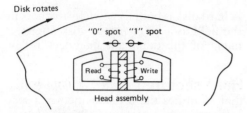

FIG. 82. Read/write head for floppy or hard disk.

Data bits are written to the *logic* 1 state by passing a pulse of current through the write winding. The absence of a current pulse writes a logic 0.

Data bits are read from the surface by electromagnetic induction in the read winding.

Refer to *Floppy disk* for a description of the method of bit storage.

Head load The action of engaging the read/write *head* of a *floppy disk* with the disk surface. When *data* transfers occur the head is actually placed in contact with the surface of the disk. See also *Floppy disk controller*.

Hex An abbreviation for *hexadecimal*.

Hexadecimal A number system that uses a *base* of 16. The sixteen symbols used are the normal *decimal* numbers 0 to 9 plus A, B, C, D, E and F.

The hexadecimal (often abbreviated to hex) system has evolved with the use of *microcomputers* because it is a convenient way of writing long *binary* numbers in shortened form,

e.g. the binary number 0100 0101 0011 1011 can be written in hex as 453B.

Table 7 illustrates the relationships between binary, hexadecimal and decimal numbers.

Decimal	Binary	Hexadecimal
0	0000	0
1	0001	1
2	0010	2
3	0011	3
4	0100	4
5	0101	5
6	0110	6
7	0111	7
8	1000	8
9	1001	9
10	1010	A
11	1011	B
12	1100	C
13	1101	D
14	1110	E
15	1111	F

Table 7. Hexadecimal number system.

For example, the 8-bit binary number 1100 0100 can be written in hex as C4.

This can be expressed as $C4_{16}$, i.e. C4 to the base of 16.

Conversely, the hex number 74E1 (or $74E1_{16}$) when expressed in binary is 0111 0100 1110 0001.

Notice that a gap is invariably inserted between 4-bit groups in binary numbers; this helps to perform the conversion to hex.

Conversion between hex and decimal numbers is a more difficult procedure and is illustrated in the following examples for 8-bit numbers:

(a) Convert hex 5D to decimal

$$\text{Hex } 5D = (5 \times 16^1) + (13 \times 16^0) \quad (D_{16} = 13_{10})$$
$$= 80 + 13 = \text{decimal } 93 \text{ (or } 93_{10})$$

(b) Convert decimal 103 to hex

Divide by 16:

$$16 \overline{)103} \quad \begin{array}{c} 6 \\ \end{array} \quad 7 \text{ (remainder)}$$

Therefore $103_{10} = 67_{16}$

High impedance state The condition of a circuit output signal when the circuit is required to be electrically dis-connected from any succeeding circuits. It is the *third state* in a *three-state circuit*, i.e. the other states are *logic* levels 0 and 1.

See *Floating* and *Three-state*.

High-level language (HLL) A

computer programming *language* that is similar to spoken language. A high-level language (often abbreviated to HLL) *program* must be converted to *machine code* before the program is run. The advantages of using high-level languages to the alternative low-level *assembly language* and machine code are:

(a) programs can be written faster and with less chance of error;
(b) programs can be transferred from one computer to another different computer with little or no altera-tion.

Programming in a low-level language requires a knowledge of the operation of that particular machine, i.e. the opera-tion of the *CPU* must be understood. A high-level language is virtually machine-independent, and novice programmers can quickly generate operational pro-grams.

A conversion program, which can be based on *backing store* or in *ROM*, is required to convert the HLL program to machine code prior to executing the program within a computer. There are two fundamentally different types of conversion program — *interpreter* (gener-ates the machine code every time the program is run) and *compiler* (generates the machine code version just once, and runs that version every time the program is called). The former is more common with *microcomputers*.

Common high-level languages that are used with microcomputers are:
(1) *BASIC* — by far the most common;
(2) *PASCAL*;
(3) *FORTH*;

(4) *C*;
(5) *FORTRAN*;
(6) *COBOL*.

High order bit The left-hand most

significant *bit* in a *word*.

High resolution graphics *Com-*

puter CRT graphics using high resolution, e.g. 500 horizontal and 200 vertical plot-ting points.

HLL See *High-level language*.

Hold The action of suspending the

operation of a *CPU* during *direct memory access* (DMA).

Hold time The time during which

data signals must be held stable when a data item is transferred into a circuit, e.g. *memory* or *input/output*.

Home computer A single-user

microcomputer that is specifically de-signed for use within the home. Support-ing *software* features are:

(a) video games;
(b) home accounts financial package;
(c) facilities to enter and run programs (invariably in *BASIC*).

A typical arrangement is shown in Fig. 83.

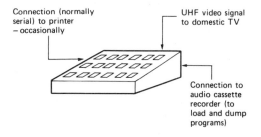

Connection (normally serial) to printer – occasionally

UHF video signal to domestic TV

Connection to audio cassette recorder (to load and dump programs)

Fig. 83. Home computer.

Keyboard quality is variable — from inconvenient membrane keys to full *QWERTY keyboard*. Low cost *floppy disk* and *printer* facilities are offered with several machines.

Several home computers offer "function" keys on the keyboard. The full

command word, e.g. RUN to run a program, or PRINT for a BASIC command, does not need to be keyed in one letter at a time — a single key performs the full function.

Typical home computers are listed in Table 8.

Model	Manufacturer	CPU	Memory
Vic 20	Commodore	6502	5–29K
Dragon 32	Dragon Data	6809	32–64K
Oric 1	Oric Products	6502	16–48K
ZX-spectrum	Sinclair	Z80	16–48K
TRS80 Model 1	Tandy	Z80	4–32K
Ti99/4A	Texas Instruments	9900	16–48K
BBC Model B	Acorn	6502	32K

Table 8. Typical home computers.

I

IBM 3740 An industry standard for the format of *data* on a *floppy disk*. This standard is used almost universally for 8-inch single density *soft sectored disks*. The format divides each *track* into several *sectors* and control data are written between each sector as shown in Fig. 84.

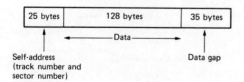

(a) Tracks and sectors

25 bytes	128 bytes	35 bytes

Self-address
(track number and
sector number)

Data

Data gap

(b) Layout of one sector

FIG. 84. IBM 3740 floppy disk format.

A preamble and a postamble define the start and end of each track. Within a sector a self-address (track number and sector number) is written, and this can be checked during read/write operations to detect any corruption or misalignment.

Each new blank disk must be formatted in this way before it can be used for data storage. This process is called "initialising" or "formatting" the disk, and is performed by calling a special program. The action of the program is to write preambles and postambles on each track and self-addresses on each sector.

Variations of the IBM 3740 format are used for smaller 5¼-inch *diskettes*.

An alternative but less common method of dividing sectors is to use a *hard sectored disk* in which index holes around the periphery of the disk mark the sector divisions.

IC See *Integrated circuit*.

Identifier A name or *label* used in a

program, e.g. an *assembly language* program.

IEEE 488 bus A *common bus* system that is used to interconnect circuit boards in a *microcomputer*. Only 24 signal connections are applied, as listed in Table 9.

Signal
8 data lines (bi-directional) 8 ground lines 8 control lines, as follows: DAV — data valid   } Control of NRFD — not ready for data} data byte NDAC — no data accepted } transfer IFC — interface clear ATN — attention   } Bus SRQ — service request } control REN — remote enable   } signals EOI — end or identify

Table 9. IEEE 488 bus signal identities.

The 8 data lines are used to carry the *microprocessor*'s *data bus* and the two halves of the *address bus*. The control signal ATN identifies data or address on the data lines. DAV is used to set *tristate* latches when data is valid on the data lines.

The IEEE 488 bus is often known by its alternative name of GPIB (General Purpose Interface Bus), and it was developed initially by Hewlett-Packard. A common application is to interconnect a *CPU* board (supporting microprocessor, *ROM* and *RAM*) to a plant instrumentation board which contains *analogue* to *digital* and digital to analogue circuitry. Additionally it is used in the Commodore PET personal computer to interconnect the various circuit boards.

Each board in an IEEE 488 system can operate in one of three modes — "talk", "listen" and "control":

(a) CPU board — operates in all three modes;

(b) *memory* board — talk and listen modes;

(c) input board — talk mode;

(d) output board — listen mode.

See *Common bus* and *S-100 bus*.

IEEE 696 bus An alternative name for *S-100 bus*.

I²L (Injection Injection Logic) A *logic* circuit family which uses *bipolar transistors* and is extremely fast in operation.

I²L circuits offer a high degree of integration, e.g. the circuit packing density is as good as *MOS*, although less than *CMOS*. Also its speed (typically 8 nsec for *gate* switching) is second only to *ECL*. I²L is not applied widely, although *dynamic RAM* devices are available. Current developments may diversify its use.

Image processing The use of a *computer* to monitor a television camera signal and to interpret characteristics of the signal to detect shapes, motion, etc.

Immediate addressing An *addressing mode* that is applied within a *program instruction*. In this particular mode the *data* value that is to be used is contained within the instruction itself — in the second *byte* of a two-byte instruction for an *8-bit microprocessor*. Therefore, no *memory* address or *CPU* register is specified to identify the data item. An example for an *Intel* 8085 instruction is:

MVI D,4

which moves the data value 4 into register D.

In-circuit emulator (ICE) A combined *hardware* and *software* system that enables a prototype *microprocessor* system to be tested. The arrangement is shown in Fig. 85.

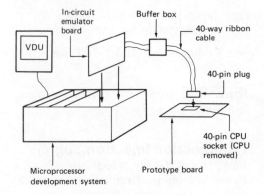

In-circuit
emulator
board

Buffer box

40-way ribbon
cable

40-pin plug

VDU

40-pin CPU
socket (CPU
removed)

Microprocessor
development system

Prototype board

FIG. 85. In-circuit emulator.

The in-circuit emulator board is plugged into a spare slot in the *microprocessor development system*. A ribbon cable connects, via a buffer box, to a plug which is inserted into the *CPU* socket in the board which it is required to test. The prototype board may be a small *microcomputer* system, e.g. washing machine controller, lift controller, etc. Software within the microprocessor development system can then be activated to perform the following functions, which test the prototype board circuit (e.g. *RAM* and *input/ output*) as well as the prototype software:

(a) full emulation, which means running the prototype program in real-time;

(b) running the program to a *break-point*;

(c) *single-step* the program (obey one instruction at a time);

(d) interrogate, i.e. examine and alter *memory* locations and *CPU* registers.

An in-circuit emulator for each main microprocessor type is an optional and expensive feature within a microprocessor development system. When the prototype program is finalised it can be written into *PROM* or *EPROM* within the microprocessor development system and transferred to the prototype board.

Increment To add 1 to a number. *Microprocessors* invariably possess an increment *instruction* which operates on the contents of a *CPU register* or a *memory* location.

Index A method of *memory* address modification that is implemented using an *index register* within *computers*. Refer to *Indexed addressing*.

Indexed addressing An *addressing mode* that is applied within a *program instruction*. A composite *memory* address is generated by adding the contents of an *index register* to a base address. For example, the following instruction for a *Zilog* Z80 *microprocessor*:

$$LD \ B,(IX+d)$$

loads register B from the memory address formed by adding the contents of the IX index register and the value d. For example,

if IX contains: 6000   (in *hexadecimal*)
         and d is: 40
composite   address _____
                is: 6040

Therefore register B is loaded with the contents of memory location 6040.

Index hole A hole in a *floppy disk* that is used to generate a synchronising signal as the disk rotates. The hole is detected using a photodiode or photo-transistor (refer to *Optoelectronic devices*).

In a *soft sectored disk* only one hole is used, and it is detected once per revolution. In a *hard sectored disk* an index hole occurs after every *sector* around the circumference of the disk.

Index register A *CPU* register that is used in an *indexed addressing instruction*.

70

Indirect addressing An *addressing mode* in which a *memory* location or a *CPU register* contains the address of the *data* item and not the data item itself. The use of a memory location for indirect addressing is not as common with microprocessors as the use of a CPU register, which is illustrated as follows for the *Intel 8085* microprocessor:

MOV C,M

moves into the C register the data value whose memory address is held in the HL register-pair (referred to by the letter M in the instruction).

Therefore, whenever indirect addressing is used in a program, the register (or memory location) that is to be used "indirectly" must be loaded previously with the appropriate memory address, e.g.

```
MVI H, 1600H ;Load HL register-pair with hex
              1600
MOV M,A      ;Move the contents of A register
              to memory address
              hex 1600
```

In this latter instruction therefore the source (A) is "direct register" addressing, and the destination (indirect on HL) is "indirect register" addressing.

Information retrieval The general name given to the *computer* science of storing and recalling *data*.

Information technology The handling, storage and transmission of *data* by automatic means. Information technology is a catch-all term that refers principally to the application of *computers* for processing data records of all types, e.g. customer accounts, bank accounts, personnel records, vehicle records, stock control, holiday bookings, travel bookings, home accounts, computer assisted learning, and many others.

Initialising Setting a system to a known state. The term is applied commonly with *microcomputers* to the following processes:

(a) Initialising a *programmable input/output chip*, e.g. a *PIO* (selecting *port* directions as input or output) and *UART* (selecting transmission speed, number of *data bits*, etc.).

(b) Initialising a *floppy disk*, i.e. setting up a blank disk in a soft sectored mode. This involves writing self-addresses at the start of every *sector* on the disk surface, normally to the *IBM 3740* format.

Injection Injection logic See *I²L*.

Input/Output Part of a *computer* that connects the machine to the outside world. The term normally applies to the circuitry that connects to the following remote *peripherals* or devices:

(a) *printer* (output);
(b) *keyboard* (input);
(c) *CRT* (output);
(d) *VDU* (input and output);
(e) *floppy disk* or *hard disk* (input and output);
(f) numerical *"segment display"* (output);
(g) instrumentation and electrical control equipment (input and output).

An individual input/output *integrated circuit*, that connects a *microcomputer* to one of these peripherals, fits into the overall *hardware* configuration as shown in Fig. 86.

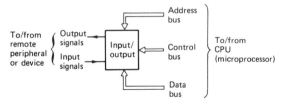

FIG. 86. Microcomputer input/output.

The input/output *chip* could be a simple *port, PIO, UART, floppy disk controller, CRT controller, keyboard encoder*, etc.

Input/output mapped input/output
Computer input/output cir-cuitry that is accessed using input and output instructions. It contrasts with memory mapped input/output in which input/output circuits are connected as memory devices and accessed using memory transfer instructions. Therefore input/output mapped devices can have the same addresses as memory devices, because they are accessed using differ-ent instructions.

Input port
A *computer* circuit that passes eight external signals into the computer. An input port to a *micro-computer* could be part of a 2- or 3-port *PIO* (Parallel Input/Output) *chip*, or it could form a single-function chip as shown in Fig. 87.

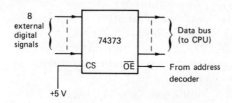

FIG. 87. Non-programmable input port.

The SN74373 is termed an "8-*bit* latch" and is described under *octal latch*. The 8 external signals, e.g. the 8 keyswitch settings, pass through the chip onto the *data bus* when the $\overline{OE}$ (NOT Output Enable) signal is set by an *address decoding* circuit during implementation of an input *instruction*. Additionally the CS (Chip Select) signal must be perma-nently set. Notice that the description "non-programmable" implies that the port is fixed in direction, i.e. it cannot be programmed or initialised to act as an input or output port.

The most common application of an input port is to connect contact-closure signals into the machine; typical examples are:

(a) keyswitches, e.g. a *keyboard*;
(b) manual on/off switches;
(c) automatic on/off switches, e.g. thermostat, limit switch, relay contact — see *Blocking diode*.

Alternatively an *A/D* converter can feed an instrumentation signal to an input port.

Instruction
A single operation which is performed by a *computer*. An instruc-tion is the most detailed command that can be given to a computer. A *low-level language program* consists of a sequence of instructions which the computer is required to execute. Some instructions may simply transfer *data* items between *CPU, memory* and *input/output*, whilst others may demand complex processing within the CPU. See *Instruction set, Fetch/execute cycle, Low-level language* and *High-level language*.

Instruction code
An instruction expressed in *machine code*, i.e. in its *binary* form.

Instruction cycle
The full sequence that is required to implement an *instruc-tion*. See *Fetch/execute cycle*.

Instruction register
A register within the *CPU* that holds the *bit* pattern for the *instruction* that is currently being obeyed within a *computer*. The role of the instruction register is illustrated in Fig. 88.

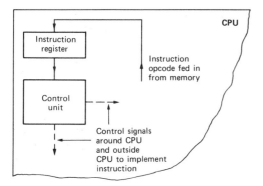

FIG. 88. Instruction register.

The instruction is fetched from *memory* in the first (fetch) part of the *fetch/execute cycle*. The instruction *"opcode"* then resides in the instruction register for the duration of the execute part of the cycle, when it is examined by the *control unit*. Control signals are sent out to implement the instruction.

The instruction register is 8-bits wide for an 8-bit *microprocessor* and 16-bits wide for a 16-bit device.

Instruction set The complete list of *instructions* that can be implemented within a particular *computer*. A *microprocessor* possesses typically 50 to 150 different instructions. A convenient way of grouping instructions is as follows:

(a) *Data* move instructions, e.g.
   Move from one *CPU register* to another
   Move from a *memory* location to a CPU register
   Move from a CPU register to an *input/output* device
   etc.

(b) Data modify instructions, e.g.
   Add two data values
   Subtract two data values
   Decrement a data value
   Logical *AND* two data values
   Logical *OR* two data values
   Shift a data value
   etc.

(c) *Jump* instructions to modify program flow, e.g.
   Unconditional jump (recommence program operation at some point other than the next instruction)
   Conditional jump (jump if a particular condition, e.g. zero number, is met) — several versions normally

(d) Miscellaneous instructions, e.g.
   Interrupt processing (enable interrupts, set *interrupt mask*)
   Subroutine call
   Stack processing (store data values on stack)

Integrated circuit (IC) An electronic circuit in which several components are integrated into the same circuit package. The term is used to contrast with a "discrete component circuit", in which each component (transistor, resistor, capacitor) is a separate device.

Several families of integrated circuits exist. The principal types are *TTL*, *MOS* and *CMOS*. See also *ECL* and I^2L. Refer to *DIL* for a description of the most common integrated circuit package.

Integrating A/D An *analogue to digital converter* that employs a voltage integration technique. The *analogue* voltage is converted into a time period that is measured by a *counter*. The "dual-ramp" integrating A/D is the most common version, and its action is illustrated in Fig. 89.

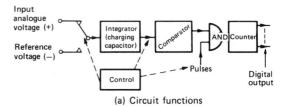

(a) Circuit functions

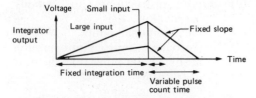

(b) Voltage waveform of integrator output

FIG. .89. Dual-ramp integrating A/D converter.

At the start of the conversion process the control unit sets the electronic switch to connect the analogue input voltage to the integrator (simply a capacitor and an *op-amp*). The integrator output voltage is allowed to ramp up for a fixed time period — the larger the input voltage the steeper is the rate of rise. The switch is then set to connect the reference voltage of opposite polarity to the integrator. The integrator output voltage then ramps down at a fixed rate, and during this period pulses are gated through to the counter. When the integrator output voltage reaches zero, the output changes from *logic* 1 to logic 0 and pulses are prevented from passing to the counter. Therefore as the analogue input voltage increases, the integrator output voltage increases and more pulses are gated to the counter.

This particular method of A/D conversion is slow (typically 50 msec), but it can give good resolution and noise rejection. Contrast with the *Successive approximation A/D* converter.

This circuit is packaged in *integrated circuit* form and is connected to an *input port* of a *microcomputer* when it is required to feed an analogue signal, e.g. an instrumentation reading, to a microcomputer.

Integrity   The accuracy and reliability of *data*.

Intel microprocessors   A widely-applied range of 8-*bit* and 16-bit *micro-processors*. Intel produced the world's first commercial 8-bit microprocessor (the 8008), and have maintained a dominant role in the manufacture of microprocessors and support *chips* ever since. The most popular Intel microprocessors are:

(a)   8080 and 8085 8-bit microprocessors;
(b)   8086 and 8088 16-bit microprocessors;
(c)   8048 and 8049 single-chip microcomputers (8-bit *CPU, ROM, RAM* and *input/output* all on one *integrated circuit*).

The 8085 is probably the widest documented microprocessor, and its internal organisation is shown in Fig. 90.

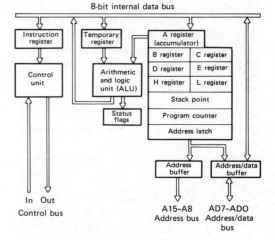

FIG. 90. Intel 8085 CPU (8-bit).

There are 7 8-bit *work registers* lettered A, B, C, D, E, H and L, but B and C, D and E and H and L can be used in pairs to provide 16-bit working for some instructions. Other modules within the device are standard for any microprocessor — refer to *CPU* (Central Processor Unit). However, the *address bus* and *data bus* are multiplexed, i.e. the data bus and one-half of the address bus share the same pins. 64K of *memory* can be accessed using the 16 address lines.

The 8085 possesses 113 *instructions*, and the time for a benchmark instruction that adds the contents of a register and a memory location is 7 msec (for a 2 MHz *CPU clock*). The device possesses *direct addressing, indirect addressing* and *immediate addressing* modes, as well as a unique feature of offering a single-bit input and single-bit output signal connection on the chip itself.

The 8085 has attained widespread use in single-board training microcomputers and for a variety of process monitoring and control tasks. Refer to *Zilog microprocessors* for a description of a device that represents a more powerful variation of this chip — the Z80 microprocessor. Notice that the Intel 8080 possesses similar features to the 8085, but three chips are required to construct the same CPU as the 8085.

The 8086 is a far more powerful microprocessor, because it is a 16-bit device and offers a wide range of enhanced features. Its internal organisation is shown in Fig. 91.

Notice that once again the address and data buses are multiplexed.

Whilst some measure of compatibility exists between the *instruction sets* for the 8085 and 8086, the latter device offers the following differences:

(1) 16-bit operation in place of 8-bit. This gives a number range of −32,000 to +32,000 approximately, compared with only 256 numbers in the 8-bit device.

(2) More registers (12 c.f. 7). Also all of the first 8 registers can be used as *accumulators*, i.e. they can be used to receive the result of *ALU* operations in most instructions.

(3) More addressing modes, e.g. *indexed addressing, segment* addressing (a variation of indexed addressing in which different 64K sections of memory can be used for program and for data) and base addressing.

(4) More instructions, e.g. multiply and divide.

(5) More address lines (20 c.f. 16). This

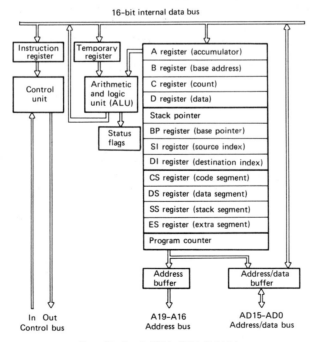

FIG. 91. Intel 8086 CPU (16-bit).

gives 1*M byte* addressing capacity.
(6) Faster instruction execution times.
(7) The 8086 possesses a 6-byte "instruction queue".

Notice that a variation of the 8086 is the 8088, which possesses almost identical features except that its external data bus is only 8 bits wide. These devices offer *minicomputer* processing power.

Intel support these microprocessors with a wide range of input/output chips, e.g. the 8155 and 8255 *PIOs*, 8251 *USART*, 8253 *counter/timer* and 8275 *CRT controller*. These devices are used with both the 8-bit and 16-bit microprocessors.

Interactive A *computer program* that is driven by operator entry. Most *microcomputer* programs require action by an operator to select and activate different responses. Normally this interactive communication uses *keyboard* entry by the operator and *data* display by the computer on a *CRT* screen.

Interface Any boundary between two systems. Normally the term is applied with *microcomputers* to indicate the connection point from machine *input/output* to remote *peripherals* and devices.

The term can also be applied in *software* applications, e.g. an area of *memory* that contains common *data*.

Interpreter A *program* that converts a *high-level language* program into *machine code* at run-time, and then executes that sequence of machine code instructions for each high level language command. Contrast with a *compiler* which generates a separate machine code version of the program before run-time.

A high-level language program which is run under an interpreter is much slower in execution time than a compiled program — typically 10 times slower. The interpreter must laboriously step through each command in the high-level language program, generate machine code and then execute that machine code, every time the program is called. *Microcomputers* invariably use interpreters rather than compilers, particularly for *BASIC* which is applied on most home and commercial microcomputers. However, slower program execution times are not a major drawback, since microcomputers are generally single-user. Programs run in an interpretive mode would be quite unsuitable in a multi-user *mainframe computer* application.

Interrogate To examine and alter the contents of *registers* and *memory* locations in a *debugger* or *monitor program*.

Interrupt A signal that suspends operation of the *program* that is currently being obeyed within a *computer*, and causes program execution to commence at a fixed *memory* location. When the interrupt service program is finished, control is returned to the interrupted program.

An interrupt is used to obtain an immediate response from a computer. The interrupt program is generally called an *"interrupt service routine"*.

The mechanism of an interrupt is illustrated in Fig. 92.

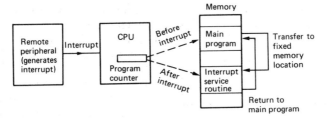

FIG. 92. Mechanism of interrupt generation and servicing.

When the *peripheral*, e.g. *keyboard* or *floppy disk*, generates an interrupt signal the current *instruction* that is being executed within the *CPU* is completed. Program control is then transferred to the interrupt service routine, which terminates with a *return* instruction (as for a *subroutine*). The main program is then re-entered. See *Interrupt vector* for a description of the method of changing the contents of the *program counter* when the interrupt occurs.

Interrupts can be prevented using the *interrupt mask* within the CPU. Also interrupt lines are assigned different priorities, i.e. a lower priority interrupt cannot interrupt a higher priority interrupt service routine.

Microcomputers possess between four and eight interrupt lines typically, and the interrupt lines form part of the *control bus*. Commonly only one or two interrupt lines are used. Typical applications of interrupts are:

(a) *restart* or *reset*;
(b) *power-up*;
(c) *keyboard encoder*;
(d) *floppy disk*;
(e) *counter/timer* (to generate a *real time clock*).

Interrupt mask A *CPU register* that is used to block *interrupts*. Figure 93 shows the action of the interrupt mask within a *microprocessor*.

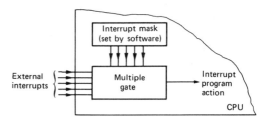

FIG. 93. Interrupt mask.

Individual external interrupt lines can be blocked by setting the appropriate *bit* in the interrupt mask register by means of a *program instruction*. Alternatively all interrupts can be blocked if all bits in the mask are set. Normally a microprocessor possesses one interrupt that cannot be masked (a "non-maskable" interrupt), and this is commonly used to *restart* the computer or to act as a *power-up* interrupt.

Notice that it is possible to use the interrupt mask to prevent a higher priority interrupt occurring when program control is within a lower priority *interrupt service routine*.

Interrupt service routine A program that is entered in response to an *interrupt* signal and that services that interrupt. Interrupt service routines are normally designed to be as short as possible to prevent an excessive amount of time taken from the main *program* that is interrupted.

Interrupt vector A fixed *memory* location that contains the start address of the *interrupt service routine* for a particular *interrupt*. Figure 94 demonstrates the application of an interrupt vector.

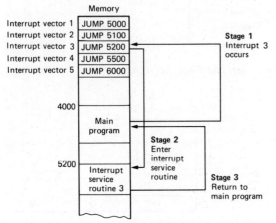

FIG. 94. Use of interrupt vector.

Each interrupt signal possesses a fixed memory location at which its vector is held. When interrupt 3 occurs, *program* control is passed to interrupt vector 3. At this location a *jump instruction* is stored, and this redirects program control to the start of the appropriate interrupt service routine. The routine ends with a *return* instruction, which transfers control back to the main program.

In some microprocessors the interrupt vectors are not jump instructions. Instead the vector simply contains the start address of the interrupt service routine; the jump *opcode* is assumed.

Interval timer An alternative name for a *counter/timer*. Strictly the term denotes the application of a counter/timer to generate a *programmable* time delay.

Invert To alter a *logic* 1 to 0, and a logic 0 to 1. An inversion process can take place on a single *bit* or on a multi-bit *data* value. Inversion can be generated by *hardware* or *software*.

The circuit symbol for an inverter is shown in Fig. 95, which also demonstrates methods of performing bit inversion using the common *NAND* and *NOR* gates.

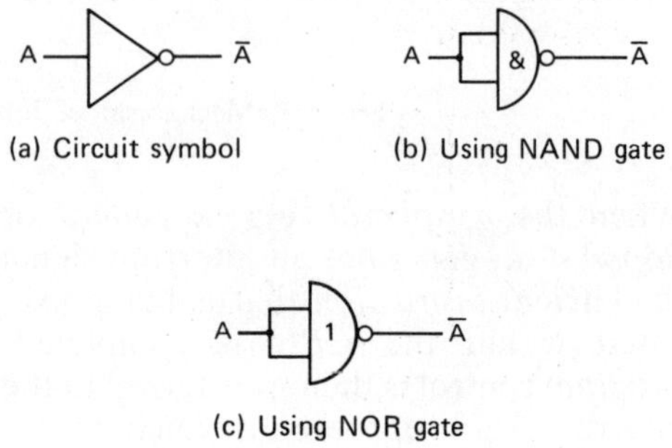

FIG. 95. Inverter.

The bubble on the output connection in each case denotes inversion, and the bar across the top of the letter A denotes that the variable has been inverted.

A simple inverter *integrated circuit* is the SN7404, which supports six separate inverters. The same function can be generated using NAND and NOR gates if the multiple inputs are connected together.

Virtually every *microprocessor* possesses an invert *instruction* so that a multi-bit data value can be inverted within a *program*.

I/O An abbreviation for *Input/output*.

IPSS (International Packet Switched Service) An international *computer data* transmission service offered by British Telecom through the telephone network.

Item A piece of *data*.

J

J-K Bistable A clocked *bistable multivibrator* or *flip-flop*. Its operation is illustrated in Fig. 96.

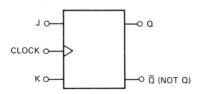

(a) Circuit symbol

J	K	Q
0	0	No change
1	0	1
0	1	0
1	1	"Toggles"

(b) Truth table

FIG. 96. J-K bistable.

The output Q only changes to the states shown in the truth table on the rising edge of CLOCK. "Toggles" means that the output changes, i.e. switches from 0 to 1, or from 1 to 0. The device is used frequently in this mode, i.e. with its J and K inputs held to logic 1, in counters. See *Counter* for a full description.

A typical J-K bistable *integrated circuit* is the SN74107, which contains two such circuits.

Joystick A manually-adjustable lever than can be applied to generate signals to *microcomputers*. Both *analogue* and *digital* input signals can be generated. The former is more common and is illustrated in Fig. 97.

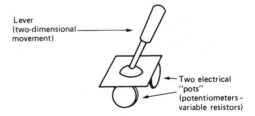

Lever (two-dimensional movement)

Two electrical "pots" (potentiometers – variable resistors)

FIG. 97. Joystick

As the joystick lever is adjusted in its two planes of movement, two variable resistance values are obtained from the two potentiometers. Often these potentiometers are connected to timing and *counter* circuits which generate variable signals in digital form for connection to *input ports* of a microcomputer. A joystick connected in this manner is often used as a game control device for a video game *program*. Versions of this device offering greater precision are the "roller-ball" and "tracker-ball".

A joystick can also be used to indicate discrete positions. In this case a set of switches replaces each of the potentiometers.

Jump A *program instruction* that alters the normal sequential execution of a program. A jump instruction can be one of two types:

(a)   unconditional jump, i.e. the jump is obeyed;

(b)   *conditional jump*, i.e. the jump is only obeyed if a condition is satisfied (the correct setting of one or more *bits* in the *status register*).

Examples of jump instructions in *assembly language* form for the *Intel 8085 microprocessor* are:

JMP 3000H	;Jump unconditionally to memory address *hex* 3000
JM 0204H	;Jump if minus to memory address hex 204
JC 6080H	;Jump if carry bit is set to memory address hex 6080

Jumper   A *hardware* link made within

a circuit to select a particular option. Jumpers are often applied on *microcomputer* circuit boards to select:

(a) addresses of *memory* or *input/output chips*;
(b) clock speed, e.g. *baud* rate of a *serial data* link.

K

K   An abbreviation for 1024. Numerically:

$$1K = 2^{10} = 1024$$

The symbol is used commonly when referring to numbers of *memory* locations, e.g. 4K *RAM* (4096 locations) or 16K *ROM* (16384 locations).

Kansas standard   A signal specification for the storage of *data* on *audio* cassette recorders. A data *byte* is stored in the format shown in Fig. 98.

(see *Frequency shift keying*) when recording data, and a *phase locked loop detector* to convert the sinewaves back to *logic* levels for data read-back.

The Kansas standard is also known by the name *CUTS*.

Kernel   The essential central circuitry that is required to enable a *microprocessor* to operate, e.g. power supply, microprocessor itself, clock circuit.

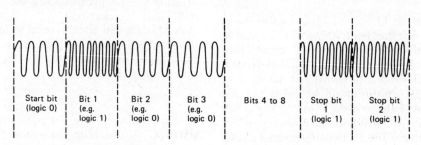

Logic 0 = 4 sinewaves at 1200 Hz
Logic 1 = 8 sinewaves at 2400 Hz

FIG. 98. Kansas standard signal waveform.

The data byte is framed by a start *bit* and two stop bits, and it is recorded at a *baud* rate of 300 (300 bits per second).

This waveform can be created by *hardware* or *software*. In the software arrangement, a *program* must pulse an *output port* pin at the frequencies required. A hardware solution involves the use of a *modem* circuit to generate the sinewaves

Keyboard   A group of pushbuttons. A keyboard, which is used for the entry of information into a *microcomputer*, can be a simple set of numerical keys, e.g. a calculator keyboard, or a full set of *alphanumeric* keys, e.g. a *VDU* keyboard. In the latter system the layout of keys is normally the *QWERTY* arrangement.

The simplest method of connecting a keyboard of, for example, 24 keys to a microcomputer is to use three *input ports* (each port carries 8 discrete *digital* input signals). However, the more popular method of connecting a keyboard is shown in Fig. 99.

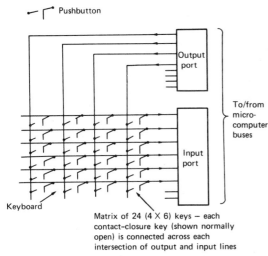

FIG. 99. Keyboard connection to a microcomputer.

In this arrangement 4 output lines and 6 input lines are combined in a "*matrix*" arrangement to connect the 24 pushbutton signals to the microcomputer. A keyboard "scanning" *program* must set just one of the *output port* lines and then read in the 6 input signals from the selected column of pushbuttons. It must then repeat this procedure for the next output line (and next column of keys), and so on, until the entire keyboard is scanned. This software action is termed "strobing in" a group of pushbutton signals.

This matrix system reduces the number of ports that are required, e.g. only 10 input/output lines are required in place of 24 for a non-matrixed arrangement. The saving is even more pronounced for a bigger keyboard.

The input lines are said to be "multi-plexed" between several groups of push-buttons — refer to *Multiplexing*.

Keyboard encoder A special-function *input/output chip* that services a manual *keyboard*. The device performs automatic *hardware* scanning of the keyboard, and it presents a *data* item to a *microcomputer* when a pushbutton (or "key") is pressed.

Figure 100 demonstrates the method of operation.

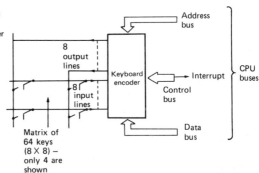

FIG. 100. Keyboard encoder.

The keyboard encoder *integrated circuit* connects directly onto the microcomputer buses (in the same manner as a *port, PIO* or *UART*). The device continually sets one of its output lines and reads in the setting of a column of 8 keys. It repeats this procedure for all 8 of its output lines. If it detects that any key is pressed it generates an *interrupt* to the *CPU* (*micro-processor*). The main *program* within the computer is interrupted, and an *interrupt service routine* is entered. This reads in the code for the pushbutton that is pressed.

In this way hardware activity by the keyboard encoder chip avoids the necessity to perform software scanning of the keyboard on a regular basis, e.g. once every 100 msec, as described under *Keyboard*.

81

L

Label A name that is assigned to a *memory* location in an *assembly language program*. A label can be given to any *instruction* or memory location, and another instruction can refer to that label. The actual address is inserted by the assembler when it converts the program to *machine code*.

Consider the following program example:

```
        LXI  H,2100H
REPEAT:MOV  A,M
        SUB  C
        INX  H
        DCR  B
        JNZ  REPEAT
```

When the assembler steps through this program creating machine code for each instruction, it remembers the memory location at which it places the MOV instruction. Later when it assembles the JNZ instruction it notes the reference to the same label (REPEAT) and inserts the memory address for it in the JNZ instruction.

The use of labels saves the programmer the task of calculating and remembering precise memory locations throughout his program.

LAN See *Local area network*.

Language A clearly-defined set of characters and symbols which is used for conveying a *program* to a *computer*. Programming languages are categorised into two levels:

(a) *high-level language* (the most common *microcomputer* language is BASIC);

(b) *low-level language* (*assembly language* or *machine code*).

It is far easier and quicker to write most programs in a high-level language, which is more like spoken language. However, low-level language programs, which reflect more how the computer executes the program, produce far smaller and more efficient programs.

Large-scale integration (LSI) A measure of the degree of integration of electronic components with a single device. An *integrated circuit* is said to be LSI if it possesses between 100 and 1000 *gates*. However the term is often used to cover *VLSI* also. See also *Small-scale integration, Medium-scale integration* and *Very large-scale integration*.

Latch A circuit that holds or staticises a set of *bits* (*logic* 1s and 0s). Whilst the term could be applied to any *register*, in *microcomputer* parlance it is normally used to describe an *output port*, i.e. a device that captures a bit pattern given to it and holds it.

A latch is a collection of *flip-flops*.

Latency The time taken for a device, e.g. *backing store*, to commence *data* transfer following addressing of the device.

LCD (Liquid Crystal Display) An extremely low-power opto-electronic display device. The principle of display is that illuminated areas are "transflective", i.e. a silvered background reflects incident light and transmits back light, whilst black opaque segments do not. Normally LCD displays are *segment displays*, as shown in Fig. 101.

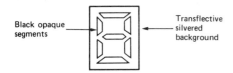

Fɪɢ. 101. LCD segment display.

Leading edge The first voltage transition in a *pulse* waveform. This transition can go from *logic* 0 to logic 1, or vice versa.

Least significant bit (LSB) The right-hand *bit* in a multi-bit number.

LED (Light Emitting Diode) An on/off indicating device. The LED has largely replaced the filament lamp for indicating purposes on domestic electronic equipment and control panels due to its reliability and lower power consumption. The principle of operation is that light is emitted from a PN *semiconductor* junction when current is passed through it.

The circuit symbol and the normal method of driving a LED from a *microcomputer* are shown in Fig. 102.

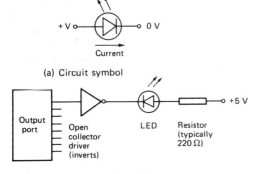

(a) Circuit symbol

(b) LED driven by microcomputer

Fɪɢ. 102. LED.

LEDS are commonly applied in red, amber and green colours. Typically 25 mA is used to drive the amber and green devices, whilst only 20 mA is required for a red LED because it is more efficient optically. *TTL* circuits can only drive 16 mA, whilst *MOS* and *CMOS* can supply even less current. Therefore a *driver*, which is normally of the *open-collector* type (i.e. a resistor must be supplied externally), is required. If a *logic* 1 is set on the *microcomputer output port* signal line the LED will illuminate — the open collector driver inverts the 1 to 0.

Ledger A data filing system that is often processed on a *computer* used for business applications. See *Purchase ledger*, *Sales ledger* and *Nominal ledger*.

LED segment display Strip LEDs can be arranged in a pattern to produce a segment display. See *Segment display* and *LED*.

Library A collection of *subroutines* or *programs* held within a *computer* for use by other programs. See *Linker*.

LIFO (Last In First Out) An area of *memory* that acts as a buffer, with the *data* value stored last being retrieved first. The most common example is the *stack*.

Light pen A light-sensing device that is pressed against a *CRT* screen to detect if the electron beam is causing an illumination at that point. The application of this pen-shaped device is to generate an input signal to a *microcomputer* when an operator wishes to highlight a particular position or area on the screen. For example, an operator can select a particular number that is displayed, or he can nominate an area of a *graphics* display that he wishes to have enlarged.

The method of operation is illustrated in Fig. 103.

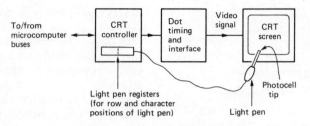

FIG. 103. Application of light pen.

Registers within the *CRT controller chip* record the position of the light pen on the CRT screen in terms of scanning row and character positions. These registers can be read by *software*, which can determine what response is required, e.g. change the display.

Line An abbreviation for "communication line", i.e. the interconnecting cable for a *data* link.

Linear A parameter that increases by equal amounts over its range. The word is often applied in place of "*analogue*" when it is required to differentiate between a *digital* and analogue signal type.

Line printer A *printer* that prints an entire line at a time. A line printer is applied with *mainframe computers* but not with *microcomputers*.

Linker A *program* that combines two (or more) separate program sections. When long or complicated *assembly language* programs are being developed it is often advantageous to write and test them in sections and combine them when they have been fully tested in isolation. Alternatively a *library* of *subroutines* can often be used within a *microprocessor development system*, and a linker is required to append subroutines to a user-program.

List To display (on a *CRT*) or print (on a *printer*) a *program*.

Alternatively, the word is used to describe a sequence of *variables* in a *high-level language* program.

Listener A device that receives *data* from a *data bus*. The term is used in the *IEEE 488 bus* system to describe a circuit board that only receives data, e.g. an output board.

Listing Abbreviation for "program listing", and describes a print-out of a *program*.

Live zero A signal range that does not possess a zero quantity. For example, common instrumentation signals that are connected to *microcomputers*, via *A/D converters*, are:

(a) 0 to 10 V (not live zero);
(b) 4 to 20 mA (live zero) — zero instrumentation signal, e.g. zero flowrate or zero weight, is represented by 4mA.

Load The action of entering a *program* into a *computer* by automatic means, e.g. using *cassette* recorder, *floppy disk* or *paper tape* reader. When applied to program development using a *microprocessor development system* the word describes the action of transferring the *machine code* version of the program from *disk* to *memory* at the correct addresses in memory.

Additionally the word is used to describe the action of engaging the read/write *head* with the disk surface in a floppy disk — see *Floppy disk* and *Floppy disk controller.*

Loader A *program* that performs the *load* function in a *microprocessor development system.*

Local area network (LAN)
An interconnected system of two or more *microcomputers* that divides the overall processing of the system into separate machines. The advantage of this arrangement is that expensive *peripherals*, e.g. *hard disk, floppy disk* and *printer*, which are only used by each machine for a small proportion of the time, can be shared by several computers. Additionally messages can be sent between individual computers in the network.

Figure 104 illustrates a typical local area network.

peripherals (Micro 1 in this arrangement).

Examples of proprietary local area networks are:

(a) Econet — up to 254 BBC microcomputers using a double twisted-pair common bus connection
(b) Z-Net — up to 255 *Zilog* Z80-based microcomputers using a coaxial common bus connection, which can be up to 2 km long and carries 800,000 *bits* per second.

Locater A program that is used to set the *memory* addresses used in another program so that the latter can run at various positions in memory. A locater is a common *software* facility in a *microprocessor development system.* Sometimes its function is combined into a "relocating *loader*". The process of changing the memory area in which a program runs is called "relocating" the program.

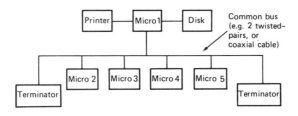

Fɪɢ. 104. Local area network.

Only one machine possesses the shared peripherals. Other machines may consist typically of only one or two circuit boards (supporting *CPU, memory* and limited *input/output*) and a *VDU.* Each machine has access to the common bus, and if any one of Micro 2 to Micro 5 requires the use of the single disk or printer then a message must be sent along the common bus to the machine that controls the

Logic A collection of simple circuit building blocks that can be interconnected to perform a wide range of switching and control functions. The basic *digital* logic functions are:

(a) *AND*;
(b) *OR*;
(c) *NAND*;
(d) *NOR*.

These circuits, which are often called "gates", operate on *binary* signals.

Flip-flops and other circuit elements are often included in full systems.

Logic can also be performed by *software*, e.g. *computers* possess *instructions* that can implement AND, OR and *EXCLUSIVE OR* logic functions on multi-*bit data* values.

Logic analyser An item of test equipment that is used for fault-finding and design work on *logic* systems. The device records *binary data* in various forms, and can be applied on complex logic systems and on *computers*.

A typical logic analyser is shown in Fig. 105.

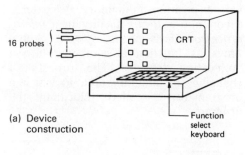

(a) Device construction — Function select keyboard

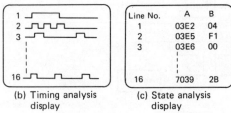

(b) Timing analysis display (c) State analysis display

FIG. 105. Logic analyser.

The 16 (or 32) probes can be connected at different points in the circuit under test. The waveforms at these points can be displayed such that the device essentially performs the role of a multi-channel CRO (oscilloscope). Some logic analysers also offer a display option that converts the setting of the test signals into *binary* or *hexadecimal* numbers. These two display options are shown in Fig. 105

(b) and (c). Display (c) is useful in *microcomputer* applications. If 16 probes are connected to the *address bus* and 8 probes are connected to the *data bus* (for an 8-*bit microprocessor*) then display (c) shows the states of these buses around the "trap" state selected by entry at the operator keyboard. Typically this trap state is a particular *memory* address setting on the 16 address lines, and so effectively *machine code program* execution can be checked.

Logic gate A circuit that performs one of the standard *logic* functions, viz. *AND, OR, NAND, NOR* and *NOT*.

Logic level The voltage value that is used to denote *logic* 0 or logic 1 in a *digital* electronic system. The normal levels are:

$$logic\ 1\ =\ +5\ V$$
$$logic\ 0\ =\ 0\ V$$

in *TTL* and *microcomputer* systems, but variations are possible. See *Positive logic* and *Negative logic*.

Logic probe A hand-held item of test equipment for use in *digital* electronic systems. The probe displays on a *LED* indicator the state (0 or 1) of any circuit node. Figure 106 shows how the device is applied.

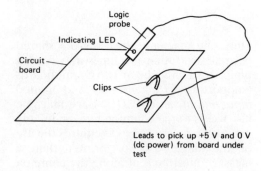

FIG. 106. Logic probe.

DC power must be supplied to the logic probe. The probe tip can be applied to any convenient test point in the circuit, and the LED indicates the *logic* state at that point, e.g.

(a) bright intensity — logic 1;
(b) zero intensity — logic 0;
(c) dim intensity — *floating* (*high impedance state*).

An additional feature of most logic probes is that of "pulse stretching". The probe slows down fast-changing pulse waveforms, e.g. a 10 MHz *CPU clock*, and the LED flashes at a rate that can be detected visually.

The logic probe is a small and cheap item of test equipment that is extremely useful for fault-finding *microprocessor* systems if logic levels can be predicted at various circuit points or if it is required to confirm *pulse* activity. Normally a different logic probe is required for use in *TTL* and *CMOS* circuits, due to the difference in signal characteristics.

Logic pulser A hand-held item of test equipment that is often applied in conjunction with a *logic probe* in *digital* electronic systems. The logic pulser generates *pulses*, which can be traced through the circuit under test by means of the logic probe, as shown in Fig. 107.

The logic pulser can be used to generate a single pulse, a burst of pulses or a continuous stream of pulses. The probe can be used to trace these pulses through a suspect *gate* or *microcomputer input/ output chip*, etc.

Look-alike A *program* that appears to the operator as if it is an alternative program. Frequently a *microcomputer operating system* (the main program in the system) is a look-alike of the *CP/M* operating system, i.e. the same operator commands are required to select the various functions of the system.

Look up To select a *data* item from a list of items.

Loop A section of program that is executed more than once until a terminal condition is satisfied. Loops occur in both *high-level language* and *low-level language* programs.

The *flowchart* for a typical low-level language program loop that outputs a series of *characters* to a *peripheral* is shown in Fig. 108.

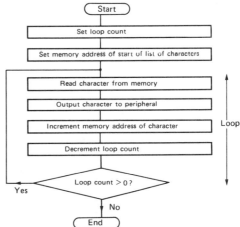

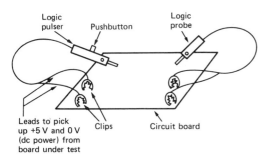

FIG. 107. Use of logic pulser and logic probe.

FIG. 108. Program loop to output list of characters.

Before the loop is entered the program sets up a "loop count". This loop count is decremented at the bottom of the loop, which is repeated until the count reaches zero.

This program is listed in *assembly language* for the *Intel 8085 microprocessor* as follows:

```
START:MVI B,8   ;Loop count of 8 in B register
      LXI       ;Memory address of 8 charac-
      H,5000H   ters in HL register-pair
LOOP:MOV A,M;Read character from memory
      OUT 10H   ;Output    to    input/output
                address 10
      INX H     ;Increment HL register-pair
      DCR B     ;Decrement loop count
      JNZ LOOP;Repeat if loop count is not
                zero
      END       ;Terminate program
```

If the END is replaced with:

JMP START

the sequence is repeated continually since the original loop resides inside an outer loop, i.e. we have a *"nested* loop" arrangement.

Loop stop
A *program instruction* that prevents program execution proceeding any further. A loop stop in *assembly language* form looks like:

```
HERE JMP HERE   ;Jump to the instruction
                labelled HERE
```

This instruction can be applied at the end of a program, or it can be inserted part way through a program during an exercise to *debug* the program.

Low-level language
A *computer* programming *language* that is close to the method which the machine uses to execute the *program*. A *microcomputer* programmer requires a good knowledge of machine operation before he can produce useful low-level language programs.

There are two classifications of low-level language:

(a) *Machine code*, which involves specifying each *instruction* in *binary* form (as held and processed within the machine).

(b) *Assembly language*, which allows the programmer to specify instructions using symbols (e.g. *mnemonics* for instruction type and *labels* for *memory* addresses) — the programmer must call an *assembler* to convert his program into machine code when it is entered into the machine.

It is far easier to program in assembly language than in machine code. There is a 1:1 correspondence between the two, i.e. one instruction in assembly language converts into one instruction in machine code, but generating the machine code by hand is a laborious and error-prone procedure.

Contrast with *High-level language.*

Low order bit
The right-hand least significant *bit* in a *word.*

Low Power Schottky
A variation of the basic *TTL* circuit family. Low Power Schottky *integrated circuits* consume one-fifth of the power of standard TTL and offer a twofold increase in speed.

The SN7400 series of integrated circuits form the standard TTL range. The Low Power Schottky equivalent range is SN74LS00, and all devices are totally pin-compatible and signal level compatible.

Refer to *Schottky TTL.*

Low resolution graphics
Computer graphics using low resolution, e.g. 100 horizontal and 50 vertical plotting points.

LSB
See *Least significant bit.*

LSI
See *Large-scale integration.*

M

M Abbreviation for mega, i.e. one million.

Machine code A *program* in *binary* form. Every program must be converted into machine code before it can be executed in the *CPU*. A machine code program for a *microcomputer* is often written in *hexadecimal* form rather than in binary — this makes the program more readable.

Consider the following program section, which is written in *Intel* 8085 *assembly language*:

MOV A,C	;Move contents of C register to A register
ADI 3	;Add 3 to A register
STA 406EH	;Store A register contents in memory location 406E (*hex*)

This converts to machine code as follows:

Memory location	Machine code	Instruction
1000	79	MOV A,C
1001	C6	ADI 3
1002	03	
1003	3A	
1004	6E	STA
1005	40	406EH

Notice that instructions for this *8-bit microprocessor* can have different lengths — 1, 2 or 3 *bytes* long. Assume that the program section commences at *memory* (*ROM* or *RAM*) location 1000. The machine code (79, C6, etc.) is listed in hexadecimal. Often the first byte of the instruction is termed the *opcode*, and any succeeding bytes are called the *operand*.

A complete program listing, which includes machine code and assembly language, normally follows the format:

Memory address	Machine code	Assembly language instruction
1000	79	MOV A,C
1001	C6,03	ADI 3
1003	3A,6E,40	STA 406EH

Machine cycle A *data* transfer operation within an *instruction cycle*. The execution of an *instruction* within a *microprocessor* requires one or more of the following types of machine cycles:

(a) *fetch opcode*;
(b) *memory* read;
(c) memory write;
(d) *input/output* read;
(e) input/output write;
(f) *interrupt* acknowledge;
(g) bus idle.

Refer to *Fetch/execute cycle*.

Machine independence The ability of a *program* to run on more than one *computer*.

Machine language Another name for machine code.

Macro-assembler An *assembler* that possesses the facility for the programmer to assign a name to a group of *instructions*. When the macro-assembler encounters that name in the *program* listing it replaces the name with the group of instructions (in *machine code* form). This feature is useful if the group of instructions must be repeated several times in a program with little or no change (although if no change is required, it is often more efficient to use a *subroutine*).

For example, the macro:

OUTPUT C

can be used at any time in a program simply by specifying its name if it is defined elsewhere in the program in the following typical manner:

```
OUTPUT MACRO REG  Define macro with a
                  name OUTPUT and a
                  "parameter" of REG
                  (register name)
        MOV A, REG
        OUT 3OH    Macro
        ENDMACRO   Specifies end of macro
                   definition
```

Thus the macro outputs the contents of register C (transfers to register A and outputs from register A).

If

OUTPUT D

is used elsewhere in the program, then the contents of register D are output.

Macroinstruction

An *instruction* within an *assembly language program* that references a macro. See *Macro-assembler*.

Magnetic tape

A *data* storage medium for use with *computers*. There are three types that are applied with *microcomputers*:

(a) *audio cassette*;
(b) *digital cassette*;
(c) *cartridge tape*.

Mailing list

A *software* function that is frequently offered with business *microcomputers*. A list of names and addresses of suppliers, customers, members, etc., can be accessed from *floppy disk* or *hard disk*.

Mainframe computer

A large *multi-user computer*. A mainframe computer traditionally handles large data filing systems for public corporations, commercial organisations, etc. Typical functions are:

(a) payroll;
(b) customer accounts;
(c) ledger;
(d) stores control;
(e) banking transactions;
(f) general information retrieval systems, e.g. police filing, personnel records, etc.;

and so on.

Typically a mainframe computer possesses dozens of *terminals* and *printers* and several *cartridge disk* systems. The overall value of such a system can be in excess of £1 million. IBM are by far the largest world-wide manufacturers of mainframe computers.

A mainframe computer can be 32-*bit*, 48-bit or 64-bit in operation and possess extremely high *software* "throughput". Although it is much smaller and slower (e.g. typical *instruction* time of 5 μsec compared with 50 nsec), the *microcomputer* is replacing some of the single functions of mainframe computers for small-scale applications, e.g. sales ledger for a small business (a few thousand accounts).

Main memory

The *memory* in a *computer* that is used to hold *programs* whilst they are running. Sometimes spare space in main memory can be used to hold additional programs that it is required to enter quickly. This is in contrast to the *backing store*, which holds programs and *data files* that are stored for subsequent transfer to main memory for execution.

In early computers the main memory was invariably *core* (magnetic toroids), but *microcomputers* use *semiconductor* memory — *ROM* and *RAM*.

Mantissa The fractional part of a *floating point* number. For example:

$$8{,}394 = 0.8394 \times 10^4$$

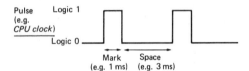

exponent

mantissa

See *Floating point* for a full description.

Mark-space ratio The ratio of times when a pulse is high and low, see Fig. 109.

Pulse (e.g. *CPU clock*) — Logic 1 — Logic 0

Mark (e.g. 1 ms) Space (e.g. 3 ms)

FIG. 109. Mark-space ratio of pulse.

The mark-space ratio is 1:3.

Mask Process of setting selected *bits* in a *data* value to 0s (or 1s). This can be performed by *hardware* or *software* using the *logic AND* and *OR* functions. A software AND *instruction* can be used to set bits to 0 (AND with 0s), and an OR instruction can be used to set bits to 1 (OR with 1s).

See also *Interrupt mask*.

Mask programmed An *integrated circuit*, normally a *ROM*, that is programmed to hold a chosen *bit* pattern by the use of a specific mask in the manufacture of the device.

Mass storage Another name for *backing store*.

Master-slave bistable A *bistable multivibrator* in which the input is not transferred immediately to the output. At the first timing stage the input is set into a master *latch*. At the second timing stage

the signal is passed through to a slave latch.

A master-slave bistable version can be built from each of the following: *S-R bistable*, *D-type bistable* and *J-K bistable*. A diagram of the latter is shown in Fig. 110 and consists of two bistables (flip-flops).

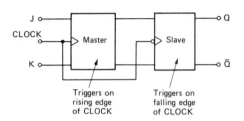

J
CLOCK
K

Master
Slave

Q
Q̄

Triggers on rising edge of CLOCK
Triggers on falling edge of CLOCK

FIG. 110. Master-slave bistable (J-K version).

A complete clock *pulse* (rising edge plus falling edge) is necessary to switch the entire bistable.

Master/slave distributed computer system A multi-*computer* system in which one machine acts as a master and the others as slaves. All *data* transfers pass through, and under control of, the master; thus a slave cannot communicate directly with another slave.

Refer to *Distributed processing*.

Matrix A two-dimensional array of rows and columns of intersecting signal connections, with *logic* elements connected at the intersections. The most common matrix system applied with *microcomputers* is a keyboard of pushbuttons. Refer to *Keyboard* for a diagrammatic description.

Matrix printer A *printer* that constructs its *characters* in a *dot matrix* manner. Typically the matrix is 5 × 7, and a column of 7 solenoid-driven printing needles is set to the required pattern at 5 different horizontal positions to construct a character. Normally a small *microcomputer* circuit within the printer converts the character code (invariably *ASCII*) sent by the *computer* into a required dot-matrix code. The character set can be altered if required by changing a character look-up *ROM* within this circuit.

Matrix printers are fast — from 30 to 300 characters per second. However, printing quality is inferior to *character printers* because of the dot construction of characters.

See also *Daisy wheel printer* and *Golfball printer*.

MDS See *Microprocessor development system*.

Medium-scale integration (MSI)

A measure of the degree of integration of electronic components within a single device. An *integrated circuit* is said to be MSI if it possesses between 10 and 100 *gates*. Much of the *TTL* range of circuits is MSI.

Memory The term can be applied generally to denote any *data* storage medium within a *computer*. Memory types are *floppy disk, hard disk, magnetic tape* and *semiconductor* memory (*ROM* and *RAM*). Normally the term is reserved for *main memory* (ROM and RAM), in which *programs* can be executed, as distinct from *backing store* (floppy disk, etc.), which stores programs for running at some later time.

Memory management unit A

slave processor that occasionally supports a *CPU* and exercises control over *memory*, particularly if *virtual memory* is applied. In this latter case the memory management unit checks each memory address that is used in an *instruction*, and if it is in *RAM* or *ROM* performs no

processing. However, if the address is on *floppy disk* or *hard disk* the unit makes space in RAM (by storing some of its contents on disk), transfers the necessary section from disk and notifies the CPU when it has completed its task.

Memory map A diagrammatic representation of the address assignments within a *computer*. A memory map can show address assignments in *hardware* terms (addresses of *memory* devices) or *software* terms (addresses of different *programs* and *data* areas) as shown in Fig. 111.

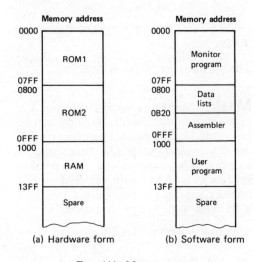

FIG. 111. Memory map.

Memory addresses are shown in *hexadecimal* form.

Memory mapped input/ output *Input/output* devices that are connected into a *microcomputer* circuit in the same manner as *memory* devices (*ROM* and *RAM*). They are then accessed using memory transfer *instructions* in place of input/output instructions. The circuit arrangement is shown in Fig. 112.

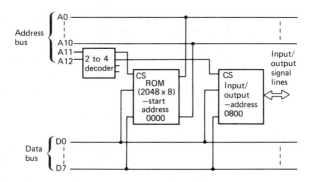

FIG. 112. Memory mapped input/output circuit arrangement.

Normally a *decoder chip* (2 to 4 in this case) is used to generate CS (*chip select*) signals for different memory devices (ROM and RAM). However, in this case one of the decoder outputs selects the input/output chip.

The *memory map* for this arrangement is shown in Fig. 113.

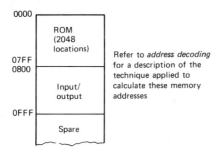

FIG. 113. Memory map for circuit of Fig. 112.

The input/output device can be accessed using the large range of memory transfer instructions therefore, and this eases programming. Also the number of decoder chips can be reduced if the chip select signal for the input/output chip is taken from a spare decoder output. However, a disadvantage is that a large block of memory addressing range (2K — 2048 locations in this example) is used up by a single input/output chip, which at most requires a handful of addresses (1 in this example).

Most *home computers* use memory mapped input/output. This makes it easier for novice programmers to perform input and output operations, e.g. in *BASIC* the *PEEK* and *POKE* commands can be used for memory transfer and for input/output operations.

Memory mapped video The arrangement in which part of *main memory* (invariably *RAM*) in a *microcomputer* is reserved to hold *data* which provides picture information to a *CRT*. This is illustrated in Fig. 114.

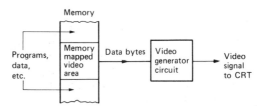

FIG. 114. Memory mapped video.

A *video generator* circuit continually extracts data *bytes* from memory (under *DMA* control) and generates a video signal which can be fed to the CRT. The picture information held in the memory mapped video area can be stored in various forms:

(a) Text in the form of *ASCII* characters, e.g. 960 memory bytes can store one character for each position on a CRT screen format of 24 lines of 40 characters per line.

(b) *Graphics* information in the form of data bytes which reflect the *dot matrix* form of shapes on the CRT screen, so that dots, lines, squares and other miscellaneous shapes can be constructed.

In (b) large areas of memory are used — typically 8K. Thus when large total RAM storage areas are quoted for *home computers* and *business computers*, the usable programmable area must be calculated by discounting memory mapped video areas as well as for space for *organiser program*, etc.

Memory organisation The description, in numerical form, of the number of *bits* in each location of a *memory* device. For example a *ROM chip* with a "memory organisation" of

$$2048 \times 8$$

has 2048 locations and 8 bits in each location. Therefore it requires 8 connections to data lines (*data bus*) and 11 connections to address lines (*address bus*) — $2^{11} = 2048$.

Menu A *computer CRT* display format that presents a list of functions available to the operator. A typical menu for a *program* that presents hotel accommodation information is shown in Fig. 115.

```
MENU

1. STREET MAP – PRESS S
2. HOTEL LIST – PRESS L
3. INDIVIDUAL HOTEL DETAILS – PRESS H
4. MENU PAGE – PRESS M
```

FIG. 115. Menu display page for menu-driven program.

Contrast with a *Command driven* program.

Message A group of *characters* or *data* items.

Microbus analyser A variation of the basic *logic analyser* that is tailored for application with only one specific type of *microprocessor*. The equipment is used for fault-finding in microprocessor systems and is normally designed to be portable, as shown in Fig. 116.

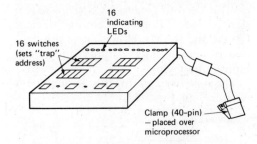

FIG. 116. Microbus analyser.

The 40-way clamp is placed over the 40-pin microprocessor in the circuit under test. A "trap" address (normally a selected *memory* address which is detected on the *address bus* lines) is set on the analyser switches, and when that address is encountered a staticising procedure is initiated. This stored data, which represents transactions on the *address bus* and *data bus*, can then be examined on the indicating LEDs. In this way *program* execution can be monitored.

An alternative name for this item of equipment is "system analyser".

Notice that this equipment is only suitable for a particular microprocessor — different microprocessors possess different layouts of pin connections and different *control bus* signals.

Microcode The detailed control actions that are required to execute an

94

instruction. The *control unit* within a *computer's ALU* contains the microcode which is referenced when each individual instruction is implemented. The microcode is not accessible to the user.

Microcomputer A complete *computer*, comprising *CPU, memory* and *input/output*, constructed using *VLSI* components. In its simplest form the entire circuit can be constructed within a single *integrated circuit*, e.g. digital watch, pocket calculator. Normally a microcomputer comprises three or more *chips*, and the circuit functions can be divided into the three blocks shown in Fig. 117.

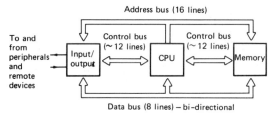

FIG. 117. Three-block diagram of microcomputer.

The numbers of lines refer to a typical 8-*bit* microcomputer. The *CPU* (or "*microprocessor*") is normally a 40-pin device, and it generates three "buses". The *data bus* carries *program instructions* into the CPU, or it carries data items between CPU and memory or input/ output. The *address bus* carries the address in memory or input/output of the data item or instruction that is carried along the data bus. The *control bus* times and activates the above actions.

Memory is commonly a mixture of *ROM* and *RAM* devices.

Input/output connects to *peripherals*, e.g. *floppy disk, printer, keyboard* or *CRT*, and to remote devices and circuits.

Microcomputers are applied in an ever-expanding range of applications, e.g.

(a)   digital watch, pocket calculator,

pocket game — one or two chips only;

(b)   washing machine controller, petrol pump controller, cash register, lift controller, industrial controller, telephone answering machine, *home computer* — single circuit board typically;

(c)   *disk*-based office and commercial system (see *Desktop computer*).

Microcomputer development system See *Microprocessor development system*.

Microelectronics The construction of electronic circuits in microminiaturised form. Tens of thousands of simple circuit functions, e.g. *gates* and *flip-flops*, can be constructed on a single *integrated circuit*.

See *TTL, MOS, CMOS, Integrated circuit, Microcomputer* and *Microprocessor*.

Microinstruction Part of an *instruction*. The execution of an instruction requires several separate *CPU* actions, which are called microinstructions. See *Microcode*.

Microprocessor A *CPU* constructed on one (occasionally two) *integrated circuits*. Refer to *CPU* for a full description of the internal organisation and operation. The principal microprocessors are listed under:

(a)   *Intel* — 8080, 8085, 8086, 8088, 8048, 8049 types;
(b)   *Zilog* — Z80, Z8001;
(c)   *Motorola* — 6800, 68000;
(d)   *MOS Technology* — 6502;
(e)   *Texas Instruments* — TMS 1000, 9900.

Other manufacturers of less-widely applied microprocessors are Fairchild, National Semiconductor, General Instruments, Western Digital, Data General and Ferranti — these are principally 16-*bit* devices.

The most common microprocessors are 8-bit in operation. 4-bit devices normally include their own limited *ROM, RAM* and *input/output* and therefore constitute single-chip *microcomputers*. 16-bit devices rival *minicomputers* in computing power.

Microprocessor development system (MDS)
A *computer* system that affords *program* development facilities for *microprocessors*. Normally the MDS is itself *microcomputer*-based, but some *minicomputers* are also used in this role.

The main physical features of a microprocessor development system are illustrated in Fig. 118.

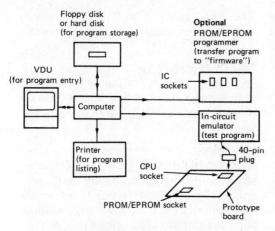

FIG. 118. Microprocessor development system.

Normally program development is performed in *assembly language* within the MDS. The programmer has access to a *VDU, disk* (*floppy disk* or *hard disk*) and a *printer* to facilitate program entry, testing, storage and listing. When the programmer is satisfied that his program is operational he can transfer it to a *PROM/EPROM programmer*, and a PROM or EPROM containing the proven software can then be inserted into the prototype board. The function of the prototype could be for lift control, industrial control, robot control, telephone answering machine, cash register, etc.

An additional stage in this procedure could be the application of an *in-circuit emulator*, which is used to test the prototype hardware board with the prototype *software* still within the MDS.

Software facilities within the microprocessor development system, which is normally based on the same microprocessor as used in the prototype board, are:

(a)   *assembler*;
(b)   *debugger*;
(c)   various other utility programs, e.g. *loader, linker, locater.*

Microprogram
Another name for *microcode.*

Microspace justification
A feature of high-quality *printers*, or a feature of the *software* that drives the printer, that stretches words across the full width of the page.

Minicomputer
An arbitrary name given to a multi-user *computer* that performs down-market applications from a *mainframe computer*. A minicomputer is normally a 16-*bit* machine, although 24-bit and even 8-bit models are common. Whilst a mainframe computer handles several commercial functions (e.g. payroll, sales invoicing, customer accounts, etc.) and employs large data filing systems, a minicomputer possesses a smaller number of *peripherals* (*VDUs* and *disks*) and lower *software* throughput. The main application areas of minicomputers are as message-switching machines (channelling messages from several *terminals*) feeding to mainframe computers, and as industrial process monitoring and control systems.

The most common ranges of minicomputers are the Digital Equipment Corporation PDP machines and the Ferranti Argus models.

Mini-diskette

Another name for a *diskette* (5¼ inch *floppy disk*).

Mnemonic

A group of letters that is used as a symbol for the *binary* code for an *instruction*. Instructions for an 8-bit *microprocessor* are normally 1, 2 or 3 *bytes* long, and the first byte carries the code that specifies the nature of the instruction, e.g. transfer from *memory*, add, output a *data* value, etc. In *machine code* this byte is termed the "*opcode*", but to assist the programmer the microprocessor manufacturer specifies a mnemonic which attempts to describe meaningfully the nature of the instruction, e.g.

Mnemonic	Meaning
STA	Store A register contents in memory
IN	Input
JNZ	Jump if not zero
SUB	Subtract

For example, the STA mnemonic is binary 0011 0010 (*hexadecimal* 32) in machine code for the *Intel 8085*.

The principal difference to the programmer between machine code and *assembly language* is that he can use mnemonics in the latter to specify the instructions in his *program*. This allows him to forget about bit patterns within instructions, and greatly eases his task. He then requires the use of an *assembler* to convert his program into machine code.

Modem

An item of equipment that converts *logic* levels to frequencies, and vice versa. The word is an abbreviation for modulator-demodulator.

Modems are used when it is required to connect a *data* link through the telephone network. The standard data communication procedure is to send *serial bits* according to the *RS 232-C* specification. The arrangement is shown in Fig. 119 for a link from a *microcomputer* to a *mainframe computer*, but the same principles apply to a serial link from a computer to a *VDU* or a *printer*.

The transmitting modem converts incoming bits (0 or 1) into two different frequency sinewaves. The receiving modem regenerates the logic levels. In this way the telephone network (cables and repeaters/amplifiers) handles data as normal speech frequency sinewave signals.

The British standard modem signals are:

Transmit logic 1 = 1180 Hz
 Receive logic 1 = 1850 Hz
Transmit logic 0 = 980 Hz
 Receive logic 0 = 1650 Hz

See also *Frequency shift keying* and *Phase locked loop detector*.

Monitor

The main *microcomputer program* that runs other programs in the system. Normally the monitor is *ROM*-based, and it possesses the following facilities:

(a) enter another program elsewhere in *memory*;

(b) examine and alter memory locations;

(c) examine and alter *CPU registers*;

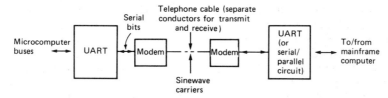

FIG. 119. Modem-driven data link.

(d) debug a program, e.g. run it to a *breakpoint, single-step* one *instruction*.

For a *disk*-based microcomputer system, in which programs can be called simply by keying in their names, the main program possesses features additional to that of a monitor, e.g. disk transfer organiser, operator command interpreter. In this case the main organiser program is called an *"operating system"* and not a monitor.

Monostable multivibrator

A two-state circuit that has only one stable state. When the circuit is triggered into its unstable state, e.g. *logic* 0, it remains in that state for a fixed time and then automatically returns to the previous state (logic 1).

Figure 120 shows the use of the ubiquitous 555 timer *chip* in a monostable circuit.

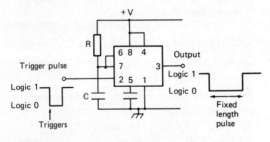

FIG. 120. Monostable multivibrator using 555 timer.

The circuit output switches from 1 to 0 on the falling edge of the trigger *pulse*, and it stays at that level for a fixed time that is determined by the values of R and C.

A monostable multivibrator can be used in the following applications:

(a) regeneration of a pulse distorted by transmission along a long *data* link, e.g. *RS 232-C* link;

(b) removing *contact bounce* on a contact closure signal that is fed to a *computer* as a *digital* input.

MOS (Metal Oxide Semiconductor)

Integrated circuits made from either P-type or N-type field effect transistors (see *FET*). The advent of the *microcomputer* and the impact of *information technology* occurred with the introduction of MOS circuits.

There are three classifications of MOS:

(a) *PMOS* (P-channel). The earliest, and slowest, *microprocessors* were constructed using PMOS.

(b) *NMOS* (N-channel). Nearly all microprocessors, *memory* (*ROM* and *RAM*) and high density *input/ output chips* are constructed using NMOS.

(c) *CMOS* (Complementary — both P- and N-channel). This possesses lower packing density than PMOS and NMOS, but its lower power and higher speed qualities make it a challenger to traditional NMOS applications.

Normally these abbreviations are applied as follows: whilst CMOS refers ony to itself, MOS implies both PMOS and NMOS.

A typical NMOS *gate* circuit is shown in Fig. 121.

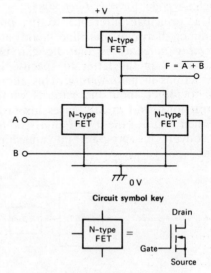

FIG. 121. NMOS NOR gate.

Notice that the circuit uses only transistors (FETs), and the elimination of resistors and other components enables the packing density to be extremely high. If either A or B is at *logic* 1 (+V), one FET conducts. This causes the output F to go low (0 V). This produces the *NOR* logic function.

Typical gate characteristics are: speed 50 nsec, power dissipation 0.2 mW/gate, *noise immunity* 1 V, *fan-out* 50 plus.

A complete microprocessor, which consists of a multiplicity of gates, registers, etc., contains tens of thousands of similar circuits within the same silicon wafer.

MOS Technology microprocessor

A range of *8-bit microprocessors* produced by the commercial firm MOS Technology. The most popular device is the 6502, which is used widely in *home computers* and some *desktop computers*, e.g. Apple, BBC, VIC 20, Oric 1 and Commodore PET *microcomputers*. Many microcomputer buffs regard the 6502 and its computing power scornfully, but it has achieved widespread application. A block diagram of the 40-pin device is basically the same as described under *CPU*, with its *register* set as shown in Fig. 122.

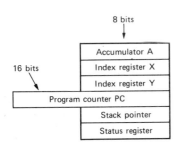

FIG. 122. Registers in 6502 microprocessor.

The device possesses only one register (the *accumulator* A) that can be generally applied for *data* storage within a *program*. Therefore data values must be stored in *memory* locations. It possesses *indexed addressing* and *indirect addressing*. Its *stack pointer* is only 8 bits long, and so the *stack* must be within the first 256 memory locations. It possesses only one *interrupt* line (apart from *RESET* and one *non-maskable interrupt*), and this means that external devices must be polled after an interrupt if they share the same interrupt line. *Input/output* must be *memory mapped*. Its *CPU clock* is on-chip; thus it only requires an external crystal or RC circuit.

Most significant bit (MSB)

The left-hand *bit* in a multi-bit number.

Motherboard

A circuit board into which subsidiary boards are plugged. Contrast with a *Backplane*.

Motorola microprocessors

A range of *8-bit* and 16-bit *microprocessors* produced by Motorola. Their most popular microprocessors are:

(a) 6800, 6803 and 6809 — 8-bit devices;

(b) 68000 — 16-bit (arguably 32-bit) device.

The 40-pin 6800 is described here and its main features are basically the same as illustrated under *CPU*, with its *register* set as shown in Fig. 123.

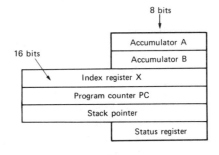

FIG. 123. Registers in MC6800 microprocessor.

The device possesses only two *work registers*, but they are both *accumulators*. It possesses *indexed addressing* but not *indirect addressing*. Apart from *RESET* and one *non-maskable interrupt* there is only one external *interrupt* line; therefore external devices that share the same interrupt line must be polled after an interrupt occurs. *Input/output* must be *memory mapped*. An external *CPU clock* generator circuit is required.

The 16-bit 68000 represents a huge jump in computing power over the 6800. It uses 32-bit registers and a far more powerful instruction set. Its register set is illustrated in Fig. 124.

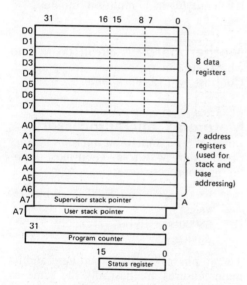

FIG. 124. Registers in MC68000 microprocessor.

The first 16 registers are all 32-bit and can be used for indexed addressing. 8-bit and 16-bit sections of the first 8 of these registers can be used individually. Input/output is memory mapped only. The device is packaged in a 64-pin *IC*, and it possesses 23 address lines. 8-bit memory devices must be used in pairs to provide 16-bit storage.

Motorola support these devices with the usual range of input/output chips, e.g. *PIO* and *UART*. Indeed the 6800 support

devices can be used in pairs in a 68000 system.

MP/M (Multiprogramming Control Program for Microprocessors)
A multi-user version of *CP/M*. The name is a registered trademark of Digital Research. MP/M possesses a time-of-day facility and *programs* can be scheduled to run at any chosen time. Messages can be sent from one operator's *VDU* to another. MP/M can be used in a *local area network*.

MSB
See *Most significant bit*.

MSI
See *Medium-scale integration*.

MTBF (Mean Time Between Failures)
The average time between failures in a component or system.

MTTR (Mean Time To Repair)
The average time to clear a fault.

Multibus
A *common bus* system that is used to interconnect *microcomputer* circuit boards manufactured by *Intel*. Multibus is a registered trademark of Intel.

Multiplexing
The technique of passing more than one signal along a single connection. Normally multiplexing is performed on a time basis, i.e. different signals use the same path at different times. The advantage of multiplexing is that it can save circuitry, and it is applied with the following systems that are commonly connected to *microcomputers*:

(a) Segment display. The same segment signals are shared by several display units — refer to *Segment display*.

(b) Keyboard. The same input signal lines are shared by several groups of pushbuttons — refer to *Keyboard*.

(c) Combined segment display and keyboard. Figure 125 shows the circuit arrangement.

This system illustrates (a), (b) and (c) multiplexing techniques. Technique (a) is the sharing of the segment lines a to p amongst all five display units; the particular unit selected is determined by the setting of only one of the five Digit lines. Technique (b) is the sharing of the six input lines by five different groups of keys; the particular group selected is again determined by the setting of only one of the five Digit lines. Technique (c) is the sharing of the five Digit lines between the segment display unit and the completely separate keyboard. An extra signal effectively distinguishes between the application of these five lines to display or keyboard. This signal is Display On, which gates the segment pattern to the display unit.

(d) Digital input system, which possesses a large number of single-*bit* input signals. A similar multiplexing system to that of a keyboard connection is applied, and is described under *blocking diode*.

(e) *Analogue* input system. A typical arrangement is shown in Fig. 126, which shows how 16 external analogue input signals are connected to a microcomputer.

The multiplexed part of this circuit is the single analogue signal feeding to an *A/D* (analogue to digital) converter which in turn connects to an *input port*. Therefore 15 A/D converters and 15 input ports are saved by multiplexing. The particular analogue input signal selected is set by the 4-bit number that *software* sends through the *output port*. The 16-channel ana-

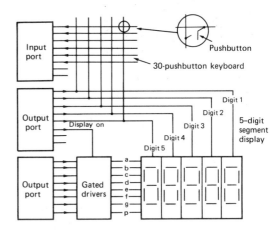

FIG. 125. Multiplexed keyboard and segment display.

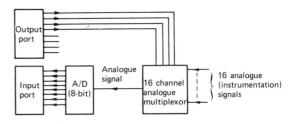

FIG. 126. Multiplexed analogue input system.

logue multiplexor *chip* passes just one of its 16 analogue input signals through to the A/D converter. Refer to *Data acquisition*.

(f) Telemetry. This involves the transmission of bits over cable links using different frequency sinewave carriers. Refer to *Telemetry* for a full description.

Multiply The normal arithmetic process of numerical multiplication, as applied in *computers* using *binary* numbers. Only 16-*bit microprocessors* possess a multiply *instruction*. Therefore in 8-bit microprocessors multiplication must be implemented by *software* as repeated addition.

Multiplication of binary numbers by hand is demonstrated as follows:

```
1100        ←Multiplicand
1001        ←Multiplier
────
1100
0000    ⎫
0000    ⎬        Partial products
1100    ⎭
────
1101100
```

Thus $1100 \times 1001 = 1101100$ (in binary)
Expressed in decimal:

$$12 \times 9 = 108$$

The computer *program* must examine each bit of the multiplier in turn. At the same time the multiplicand is shifted one place to the left, and if the multiplier bit is set to 1 the shifted "partial product" is added to a running total. The final running total is the answer, which can be twice as long as the two original numbers.

Multi-programming   The arrangement in a *computer* system in which a large number of *programs* can be run automatically at various times or on command, e.g. from other programs. The overall system of programs is under control of one master program — called the *"operating system"* or *"executive"*. Multi-programming is far more common in *minicomputers* and *mainframe computers* than in *microcomputers*.

Multi-user   A *computer* system that possesses more than one operator *terminal*. In a multi-user *microcomputer* two or more operators can use a single *CPU* and *memory* to run *programs* that they select, but if more than one program is active at one time then the main control program (the *"operating system"*) must assign a priority arrangement to those programs. Most microcomputers are single-user, whilst *minicomputers* and *mainframe computers* are invariably multi-user.

Multivibrator   A circuit that can be set in one of two states — *logic* 1 or logic 0. There are three versions:

(a)   *monostable multivibrator* — possesses only one stable state;

(b)   *bistable multivibrator* (or *flip-flop*) — possesses two stable states, and is used to store a logic 1 or 0;

(c)   *astable multivibrator* — possesses no stable states, and is used to generate a *pulse* stream by continually switching from one state to the other.

MUX   Multiplexor — see *Multiplexing*.

N

NAND   The inverse of the *logic AND* function. It operates on two *bits* as shown in Table 10.

A	B	$\overline{A.B}$
0	0	1
1	0	1
0	1	1
1	1	0

Table 10. Truth table for NAND function.

The function "NOT A AND B" is represented by $\overline{A.B}$ — the dot (period) symbol indicates the AND function and the bar above the whole expression indicates inversion (i.e. changes 1 to 0 and 0 to 1).

A *hardware* NAND *gate* is represented by the circuit symbols shown in Fig. 127.

(a)   (b)

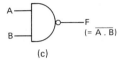

FIG. 127. Circuit symbols for NAND gate.

The first *chip* in the familiar *TTL* SN7400 range of *digital integrated circuits* supports four such gates and is illustrated in Fig. 128.

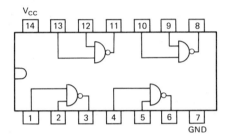

FIG. 128. Quadruple 2-input NAND gate (SN7400).

Other chips in this range offer 3-, 4- or even 8-input NAND gates. Clearly each input must be set to 1 to cause the gate output to be set to 0.

A *software* NAND function is not normally available with *microprocessors*. An AND *instruction* followed by an invert (or *complement*) instruction performs a NAND function on a multi-*bit data* value.

National Semiconductors microprocessors
A range of 16-*bit microprocessors* offered by National Semiconductors. The main device is the 16032, which offers 32-bit *registers* and 16M *byte* addressing range.

Negative logic
The representation of *logic* 1 by a low voltage and logic 0 by a high voltage. Normally in negative logic:

$$\text{logic } 1 = 0 \text{ V}$$
$$\text{logic } 0 = +5 \text{ V}$$

but other voltage levels are used, e.g. +9

V, for logic 0 in some electronic systems.

Contrast with Positive logic.

Nested
The insertion of one *program* section within another. Program nesting can occur with:

(a) Program loops (an example is given under *Loop*) — one loop is inserted inside another loop; see Fig. 129.

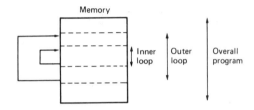

FIG. 129. Nested program loops.

(b) Subroutines — one *subroutine* can call another; see Fig. 130.

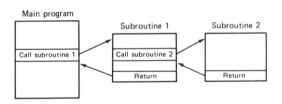

FIG. 130. Nested subroutines.

(c) Interrupts — one *interrupt service routine* can be interrupted by a second *interrupt* causing entry to a second interrupt service routine; see Fig. 131.

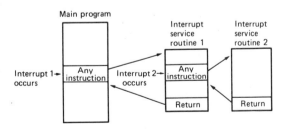

FIG. 131. Nested interrupts.

Network A system of several inter-connected *computers*. These could be any combination of *mainframe computers*, *minicomputers* or *microcomputers*. A network of microcomputers is generally termed a *local area network*.

NMOS One of the three classifications of *MOS integrated circuits*. The others are *PMOS* and *CMOS*. NMOS is the most common and is used to construct most high packing density (*VLSI*) *micro-computer chips*, e.g. *microprocessor*, *ROM, RAM* and *input/output*.

NMOS circuits utilise N channel FETs. Refer to *FET* for a description of the basic circuit component, and *MOS* for an outline of the application of the family of logic circuits.

NODE An intersection point in an electronic circuit at which more than one signal path exists, e.g. the output connection of one *integrated circuit* that feeds into two succeeding integrated circuits.

Noise Undesirable electrical signals. The most common sources of noise in a *digital* electronic system are:

(a)   radiation from electrical equipment that generates sparks, e.g. arc welding equipment, heavy current switch, motor commutator, non-suppressed car ignition, etc.;
(b)   crosstalk from adjacent conductors;
(c)   supply voltage variations.

These are termed *series mode* noise signals. *Common mode* noise signals can also occur, particularly in industrial applications in which instrumentation signals are connected to *computers*.

Noise immunity A measure of the ability of a circuit to reject *noise*. A circuit with a quoted noise immunity of 1 V does not respond erroneously if noise signals of less than 1 V occur on the input signals.

See also *Noise margin*.

Noise margin The difference between the output voltage and the input threshold voltage of a circuit. The noise margin gives an indication of the tolerance of a circuit to *noise*. For example, a typical *TTL* gate produces outputs of 3.3 V and 0.2 V for the logic 1 and 0 states, and the input threshold is 1.4 V. Therefore the noise margin in the logic 1 state is 3.3 V $-$ 1.4 V = 1.9 V, and in the logic 0 state it is 1.4 V $-$ 0.2 V = 1.2 V.

Nominal ledger A *software* function that is frequently offered with business *microcomputers* to maintain records of nominal accounts over a time period for a small commercial organisation. Printed nominal postings, reports of transactions, details of accounts, balance sheet, asset and liability information are produced. Typically several hundred nominal accounts can be recorded on a single *floppy disk*, and several disks can enable over 1000 nominal accounts to be processed.

Non-destructive read-out A *memory* medium in which *data* is not destroyed when a read operation is implemented. *Microcomputer* memory (*main memory* and *backing store*) can be categorised as follows:

(a)   Non-destructive read-out — *ROM, RAM, floppy disk, hard disk, magnetic tape*.
(b)   Destructive read-out — *core* and *bubble*.

Non-impact printer A *printer* in which the print head does not come into contact with the paper. Examples are thermal and electrostatic systems. The disadvantage of these methods is that special and expensive paper must be used.

Non-maskable interrupt
An *interrupt* signal that is not subjected to a masking operation. A typical *microprocessor* normally possesses between 1 and 8 interrupt lines that pass through the *interrupt mask*, which can be set by *software* to block an individual interrupt. Additionally one interrupt line by-passes this mask system, and when it is set it must be serviced — refer to *interrupt service routine* and *interrupt vector*. Commonly this interrupt performs a *reset* function, i.e. it clears one or two *CPU registers* including setting the *program counter* to zero. Therefore if a timing circuit is connected to this non-maskable interrupt line, then after a short time has elapsed after switch-on an interrupt occurs and *program* execution commences at *memory* location 0. A second non-maskable interrupt is available with some microprocessors.

Non-volatile memory
Memory that does not lose its stored *bit* pattern when power is removed.

NOR
The inverse of the *logic OR* function. It operates on two *bits* as shown in Table 11.

A	B	$\overline{A+B}$
0	0	1
1	0	0
0	1	0
1	1	0

Table 11. Truth table for NOR operation.

The function "NOT A OR B" is represented by $\overline{A+B}$ — the + (plus) symbol indicates the OR function and the bar above the whole expression indicates inversion, i.e. changes 1 to 0 and 0 to 1.

A *hardware* NOR *gate* is represented by the circuit symbols shown in Fig. 132.

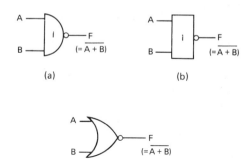

FIG. 132. Circuit symbols for NOR gate.

A *chip* in the familiar *TTL* SN7400 series range of *digital integrated circuits* that offers four such gates is the SN7402, which is shown in Fig. 133.

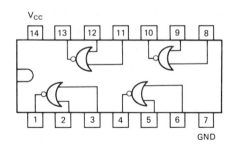

FIG. 133. Quadruple 2-input NOR gate (SN7402).

Triple-input NOR gates are also available. Clearly each input must be set to 0 to generate a 1 at the gate output.

A *software* NOR function is not normally available with *microprocessors*. An OR *instruction* followed by an invert (or *complement*) instruction performs a NOR function on a multi-*bit data* value.

Normalise
To remove leading zeros in a number. The *mantissa* in a *floating point number* is normalised to provide maximum resolution.

NOT The *logic* name for an *invert* function. A NOT gate changes a 1 to 0 and a 0 to 1. Refer to *invert* for a description of a NOT circuit ("inverter").

N-type FET A *FET* constructed using an N-type conduction channel. Such a device is the principal circuit element in *NMOS* circuits, which are the most common *integrated circuits* used in the construction of *microprocessors*, *ROM* chips, *RAM* chips, etc.

Refer to *FET* for a description of the construction of an N-type FET.

Number crunching The action of performing lengthy numerical operations by *computer*. An example of a number crunching *program* is one that is required to calculate statistical figures, e.g. total, average, maximum, minimum and standard deviation, from numbers held in a large *data file*.

Numerical control Automatic control of machine tools. Modern numerical control systems are *computer*-based — refer to *Computer numerical control*.

Numeric display An optoelectronic display system for *decimal* numbers. Normally such systems are *segment displays*, and the display techniques are based on one of the following:

(a) *LED* (light emitting diode);
(b) *LCD* (liquid crystal display);
(d) discharge tubes — almost totally superseded by (a) and (b).

Numeric keypad A small *keyboard* that supports only numbers and not letters. A numeric keypad can be connected to a *microcomputer* if only limited operator entry facilities are required.

Nybble Group of 4 *bits*. Therefore 1 nybble = ½ *byte*.

O

OCR See *Optical character recognition*.

Octal A number system that uses the *base* of 8. Although no longer used with *microcomputers*, the octal numbering system is used with *minicomputers* and *mainframe computers* to express long *binary* numbers in a shortened form.

For example, the 16-*bit* binary number 0 101 011 100 010 001 can be written in octal as 053421.

Thus three bits are represented by a single octal character (0 to 7).

Example: Convert octal 437 to *decimal*.

Octal 437 = 437_8 = $(4 \times 8^2) + (3 \times 8^1) + (7 \times 8^0)$
= 256 + 24 + 7
= 287_{10} (= decimal 287)

Octal latch An 8-*bit register* mounted on a single *integrated circuit*. This particular *chip* within the standard SN7400 range of *TTL* devices is worthy of highlighting because of its common application as an *input port* or an *output port*. Consider Fig. 134.

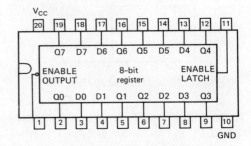

Fig. 134. Octal latch (SN74373).

The 8 input signals (D0 to D7) are latched into the register if ENABLE LATCH is set (to 1), and they appear on the *three-state* output lines (Q0 to Q7) only if ENABLE OUTPUT is set (to 0). If this latter condition is not met the output lines are in the "floating" state. This makes the device suitable as an input port, which passes 8 external signals onto the *microcomputer data bus*, which is three-state.

Refer to *Input port* and *Output port* for descriptions of the applications of this device.

An alternative to this component is the SN74374. A simpler version, which again is pin-compatible, is the SN74273. However, this is not a three-state output device, and therefore can be used as an output port but not as an input port.

Off-line The state of a *computer* when it is disconnected from the devices or process that it is controlling.

One's complement The complement of a *binary* number, e.g.

Original number: 0010 1101
One's complement: 1101 0010

A one's complement representation of a number occurs when the negative version of a number is being generated. Negative binary numbers are described under *Two's complement*.

On-line The state of a *computer* when it is connected to the devices or process that it is controlling.

Op-amp An amplifier for an *analogue* voltage. An op-amp, or "operational amplifier", possesses a feature that distinguishes it from audio amplifiers or television amplifiers — it amplifies extremely low-frequency signals, including steady dc signals. This is required be-

cause its main area of application is to amplify instrumentation signals, which are typically slow-drifting dc levels.

Op-amps are constructed in *integrated circuit* form, and the most common circuit arrangement is shown in Fig. 135.

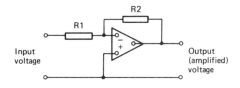

FIG. 135. Op-amp circuit.

Two resistors must be included in the circuit as shown in order to select the voltage gain required, as follows:

$$\text{Voltage gain} = \frac{R2}{R1} (\text{typically } 10 \text{ to } 100)$$

The op-amp can be used in alternative circuits that produce different circuit functions, e.g. *comparator* (compares two voltages), summer (adds two voltages), oscillator (generates a *pulse* stream), integrator (sums a voltage value with time), etc.

The most common op-amp is the 741 circuit, which is an 8-pin *integrated circuit* and can be purchased for less than £1.

Commonly an op-amp is connected between an instrumentation transducer and an *A/D* converter *chip*, which in turn feeds an *input port*, when an instrumentation signal is connected to a *computer*.

An op-amp circuit consists of several *transistor differential amplifiers* connected in *cascade*.

Opcode Part of the *machine code instruction* that specifies the function of the instruction, e.g. add, output, jump, etc. For example:

SUI 9   ;Subtract 9 from A register

is a two-*byte* instruction for the *Intel* 8085

microprocessor, and the bytes are held in *memory* as:

Memory bytes   Opcode (SUI)

SUI 9 {
1101 0110
0000 1001   Operand (9)

The first byte (*hexadecimal* D6) is the opcode, whilst the second byte contains the number that is to be used in the subtraction process and it is termed the *"operand"*.

Open

The action by an *operating system* of setting a *data file* accessible to a *program*.

Open collector driver

A *TTL* circuit in which the output signal requires an external load resistor. This circuit arrangement is applied in the following applications:

(a)   Open collector TTL *integrated circuits*, e.g. *NAND, NOR, AND* and *OR gates*. One benefit of this open collector connection is that several gate outputs can be connected together to give a *wire AND* arrangement.

(b)   *Darlington driver*, which gives a high current drive, e.g. to switch a solenoid. Figure 135 shows a typical arrangement.

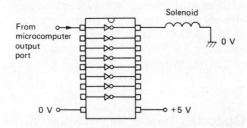

FIG. 136. Open collector (Darlington driver) connection to solenoid.

Refer to *Totem pole* for a description of the output circuit in an open collector TTL device.

Operand

Part of the *machine code instruction* that specifies the *data* value, or *memory* address of the data value, that is to be processed in an instruction. For example:

STA 80E3H   ;Store contents of A register in memory location 80E3

is a three-*byte* instruction for the *Intel* 8085 *microprocessor*, and the bytes are held in memory as:

Memory bytes

STA 80E3 {
0011 0010   Opcode (STA)
1110 0011
1000 0000 }   Operand (80E3)

The first byte is the *opcode*, which defines the function of the instruction. The memory address *hexadecimal* 80E3 is stored in the next two bytes, and is called the "operand". Sometimes the operand is only one byte long in an 8-*bit* microprocessor — an example is given under *Opcode*. Many instructions do not possess an operand if they do not need to specify a data value or its memory address.

Operating system

The master *program* in a *disk*-based *computer*. The operating system resides permanently in *main memory* and it is used to call other programs. It implements commands that the operator enters using his keyboard, e.g. run a program, print a program, erase a program, and it administers all necessary *data* transfers to and from the system *peripherals* (e.g. *floppy disk, printer*).

Normally the operating system must be transferred from disk into memory when the computer is switched on; this is called *"bootstrapping"* the system.

The most common operating system that is used with *microcomputers* is *CP/M*, and this can be run on machines from many different manufacturers.

Operational amplifier

See *Op-amp*.

Operation code Better known by the name of *opcode*.

Operator An alternative name that is used occasionally for *mnemonic*.

Optical character recognition (OCR) *Computer* identification of printed characters by the use of light-sensitive devices.

Optoelectronic devices Electronic components that employ optical techniques at their input or output. A wide range of optoelectronic devices is applied particularly with *microcomputers* and supporting systems, e.g. sensors and emitters (visible and infrared), displays and couplers. Refer to:

(a) *LED* — light emitting diode for on/off indication purposes;
(b) *segment display* — numeric display and *character* display;
(c) *LCD* display — numeric display (low power);
(d) *light pen* — detect light on a *CRT*;
(e) *optoisolator* — to transfer a signal with electrical isolation;
(f) *fibre optics* — for *data* transmission.

One particular type of device is worth mentioning here, because it forms the principal component in (d) to (f) above — the photodetector. This can take several forms as shown in Fig. 137.

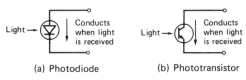

(a) Photodiode   (b) Phototransistor

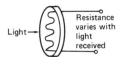

(c) Light dependent resistor

FIG. 137. Photodetector.

Refer also to *Optical character recognition* and *Image processing*.

Optoisolator A device that transfers an electrical signal using an optical medium such that electrical isolation between input and output is achieved. An optoisolator is particularly useful for passing a *digital* output signal from a *microcomputer output port* to a remote circuit, as shown in Fig. 138.

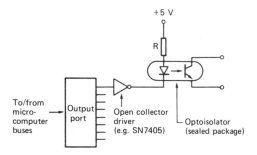

FIG. 138. Optoisolator.

The optoisolator possesses two input and two output connections. When current passes through the input connections an internal *LED* transmits light within the package to a phototransistor (see *Optoelectronic devices*). The phototransistor conducts, and provides a circuit path for an electrical device or system to become energised.

This particular arrangement is attractive if it is recommended that the remote equipment should not be connected electrically to the microcomputer circuitry.

OR The *logic* OR function operates on two *bits* as shown in Table 12.

A	B	A+B
0	0	0
1	0	1
0·	1	1
1	1	1

Table 12. Truth table for OR function.

The function "A OR B" is represented by A+B, where the + (plus) symbol indicates the OR function. Therefore, if either A or B is set to 1, then the result of the OR operation is also set to 1.

The OR function can be implemented by *hardware* (electronic circuitry) or *software* (computer program). The hardware OR *gate* can be represented by the circuit symbols shown in Fig. 139.

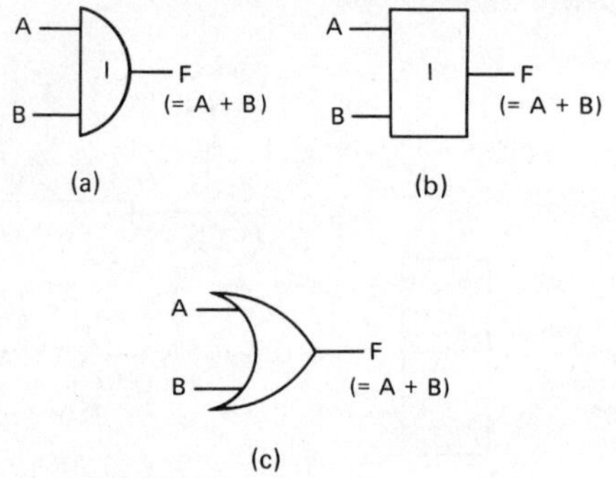

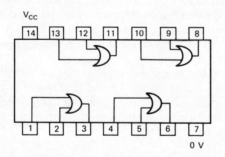

FIG. 139. Circuit symbols for OR gate.

An *integrated circuit* in the *TTL* SN7400 range that offers four such gates is the SN7432, and it is illustrated in Fig. 140.

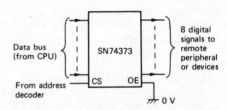

FIG. 140. Quadruple 2-input OR gate (SN7432).

A software OR function can be performed on multi-bit *data* values. Each *microprocessor* contains an *instruction* that performs the OR function. For example, the OR instruction for an 8-bit microprocessor may be:

ORA C   ;OR the contents of registers A and C

The effect of this instruction is, e.g.:

$$\begin{array}{ll} \text{A register}= & 1111\ 0000 \\ \text{C register}= & 0110\ 1001 \\ \hline \text{Result}= & 1111\ 1001 \end{array}$$

Therefore the instruction effectively adds 1s into bit positions in the second word if 1s are set in the corresponding bits in the first word.

Output port   A *computer* circuit that passes eight discrete *digital* signals out to remote devices and equipment. An output port in a *microcomputer* could be part of a 2- or 3-port *PIO* (Parallel Input/Output) *chip*, or it could form a single function chip as shown in Fig. 141.

FIG. 141 Non-programmable output port.

The SN74373 is termed an "8-bit latch" and is described under *Octal latch*. 8 single-*bit* signals, e.g. the settings for 8 remote *LEDs*, pass out from the *data bus* through the chip when the CS (*Chip Select*) signal is set by an *address decoding* circuit during implementation of an output *instruction*. Additionally the OE (*NOT* Output Enable) signal must be permanently set. Notice that the description "non-programmable" implies that the port is fixed in direction, i.e. it cannot be *programmed* to act as an input or as an output port.

The most common applications of an output port are to drive the following items:

(a) *segment display*;
(b) indicating *LED*;
(c) electrical relays, solenoids, motors, etc.;
(d) *D/A* converter.

Overflow A condition generated in a *computer* when an arithmetic operation creates a quantity beyond the capacity of the *register* that holds the result. An overflow *flag* in the *CPU*'s *status register* is set if an arithmetic *instruction* causes an overflow condition.

Overlay The action of running one half of a *program* firstly, then loading and running the second part on top of the first. If *memory* space is limited within a *computer* and a program cannot fit into the available area, the program can be stored on *backing store* in two or more parts. When the first part has been transferred and run to completion, it calls the next part.

P

Pack To compress *data* items in a storage medium by removing superfluous information, e.g. "space" characters or leading zeros.

The name is also used to describe a *cartridge disk*, or "disk pack".

Package A *program*, or set of programs, that performs a particular *computer* function, e.g. *payroll*, computer aided design (see *CAD*) of electronic circuits, etc.

Packing density The amount of *data* that can be stored in a given space — normally expressed in *bits* per inch (bpi). Packing densities for individual *backing store* devices are discussed under *Floppy disk, Hard disk, Cartridge tape* and *Digital cassette*.

Paddle A simple manually-operated games input to a *microcomputer*. The device is normally an electrical potentiometer which is altered by knob adjustment. The variable electrical resistance adjusts a timing circuit within the microcomputer in order to simulate an *analogue* input for use by a games *program*, e.g. to move a games symbol on the *CRT* screen.

Page An area of *memory* — usually 256 addresses (or *bytes*). In a 16-*bit* address line system, i.e. most 8-bit *microprocessors*, this allows interpretation of an address as shown in Fig. 142.

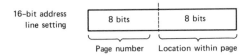

FIG. 142. Memory page selection.

Paged addressing A *computer addressing mode* that allows a *program* to switch from one area of *memory* to another simply by changing the contents of a page register. It is uncommon with microprocessors.

Paper tape A non-magnetic *data* storage medium that stores data as punched holes on paper tape. It is uncommon with *microcomputers* but is used frequently for storing secure copies of *programs* and data *files* with *minicomputers* and some *mainframe computers*.

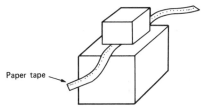

FIG. 143. Paper tape punch (or reader).

Figure 143 represents a paper tape punch; a tape reader has much the same physical appearance. The former represents *bits* as punched circular holes across the width of the tape, whilst the latter detects the holes using light sources and photodetectors. The layout of data on the paper tape is illustrated in Fig. 144.

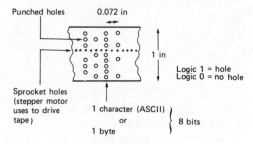

FIG. 144. Paper tape.

The use of paper tape as a storage medium offers the advantage of security of storage — magnetic storage media can deteriorate and bit magnetic polarisation can be corrupted. However, paper tape punches and readers are expensive, noisy and slow.

Parallel The use of separate signal paths for each *data* item, e.g. 8 signal connections are used for an 8-*bit* data value. Contrast with *Serial*.

Parallel input/output The arrangement of connecting external signals to a *computer* using *parallel* paths. In a *microcomputer* such connections are made via *ports*, which can be *input* or *output* in direction and carry 8 discrete signal lines. A *programmable* parallel input/output *integrated circuit* is offered by most *microprocessor* manufacturers and is described under *PIO*.

Parameter A value that is used within a *program* and is passed from one program (or section of program) to another. Commonly the *data* value is

passed in a *memory* location or in a *CPU register*.

Parity The numbers of 1s in a *word*— the number can be even or odd. An additional *bit* is often appended to a group of bits to make the total number of 1s an even or an odd number — see Fig. 145.

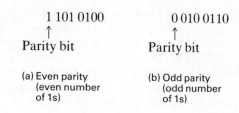

FIG. 145. Parity bit.

A parity bit is added to each *character* (7 bits) in the standard *ASCII* code for representing characters.

The parity bit facilitates a limited error-checking feature — a single-bit error is indicated, although its location is not highlighted.

Pascal A *high-level language*. Pascal lends itself to *structured programming* well, and is becoming increasingly popular with *microcomputers*.

Pass A single execution of a *program loop*. Alternatively the term is used to describe one of the two stages in the process of generating a *machine code* program from a *source program* (*high-level language* or *assembly language*).

Password A string of *characters* that an operator must enter to obtain access to a particular function within a *program* if some measure of data security is required.

Patch A section of *program* that is

inserted into a working program to correct an error or change the function of the program in some way. The patch is added outside the bounds of the program, and a *jump instruction* is inserted at the required point in the program. Clearly the instruction that is overwritten by the jump instruction must be the first instruction in the patch.

Payroll A *software* function that is frequently offered with business *microcomputers* to maintain records of employee wages and salaries. Payslips can be printed by the system, and data for several hundred employees can be recorded on a single *floppy disk*.

PC See *Program counter.*

PCB See *Printed circuit board.*

PCM (Pulse Code Modulation) A method frequently used in telephone telecommunications to transfer speech signals in a *binary pulse* coded manner. A typical sinewave voltage waveform is sampled at regular intervals, and the amplitude of the signal at each point is represented by a binary number (see *Quantisation*). These binary numbers are transmitted as a series of pulses (pulse present = *logic* 1, no pulse present = logic 0).

Peek A special command within *BASIC* that allows the *high-level language* programmer to examine precise *memory* locations.

For example

160 EDWARD=PEEK(512)

causes memory location 512 (in decimal) to be read, and the contents are given the *variable* name EDWARD.

This command is particularly useful if

memory mapped input/output is used (as in most *home computers*), because the same command can be used to read a data value through an *input port*.

Refer also to POKE.

Period The name given to a full-stop *character* on a *keyboard* or *CRT*.

Peripheral An item of *input/output* equipment that is connected to a *computer*. The following peripherals are commonly connected to *microcomputers*:

(a) *floppy disk*;
(b) *hard disk*;
(c) *printer*;
(d) magnetic tape devices, e.g. *audio cassette* and *digital cassette*;
(e) *paper tape* reader and punch — uncommon;
(f) *plotter* — uncommon.

All of these devices are used for *program* and *data file* storage except the printer, which is for program/data listing, and the plotter, which is used to record results of programs in a graphical form.

Personal computer A single-user *computer*. A personal computer comprises a *microcomputer* with *CRT* and *keyboard* (perhaps in the form of a *VDU*) plus some form of *backing store* (normally *floppy disk* or *audio cassette* recorder).

Personal computers can be divided into two categories, depending on the application of the system:

(a) *Home computer* — normally costing less than £200, comprising microcomputer and keyboard, with interfaces to domestic television receiver and *audio cassette* recorder; used for games, programming tuition, home accounts, etc.
(b) *Desktop computer* — more than £500 normally, comprising micro-

computer with CRT and keyboard (possibly combined within a separate VDU), plus floppy disk; used for commercial functions, e.g. *word processor, sales ledger, payroll*, etc.

Personality module

An item of hardware designed for application with a specific piece of equipment. An example of the use of a personality module is a small board that fits into a *PROM programmer* to determine the type of *PROM* or *EPROM* that can be programmed. A different personality module is required for each different PROM or EPROM *chip* to adapt the programmer to the unique collection of voltages, currents and pin configurations.

PERT (Programme Evaluation and Review Technique)

A *software* function that examines the deployment of resources, normally within a capital investment project, and uses network analysis techniques to predict project timescales and to highlight the "critical path".

Phase encoding

A technique of storing *data bits* on *magnetic tape* for *digital cassette* or *cartridge tape* recorders. The technique is illustrated in Fig. 146.

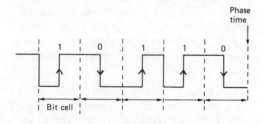

FIG. 146. Phase encoding.

Each data bit is represented by a flux change, e.g. south to north represents 1, and north to south represents 0, half-way through a "bit cell". Notice that a flux change must occur at the boundary between bit cells if the following bit is the same as the previous bit.

Phased locked loop detector

An *integrated circuit* that generates a predetermined *logic* level at its output only if a precise frequency sinewave is present at its input. It is the component that is used commonly to interpret logic 1 and logic 0 *bit* signals from a *Kansas standard* signal when a *program* is read from an *audio cassette* recorder into a *microcomputer*. See Fig. 147.

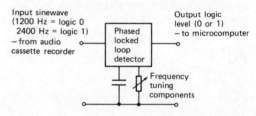

FIG. 147. Use of phase locked loop detector for signal from audio cassette recorder.

A typical device is the NE567 *chip*.

Photocell

A device that generates a voltage when light is absorbed. Therefore it is a "photovoltaic" device, and it can be used to power low-current electronic systems, e.g. pocket *microcomputer* games.

Simply the device is a silicon *pn junction*. Charge carriers cross the junction as light is absorbed, and a small emf (voltage) is generated at the terminals. A typical commercial device generates 0.55 V at 22 mA when exposed to bright sunlight. Cells can be used in series connection to increase the voltage, or in parallel connection to increase the current.

Photodiode

See *Optoelectronic devices* for a description of the photodiode, phototransistor and photoresistor (light dependent resistor).

Photomask A mask that is used in the *planar* process of constructing *integrated circuits* at each of the masking and diffusion stages.

Piggy backing The technique of placing an *integrated circuit* (IC) on top of another identical IC. Piggy backing is often applied as a fault-finding aid, and can help to highlight a faulty IC which exhibits an open-circuit input or output connection.

PIO (Parallel Input/Output) A *parallel input/output chip* that provides two or three programmable ports. The manufacturer of a *microprocessor* invariably supports his *CPU* chip with a PIO, which can be almost as complex and expensive as the microprocessor itself.

The PIO is an extremely flexible and powerful component. It enables input/output connections to be made from a *microcomputer* to a wide range of *peripherals* and external circuits. Its programmable feature allows the user to select the direction of each of its ports, e.g. input or output. Figure 148 shows a typical PIO, which is normally a 40-pin device.

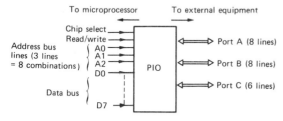

FIG. 148. Typical PIO (Parallel Input/Output).

The *chip select* signal is generated by an *address decoder* circuit and the read/write *control bus* signal selects direction of *data* transfer along the *data bus* (D0 to D7). Normally three *address bus* lines (A0 to A2) are connected to provide eight addresses on the chip. These addresses may be:

(a) Port A — 8 input/output lines;
(b) Port B — 8 input/output lines;
(c) Port C — 6 input/output lines (commonly a full port is not available);
(d) *Control register* — to program or "initialise" the ports to act as input or output ports (see *Initialising*);
(e) *Counter/timer* — this is an additional bonus circuit within many PIOs and it can be used to count external *pulses* or to generate precise time delays;

plus three unused addresses.

Widely used PIOs are the *Intel* 8155 and 8255 (both provide limited *ROM* and *RAM* also), *Zilog* Z80 PIO, *MOS Technology* 6522 and *Texas Instruments* 9901.

PIP (Peripheral Interchange Program) A *utility program* that is provided with the *CP/M operating system* and which is used principally to copy *disks*, e.g. to generate a security back-up of a *floppy disk*.

Pixel A dot position on a *CRT* screen that is divided into a *dot matrix* array. In a *microcomputer* system that generates *graphics* displays on a CRT, the screen may be divided into a 260×160 matrix. Each point on that matrix is called a pixel. Generally in a colour display that is applied with most *home computers* and many commercial *desktop computers*, lines can be drawn between pixels and a range of different colours can be assigned to each pixel dot or inter-pixel line. In the *memory mapped video* area in *main memory RAM*, a single *bit* is used to denote the illumination of a single pixel in a monochrome display; however three more bits may be necessary for a colour display to denote the colour of the point in coded form (3 bits = 8 combinations/colours).

Pixel graphics The construction of lines and shapes on a *CRT* display by *computer*, using illumination of adjacent *pixels*. *Raster scan* is applied to generate the display picture.

Pixel *graphics* are applied widely in *home computers*.

PLA See *Programmable logic array*.

Planar The fabrication process that is used generally to construct *integrated circuits*. The planar process consists of a series of photo mask and diffusion processes on a wafer of *silicon*.

Consider the construction of a simple *bipolar transistor* in a *TTL* circuit. The initial stages in the procedure are to deposit an *epitaxial* layer (into which the transistor will be later diffused) of silicon on top of a silicon substrate, and to cover this firstly with a layer of insulating silicon oxide and secondly with a thin layer of light-sensitive photoresist. This whole wafer is then exposed to UV light through a mask, as shown in Fig. 149.

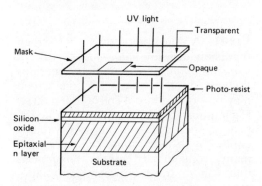

FIG. 149. Photoresist process.

The photoresist areas exposed to the UV light harden, and these areas remain after development. The unexposed photoresist area and the silicon oxide beneath it are etched away.

The photoresist is then fully etched away, and the surface of the wafer is exposed to a vapour containing boron, such that boron "diffusion" takes place through the etched window as shown in Fig. 150.

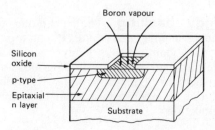

FIG. 150. Diffusion process.

A p-type region is established due to boron diffusion. The surface is then re-oxidised to create a silicon oxide layer and the entire photoresist and diffusion (using phosphorus in place of boron) procedure is repeated to create a second n-type region. Three regions now exist — n (the epitaxial layer itself), p and n. This constitutes a single transistor. Thin metallic layers are now deposited to enable connections to be made to the three layers, as shown in Fig. 151.

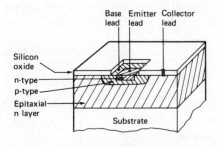

FIG. 151. Complete planar transistor.

Clearly many transistors are fabricated simultaneously on a single silicon wafer. The wafer is then scored and broken into individual "chips". Each chip can itself contain many transistors (and other components) constituting an "*integrated circuit*".

PLC (Programmable Logic Con-

troller) A *logic* system that generates a series of output signals in response to the settings of a series of input signals. The system can be "programmed" to perform different logic sequences.

PLCs are applied commonly in industrial applications to provide sequence control of complex processes, e.g. interlocked conveyor drive system, electrical crane hoist system, etc. Early PLCs were built using a large array of *gate* circuits, with a facility to rewire the interconnections between gates in order to "program" the system to perform a different overall function. Recent PLCs are *microcomputer*-based, and normally possess a *CRT* display which attempts to simulate an electrical drawing of the control system function using conventional relay logic, as shown in Fig. 152.

each row by manual entry on the keyboard. This reprogramming facility is extremely flexible and does not require any rewiring of the circuit. The current "program" of control sequence for the entire system can be dumped to *floppy disk* or magnetic card for reload after system start-up or corruption.

PLM A *high-level language* developed for *microcomputers* by *Intel* but not commonly applied.

Plotter A *peripheral* device that draws graphical representations of *data*. When connected to a *computer* a plotter can be used for the following applications:

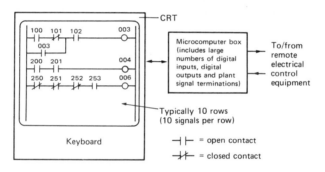

Fɪɢ. 152. Microcomputer-based PLC.

The CRT display is a "ladder network" which shows the manner in which several signals are combined across a horizontal row on the CRT to generate an output signal (denoted by the circle symbol), which typically activates a remote electrical motor. These signals are principally *digital* input signals from remote pushbuttons, limit switches, etc., but they can also be dummy inputs, i.e. a signal effectively generated by the setting of another digital output signal. The operator can monitor the setting of signals across each row as input signals change. Additionally he can redesign the logic of

(a) plot plant instrumentation data against time;
(b) plot commercial data, e.g. sales figures, histograms;
(c) draw electrical circuits, mechanical machined parts or civil engineering designs as part of a *CAD* (Computer Aided Design) *package* etc.

Plotters are rarely applied in *microcomputer* applications due to the high price — £5000 to £20,000.

There are two common interfaces between computer and plotter: *serial* (*RS 232-C*) and double *analogue* signal (one signal for each dimension in the XY plot).

PMOS
One of the three classifications of *MOS integrated circuits*. The others are *NMOS* and *CMOS*. PMOS has been almost totally superseded by NMOS, principally because the latter has a speed improvement of a factor of 10, but it was applied in the manufacture of early *microprocessors*.

P channel *FETs* are used in the manufacture of these devices — refer to *MOS* and *FET* for fuller descriptions.

PN junction
The junction of two different types of *semiconductor* material (usually *silicon*); one is p-type and the other is n-type. *Transistors* and *integrated circuits* contain numbers of pn junctions. A symbolic representation is shown in Fig. 153.

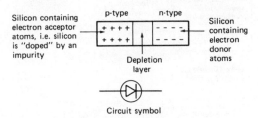

FIG. 153. Silicon pn junction.

The depletion layer is electrically neutral, and if an electric voltage is applied across the junction such that the n layer is made more positive than the p layer then the depletion layer widens and no current flows. If a voltage of opposite polarity is applied, the depletion layer narrows and current flows across the junction. This simple device is called a "diode".

If an additional layer is included a transistor is formed. An integrated circuit of the *TTL* family consists of dozens or hundreds of such junctions, whilst a *MOS* circuit contains thousands or tens of thousands of such junctions.

Pointer
The name given to a *register* when it is used in an *indirect addressing* mode.

Poke
A special command within *BASIC* that allows the *high-level language* programmer to insert *data* values into specified *memory* locations. For example

540 POKE 256,13

causes the number 13 (*decimal*) to be loaded into memory address 256 (decimal).

This command is useful if *memory mapped input/output* is used (as in most *home computers*), because the same command can be used to output a data value or *bit* pattern through an *output port*.

Refer also to *PEEK*.

Poll
A *software* action that involves checking the status of an external *peripheral* (or peripherals), e.g. to check if the peripheral wishes to transfer *data*. Examples of software polling are:

(a) repeatedly check the state of an *input/output chip* (a *UART*) that is used to transfer *characters* to a *printer*, e.g. to detect when a "busy" *bit* in the UART confirms that the previous character has been cleared;

(b) regularly scan a *keyboard* to examine if a pushbutton is depressed;

(c) examine the status of an *A/D* converter to check if it has finished a conversion process;

(d) read a collection of peripheral devices to determine which device generated an *interrupt* request if they share the same interrupt line.

Often repeated software polling is an inefficient way of examining if an external device wishes to transfer data, and an interrupt system is preferred.

POP   The action of reading a *data* value off a *microcomputer stack*. Sometimes the word "pull" is used instead. The *program instruction* POP causes a data value, which was stored initially on the stack with a *PUSH* instruction, to be removed from the stack and placed in a selected *CPU register*.

The principal role of the stack is to store return addresses automatically for *subroutines* and *interrupt service routines*, but the PUSH and POP instructions allow manual operation of the stack.

Port   The point at which *input/output* devices are connected to a *computer*. A *microcomputer* port carries eight *parallel* discrete signals, and it can be:

(a)   an *output port*, connecting to a *printer, segment display*, etc.;
(b)   an *input port*, connecting from a *keyboard*, remote instrumentation, etc.

A port can be a single *integrated circuit*, or it can be part of a *programmable* multi-port integrated circuit — a *PIO*.

Positive logic   The representation of *logic* 1 by a high voltage and logic 0 by a low voltage. Normally in positive logic:

$$\text{logic } 1 = +5 \text{ V}$$
$$\text{logic } 0 = 0 \text{ V}$$

but other voltage levels are used, e.g. +9 V, for logic 1 in some electronic systems.

Contrast with the less common *Negative logic*.

Post mortem dump   A *data* dump (to a *printer* or *backing store*) of the values of *registers* and data locations following a *program* error.

Power-down interrupt   An *interrupt* signal that is generated when a

detection circuit identifies a loss of dc power — perhaps due to loss of ac mains. A special *interrupt service routine* is entered and this performs essential housekeeping tasks that may be necessary to preserve important *data*, possibly by storing it on *backing store*. Short-term battery back-up is often necessary to allow this function to operate.

It is not used as frequently with *microcomputers* as a *power-up interrupt*.

Power-up interrupt   The *interrupt* signal that is generated by a timing circuit after *computer* switch-on, or "power-up". This signal is used to cause *program* execution to commence at a particular *memory* address, viz. the start address of the main program. Figure 154 demonstrates the action of the signal.

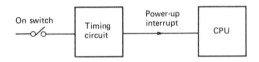

FIG. 154. Power-up interrupt.

The timing circuit allows typically ½ sec to elapse after the machine is switched on to allow time for the dc supply voltages to rise and settle. An interrupt is then generated — see *Interrupt vector*.

In some microprocessors the *Reset* signal line is used as a power-up interrupt. In addition to forcing program execution to commence at a particular memory location (often 0000), the reset action can cause certain *CPU registers* to be reset, e.g. set the *status register* to 0.

Prestel   An information system based on the British national telephone network. Pages of information, e.g. weather, travel information, entertainments, etc., can be selected for display on a domestic television receiver. Also known as "Viewdata".

Printed circuit board A board that supports an electronic circuit with component interconnections made by etched copper tracks.

Printer A *peripheral* device that produces a printed copy of *alphanumeric characters*. Printers are connected to *computers* to record *program* listings and operator messages, e.g. a summarising "log" of daily transactions. A good quality printer is the central element in a *word processor*.

Categories of printers are:

(a) *matrix-printer* — creates characters by an array of printed dots;
(b) moving-head printer — a *daisy-wheel printer* or a *golfball printer*;
(c) *non-impact printer* — thermal or electrostatic operation.

Priority The significance, normally expressed as a number, given to each of several signal lines or devices to determine the order in which they are serviced. The most common application of a priority system that is applied to *microcomputers* is with *interrupt* lines. Each interrupt signal line is assigned a priority level, such that a lower priority interrupt is ignored by the *CPU* if a higher priority is being serviced currently.

Priority coded interrupt An *interrupt* request that generates a code that represents its *priority*.

Problem oriented language A *programming language* that is tailored for a specific class of problems, e.g. scientific or mathematical functions.

Procedure A section of *program* that performs a specific task. A procedure call within some *programming languages* causes entry to a separate sequence of *instructions*, which perform an identifi-

able action. When the procedure is completed, return is made to the instruction following the call. An example of a procedure-driven language is CORAL, which is used mainly with *minicomputers*.

Processor Another name for *CPU* (Central Processor Unit). The word is also used in *software* parlance to describe a *compiler* or *assembler*, e.g. a *Cobol* processor.

Program A series of processing steps that a *computer* is required to perform. An operator who prepares this sequence of steps is called a "programmer". The program can be one of the following types:

(a) *high-level language* program — each step is called a "*command*";
(b) *low-level language* program — each step is called an "*instruction*".

Program counter A *register* within a *CPU* that holds the *memory* address of the next *instruction* that is to be obeyed. Its position within the CPU is illustrated in Fig. 155.

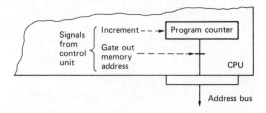

FIG. 155. Role of program counter within CPU.

The program counter is normally 16 *bits* wide with 8-bit *microprocessors*, but it can be 20 bits or more with some 16-bit microprocessors. A 16-bit program counter feeds onto the *address bus*, giving 64K memory addressing range.

The *control unit* gates out the contents of the program counter onto the address bus when an instruction is fetched from memory. Normally the program counter is incremented automatically after each instruction is obeyed, in order to point to the memory address of the next instruction. The sequence is broken if one of the following occurs:

(a) *jump* instruction is obeyed;
(b) *subroutine* call instruction is obeyed;
(c) *interrupt* occurs;

in which case the program counter is overwritten with a different memory address.

See *Fetch/execute cycle.*

Program counter relative addressing See *Relative addressing.*

Programmable An item of *hardware* that can have its function altered. The most familiar programmable *integrated circuits* are:

(a) *PIO* (parallel input/output), which can have its *ports* set by *software* to act as input or output in direction;
(b) *UART* (serial input/output), which can have its transmission speed (*baud rate*) and other transmission options set by software;
(c) *counter/timer*, which can be programmed to generate different time delays.

In each of these cases, the device is programmed by software which sends control data to the "*control register*" within the *chip.*

Refer also to *PLC* (Programmable Logic Controller), *Programmable logic array* and *PROM* (programmable *ROM*).

Programmable logic array (PLA) An *integrated circuit* that provides a *logic* network of *AND* and *OR*

gates. The overall logic function is *mask programmed*, i.e. set during the manufacturing process, or occasionally "field programmed". A typical device (DM7575) possesses 14 inputs, 96 product terms and 8 outputs. A simpler example is the SN7448, which is a *BCD* to 7-segment decoder, as shown in Fig. 156 (see *Segment display*).

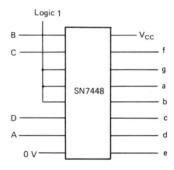

FIG. 156. Example PLA — BCD to 7-segment decoder (SN7448).

Programmable logic controller See *PLC.*

Programmable read only memory See *PROM.*

Programmable timer See *Counter/ timer.*

Programming language See *Language.*

PROM (Programmable Read Only Memory) A *ROM integrated circuit* that is programmed by the customer. Contrast with a ROM, which is *mask programmed* by the *chip* manufacturer.

A PROM is programmed in a *PROM programmer.* PROMs are more expensive than ROMs, but are cheaper than *EPROMs.* However the reprogrammable (after erasure by UV light) feature of

121

EPROMs makes them more popular devices.

Figure 157 shows how a single *bit* is stored in a matrix arrangement within a PROM using a "fusible-link" arrangement.

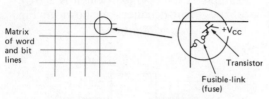

FIG. 157. Fusible-link PROM.

A bit is stored across each intersection in the matrix using a *transistor* or diode in series with a fusible link. When the PROM is programmed and a 0 is to be stored in a particular bit position, the fuse for that bit is "blown", or open-circuited, by a large current. Clearly this process cannot be reversed, and so unlike an EPROM, a PROM can only be programmed once.

PROM programmer

A device that programs (writes *data* into) *PROMs* and *EPROMs*. A PROM programmer can take one of two common forms:

(a) a *printed circuit board* that fits into a multi-board *microprocessor development system* (MDS) and allows *software* to transfer a fully tested *program* into PROM or EPROM;

(b) a stand-alone device, as shown in Fig. 158.

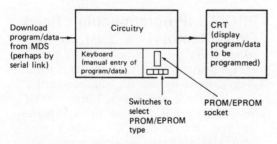

FIG. 158. Stand-alone PROM programmer.

In both (a) and (b) the program, which transfers the fully tested program/data to PROM or EPROM, usually performs a verify operation, i.e. confirm that each *byte* is programmed correctly.

Prompt

A message from a *program* to the *computer* operator to request some action from him. A prompt may take the form of a *CRT* message such as:

(a) a unique symbol by the *operating system* (e.g. by CP/M) informing the operator that the previous action is complete and that a further entry on the *keyboard* can now be made;

(b) a descriptive word or phrase, e.g. "ENTER TWO NUMBERS", by an *interactive* program.

Propagation delay

The time for a *logic* level change to propagate through a circuit.

Protocol

A fixed set of rules that must be obeyed when information is passed from one system to another. The most common application is in a *computer*-to-computer link, in which the "protocol" describes both *hardware* and *software* requirements. The former may simply specify that a *RS 232-C serial* link is to be used, at a *baud rate* of 9600, with even *parity*, etc. The latter may demand a more rigorous specification, e.g.

(a) header message, i.e. several initial *characters* must be transmitted at the start of a transmission block;

(b) trailer message must be sent, perhaps with a *cyclic redundancy check* character;

(c) a reply message must be sent by the receiving computer to signify correct reception;

(d) the transmitting computer repeats the block transmission up to three times after transmission failures before aborting the transfer.

Pseudo-instruction
An *instruction* in an *assembly language program* that does not cause the generation of a *machine code* when the program is assembled. A pseudo-instruction is a command to the *assembler* and is not strictly part of the program. Common assembler "pseudos", using typical *mnemonics*, are:

(a) ORG — start assembling at a specific *memory* location;
(b) END — program is completed;
(c) EQU — give a *label* name to a memory address or *data* value;
(d) DB — enter data values, not instructions.

A sample assembly language program for the *Intel* 8085 *microprocessor* using pseudo-instructions is:

Label Instruction Comment

      ORG 100H   ;Pseudo — start loading program at memory address 100

MARY EQU 200H   ;Pseudo — set label MARY to have value hex. 200

    LDA MARY   ;Load A register with contents of memory address 200

    OUT 10H   ;Output A register to input/output port address 10

HERE:JMP HERE   ;Loop stop — jump to itself

    ORG MARY   ;Pseudo — transfer assembly to memory address 200

    DB 4   ;Pseudo — load data value 4 into memory address 200

    END   ;Pseudo — finish program

P-type FET
An *FET* constructed using a P-type conduction channel. Such a device is the principal circuit element in *PMOS* circuits.

Pull-up resistor
A register that pulls the voltage level for a signal line to a high voltage (normally *logic* 1). A pull-up

resistor can be applied in the following cases shown in Fig. 159.

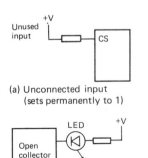

(a) Unconnected input (sets permanently to 1)

(b) Open collector output (provides current path for load)

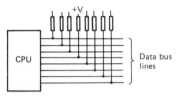

(c) Microprocessor (CPU) data bus (pulls data bus lines, when unused, to 1)

KEY
Resistor symbol is:

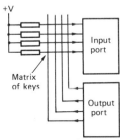

(d) Matrix keyboard input (holds input to 1 until set to 0 when a closed key is scanned)

FIG. 159. Applications of pull-up resistor.

Pulse
An electrical signal that switches between two *logic* levels and then returns to its original state — see Fig. 160.

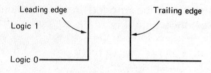

Fig. 160. Pulse.

The *leading edge* and the *trailing edge* can each be either a *rising edge* or a *falling edge*. A voltage pulse is the common trigger signal for a wide variety of electronic circuits, e.g.

(a) *flip-flop*;
(b) *counter*;
(c) *microprocessor*, using the *CPU clock* stream of pulses;
(d) *A/D* converter;
etc.

A pulse stream is generated by an *astable multivibrator*.

Pulse generator See *Astable multivibrator*.

Purchase ledger A *software* function that is frequently offered with business *microcomputers* to maintain records of supplier accounts for a small commercial organisation. Printed cheques, credit notes and debit/credit adjustments are produced. Typically several hundred supplier accounts can be recorded on a single *floppy disk*, and several disks enable over 1000 accounts to be processed.

Push The action of entering a *data* value on a *microcomputer stack*. The *program instruction* PUSH causes a data value to be transferred from a *CPU register* to the next free location on the stack, and the data value can be retrieved later in the program using the *POP* instruction.

The principal role of the stack is to store return addresses automatically for *subroutines* and *interrupt service routines*, but the PUSH and POP instructions allow manual operation of the stack.

Pushdown list A list of *data* values in which the last data item stored is the first to be retrieved. An alternative name is "last in, first out". See *LIFO* and *Stack*, which is an example of a pushdown list.

Pushup list A list of *data* values in which the last data item stored is the last to be retrieved. An alternative name is "last in, last out".

Q

Quantisation The setting of a *continuous* signal into one of several possible discrete ranges. The term is applied to *A/D* converters, e.g. the quantisation of an *analogue* signal in an 8-bit A/D converter involves setting the signal at one of 256 levels ($2^8 = 256$). If the analogue voltage range is 0 to 10 V, each "quanta" therefore

$$= \frac{10 \text{ V}}{256} = 0.039 \text{ V}.$$

The "quantisation error" is half this amount, i.e. 0.0195 V.

Quartz crystal See *Crystal*.

Quiescent state The normal setting of a *logic* signal within a circuit when that particular part of the circuit is not performing its active function. For example, the quiescent state of a *chip select* signal that conforms to *positive logic* is logic 0.

Qwerty keyboard A *keyboard* in

which the pushbuttons are arranged in the manner of a traditional typewriter, i.e. with the top left-hand block of pushbuttons forming the letters "QWERTY". Contrast with *Numeric keypad*.

R

Rack-up A method of displaying information on a *CRT* such that when the display screen is full the entire format is moved up by one line position when a new line is added at the bottom.

Radix Another name for *base*.

Rail voltage The dc voltage supply lines in an electronic circuit.

RAM (Random Access Memory) *Semiconductor memory* that can be written to and read from. Strictly the term "random access" means that locations can be accessed in a random manner without the need to step through preceding locations, but this description applies also to the other type of semiconductor memory — *ROM* (Read Only Memory). Hence the name is misleading, but it is generally accepted. An alternative and better name is Read/Write Memory (RWM), but this has achieved only limited application.

Most *microcomputers* possess a mixture of ROM and RAM in their *main memory*. ROM contains *programs* and *data* which are permanent, whilst RAM allows the user to enter a program. The program can be manually entered into RAM from the operator *keyboard*, or transferred from *backing store*.

RAM memory is "volatile", i.e. it loses its stored *bits* when dc power is removed — bits are set unpredictably on switch-on.

A typical RAM *integrated circuit* is shown in Fig. 161.

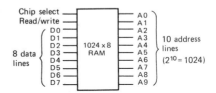

FIG. 161. Typical RAM integrated circuit (1024 × 8).

The 10 address lines give 1024 (2^{10}) combinations, and so the device contains 1024 locations. The 8 bidirectional data lines indicate that 8 bits are stored in each location. The *chip select* signal must be set to 1 to activate the *chip*, and the setting of the read/write signal determines if data is to be read from the chip or written to it.

Unfortunately the majority of RAM chips do not give *byte* (8-bit) storage to enable straightforward connection to a *microprocessor's data bus* like ROM devices. Often RAM is offered in 4-bit and 1-bit form, and two or eight devices respectively must be connected to the 8-bit data bus.

There are two categories of RAM as follows:

(a) *static RAM* — stored bits are held until dc power is removed;
(b) *dynamic RAM* — as for static RAM, plus the characteristic that bits are lost, unless the device is refreshed, after a short time period (typically 2 msec).

The most common static RAM chip is probably the 2114 (1024 × 4), and Fig. 162 shows two such devices combined to provide 1K of byte storage in an 8-bit microcomputer.

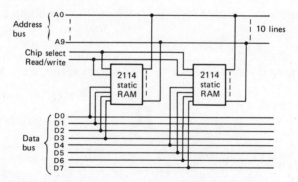

FIG. 162. Static RAM — 2 off 4-bit chips combined for byte storage.

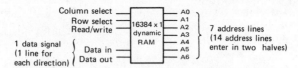

FIG. 163. Dynamic RAM (4116 — 16384 × 1).

Figure 163 shows the pin connections for a typical dynamic RAM chip — the 4116.

Features which distinguish this device from a typical static RAM chip are:

(1) Separate input and output data lines for the single bit that is stored — data lines are bidirectional with static RAM.

(2) Only 7 address lines are used in place of the expected 14 lines; the two halves of the address are entered one after the other — "row select" is set with the first half, and "column select" is set with the second half.

(3) Refresh is accomplished by setting all combinations on the 7 address lines together with "row select" faster than once every 2 msec.

Dynamic RAM is lower powered, smaller, faster and cheaper than static RAM. However, it is normally only justified in large memory systems due to the cost of the additional circuitry to provide the refresh facility and the "time-multiplexing" of the two halves of the address bus.

A typical circuit arrangement for a CMOS static RAM memory bit is described under *CMOS*. A dynamic RAM in *MOS* form uses a simpler circuit for bit storage, e.g. a capacitor (from which electric charge leaks, thus necessitating refresh) and a couple of *FETs*.

Random access Method by which *data* can be retrieved in a random manner without the necessity to step through all locations before the selected one. Contrast with *Sequential access*.

Most *memory* systems applied with *microcomputers* are random access, e.g. *ROM* and *RAM* (*main memory*), and *floppy disk* and *hard disk* (*backing store*). *Magnetic tape* devices are not random access.

Random access memory See *RAM*.

Random logic Another name for *combinational logic*.

Raster scan The technique of deflecting the electron beam across a *CRT* in a succession of horizontal lines, or "scans", to produce a complete picture "raster". When the CRT is connected to a *microcomputer* to display data directly fed out of microcomputer *memory*, the normal raster scan electron beam intensity is modulated by the data from memory. The method of modulation is described under *Memory mapped video*, *Video signal* and *Video generator*. A raster scan is the normal method of deflecting the electron beam across the face of the CRT, and is in contrast with the less common technique that draws graphical symbols by deflecting the beam from any specific point on the CRT screen directly to another.

A typical raster scan is shown in Fig. 164.

nature of a *memory* device, and in particular of *RAM chips*.

Read/write signal Another name for *write enable*.

Real time clock A time-of-day count that is held in a *computer memory* and updated by *software*. This real time clock can be referenced so that certain software functions can run at specific times in the day, e.g. a reporting *program* can run at 11 o'clock, or a *data* storage program can run every ·hour.

A typical arrangement is shown in Fig. 165.

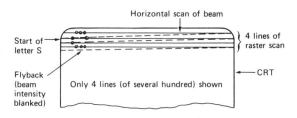

FIG. 164. Raster scan.

Read The action of transferring a *data* value from a device. The term is normally applied with *microcomputers* to the process of transferring the contents of a *memory* location into the *CPU*. Alternatively a *register* (e.g. *status register*), *input port*, *keyboard*, *counter/timer*, etc., can be read, and the value placed in a CPU register for subsequent examination and processing by *software*.

Read only memory See *ROM*.

Read/write The description of a device that can be read from and written to. Normally the word is used to define the

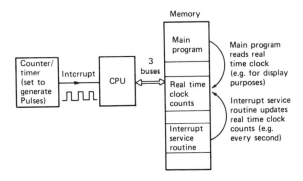

FIG. 165. Real time clock.

A real time clock is more commonly applied with *mainframe computers* and *minicomputers* than with *microcomputers*.

127

Refer to *Counter/timer* and *Interrupt*.

Real time programming   A *software* arrangement in which programs are run with reference to the time of day or at regular timed intervals. Examples are:

(a)   programs run at end of day, end of working shift, at precisely 09.30, etc.

(b)   programs run with a timed interval, e.g. a *keyboard* scanning program runs every 100 msec, a plant instrumentation scanning program runs every 10 sec, one program is run 5 sec after a program that calls it.

Real time programming is applied particularly with process monitoring and control applications — see *Minicomputer*.

Record   A block of *bytes* in a storage medium. Normally a record is a subdivision of a *file*, and applies to *floppy disk* or *magnetic tape* storage devices. *CP/M* uses the word to describe a *sector* (128 bytes) on *backing store*.

Recovery time   The time required to change a *memory* device from write to read mode, and to obtain correct *data* at the output connections.

Recursive routine   A *program* section, e.g. a *subroutine*, that calls itself.

Redundancy   The application of additional *characters* or *bits* in a *data* list to assist in the detection of data corruption, e.g. a *parity* bit or a *cyclic redundancy check* character.

Alternatively the word is used to describe the situation in which additional or duplicate *hardware* units are applied, normally to assist the security of the overall system function in the event of a breakdown.

Re-entrant subroutine   A *subroutine* that is used both by a main *program* and by an *interrupt service routine*. Assume that a subroutine is being executed as a result of a call from the main program, and an *interrupt* occurs. The interrupt service routine which is then entered may call the same subroutine, which is then said to be "re-entered". Great care must be taken when programming such a subroutine to prevent data corruption occurring during re-entry.

Refresh   The process of reinstating *data* of the following forms:

(a)   stored *bits* in a dynamic *RAM* — caused by leakage of the capacitor charge;

(b)   *CRT* display — repeating a *raster scan*, e.g. 50 screen updates every second;

(c)   *multiplexed segment display* — each digit display in a multiplexed multidigit segment display system is updated in turn, and the whole display system must be updated (or "refreshed") at a rate that is fast enough so that it appears as constantly on to the human eye.

Register   A multi-*bit hardware* storage device. When applied in *microcomputer* terminology the word frequently refers to a *CPU* work register which is used to provide temporary storage of *data* within a *program*, e.g. the A (accumulator), B, C, D, E, H and L registers in the *Intel* 8085 and *Zilog* Z80 *microprocessors*. The bit-size of the CPU registers is the same as the *word* length of the microprocessor, i.e. 8-bit or 16-bit normally.

Register indirect addressing

See *Indirect addressing.*

Register pair

Two *CPU registers* used as a single unit. In some 8-*bit microprocessors* two of the *work registers* within the CPU can be used to process 16-bit *data* values in some *instructions.* For example, the B and C registers in the 8-bit *Intel* 8085 can be combined by an instruction that loads a 16-bit data value into the register pair, and by another instruction that decrements (subtracts 1) from the contents of the pair.

Relative addressing

An *addressing mode* which is used normally with *jump instructions*, i.e. *program* instructions that transfer control to a different part of the program. The jump is made "relative" to the current instruction, i.e. a certain number of *words* backwards or forwards in *memory.* For example, the instruction

$$JZ +7$$

jumps (on zero) forwards 7 words.

Many *microprocessors* do not possess relative addressing; they possess *absolute addressing* alone for jump instructions.

Notice that relative addressing involves a limit to the magnitude of the step that can be demanded, e.g. if an 8-*bit field* is used in the *machine code* for the number of words to be jumped then the limit is 255 words forwards and backwards.

Relocate

To amend a *program* so that it runs in a different area of *memory.* A relocater program is often applied in a *microprocessor development system* in order to process a program under development such that the latter can be scheduled to run in a different memory area. This process involves altering any absolute memory addresses that are used in the program.

Report generator

A *program* that allows the operator to select the format or lay-out of information that is produced (normally on a *printer*) by a *computer.*

Reserved word

A *word* or group of *characters* that cannot be used for certain functions in a *programming language* because it carries a special significance. For example:

(a) a *label* in an *assembly language program* cannot carry the same name as the *mnemonic* for an *instruction* or a *pseudo-instruction*;

(b) a variable name in a *high-level language* program cannot be the same as a special function word, e.g. DATA, PRINT (in *BASIC*).

Reset

A signal that is applied with many *microprocessors* in order to clear several of the *registers* within the device. In particular the *program counter* is set to a fixed address (normally 0). The particular application of this signal is as a *power-up interrupt*, i.e. when the machine is switched on a timing circuit sets the Reset signal after a delay in order to force *program* execution to commence at a fixed *memory* location (normally 0).

Often a manual pushbutton is also connected to this signal line, so that the operator can cause re-entry into a start-up program if a *software* "crash" occurs or if he wishes to break out of a user program that loops continuously.

Refer also to *Non-maskable interrupt* and *Interrupt service routine.*

Resistor ladder D/A

A *digital to analogue converter* circuit that employs a "ladder" of different resistors, each of which is used to switch in a scaled value of a reference voltage. It represents the most popular technique for D/A conversion and is available in *integrated circuit* form. Figure 166 demonstrates the principle of operation.

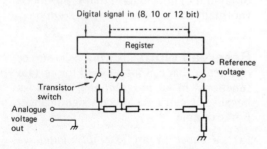

Digital signal in (8, 10 or 12 bit)

Register

Reference voltage

Transistor switch

Analogue voltage out

FIG. 166. Resistor ladder D/A.

The *digital* representation of the signal is connected to the 8, 10 or 12 digital input connections, and typically fed from a *microcomputer output port*. If any *bit* in this representation is set to 1 then a resistor is switched in to the circuit to generate a weighted value of a reference voltage. Each bit switches in descending proportions of this reference, e.g. ½, ¼, etc. The sum of these components is passed out of the device as an *analogue* voltage signal. This signal may feed to a *plotter*, *servo* (e.g. for a *robot*), chart recorder, or any other analogue device. Conversion speed is typically 1 μsec.

Resources
The *memory* and *peripherals* within a *computer* system.

Restart
The action of restoring a *computer* to its normal operational state, usually after a failure. A *microcomputer* can generally be restarted in the following ways:

(a) switching the machine off and on — this generates a *power-up interrupt*;
(b) pressing a restart pushbutton — commonly this is connected to a *Reset interrupt*.

Restore
To set a *data* value used in a *program*, or the contents of a *CPU* *register* or *memory* location, to its original state.

Return
An *instruction* that is used at the end of a *subroutine* or an *interrupt service routine*. The action of a return instruction is to restore the contents of the *program counter* within the *CPU* to enable *program* control to return to the main program at the correct point, e.g.

(a) the instruction following the *call* instruction in the case of a subroutine;
(b) the instruction following the point at which the main program was interrupted in the case of an interrupt service routine.

Normally the return address is removed from the *stack*, as illustrated in Fig. 167.

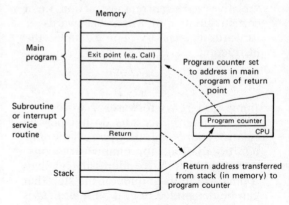

Memory

Main program

Exit point (e.g. Call)

Program counter set to address in main program of return point

Subroutine or interrupt service routine

Return

Program counter

CPU

Return address transferred from stack (in memory) to program counter

Stack

FIG. 167. Action of return instruction.

The *assembly language mnemonic* for the return instruction is commonly RET.

RGB monitor
A colour *CRT* that requires separate input signals for red (R), green (G) and blue (B). Although expensive and not commonly applied with *microcomputers*, an RGB monitor offers high quality and good resolution displays. Figure 168 shows the general method of connection.

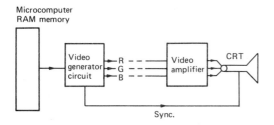

FIG. 168. Connection of RGB monitor to a microcomputer.

Ripple through counter
A *counter* in which the output of one stage is connected as the input to the succeeding stage, as shown in Fig. 169.

The advantages of robots over human control include lack of fatigue and fallibility, speed of operation and their flexibility (they can be reprogrammed to perform a different sequence).

A typical robot which is driven by a *microcomputer* is shown in Fig. 170.

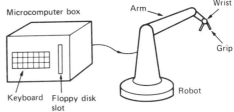

FIG. 170. Microcomputer-driven robot.

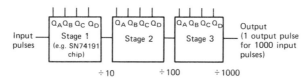

FIG. 169. Ripple through counter.

Each stage counts 10 *pulses*, i.e. it is a decade counter. The Q outputs from each stage can be used to drive a *numeric display* to give visual indication of the count achieved.

Rising edge
The transition of a *logic* level from 0 to 1. The term is normally applied to *pulse* signals — the pulse possesses a rising edge and a *falling edge*. See *Edge triggering*.

Robot
A mechanical device that performs an automatic sequence of movements. *Microprocessor*-based robots are used in the following applications:

(a) automatic welding in a car assembly line;
(b) automatic paint spraying;
(c) "pick-and-place" applications, e.g. passing a machined piece from one manufacturing process to the next, e.g. from one *computer numerical control* machine tool to the next.

An industrial robot possesses five or six degrees of freedom to give flexible movement. This means that five or six electric or hydraulic (for more power) drives are required within the robot. In an electrically actuated device, these drives are either:

(a) *servos* — for better resolution of positioning;
(b) *stepper motors* — simpler to drive from microcomputer.

A storage device, e.g. a *floppy disk*, is required to store and reload a movement sequence, and this allows the sequence to be reprogrammed.

High technology robots can use a wide range of external sensors, e.g. infrared and tactile (touch) sensors, *image processing* using a video camera, etc.

Roller-ball
A manually-adjustable input device that is applied to generate a variable signal to a *computer*. It is a variation of the *joystick*.

Rollover The situation when two keys in a *keyboard* are pressed together. Problems can occur in the scanning *software*, and two methods can be adopted to handle this situation:

(a) accept the first key closure that is detected in the scan procedure (described under *Keyboard*), process it (e.g. display the symbol for the key), and then accept and process any further keys that are pressed simultaneously — this is called "N-key rollover";

(b) accept only one key closure and ignore the keyboard until that key is released — this is called "two-key rollover".

ROM (Read Only Memory)

Semiconductor memory that can only be read. Once a *program* and/or *data* is written into ROM it cannot be altered. There are several different categories within the generic name of ROM:

(a) ROM (Read Only Memory) — the device is programmed during *chip* manufacture;

(b) *PROM* (Programmable ROM) — manufactured in a "blank" form and programmed by the user;

(c) *EPROM* (Erasable PROM) — PROM that can be erased by exposure to UV light and re-programmed;

(d) *EAROM* (Electrically Alterable ROM) — ROM that can be altered when located in its final circuit.

ROM possesses one big advantage over *RAM*, which is read/write memory. It is non-volatile, i.e. when dc power is removed the chip retains its stored *bit* pattern. For this reason, ROM is used to hold *microcomputer* programs that are required when the machine is switched on. The user can enter programs, or call them off *backing store*, into RAM. A program and/or data held in ROM is

often called "firmware". A typical ROM is the 2316, which provides *2K bytes* storage, and is illustrated in Fig. 171.

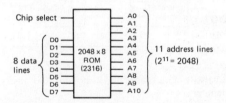

FIG. 171. Typical ROM integrated circuit (2048×8, e.g. 2316).

The 11 address lines give 2048 (2^{11}) combinations, and so the device contains 2048 locations. The 8 data lines indicate that 8 *bits* are stored in each location. The *chip select* signal must be set to 1 to activate the chip and to cause the contents of the addressed location to be placed on the data lines.

In a practical microcomputer circuit the address lines are connected to the least significant 11 lines in the *address bus*, the data lines are connected to the *data bus* and the chip select signal is connected from an output from an address decoder circuit (see *Address decoding*).

Rotate The act of shifting a *data* item in an *instruction* such that a *bit* which is shifted out of one end is shifted in to the other end. A typical 8-bit *microprocessor* possesses several instructions that perform *shift* operations. A small number of these instructions cause a rotate action — Fig. 172 demonstrates the action of a rotate left instruction.

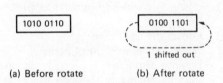

(a) Before rotate   (b) After rotate

FIG. 172. Contents of accumulator for rotate instruction.

The bit that is rotated from one end of the *accumulator* to the other normally sets the *carry flag* in the *status register*.

Routine The name given to a short *program*, or section of program, that performs a well-defined function, e.g. error routine, output routine. A group of standard program sections that can be appended by user programs when they are under development is often called a set of "library routines".

Two special types of routines are *subroutines* and *interrupt service routines*.

RS 232-C A world standard that is applied for *serial data* transfer. The RS 232-C specification defines the signal characteristics for serial communication between *computer* and remote *VDU*, *printer* or other computer. The signal waveform for the transmission of one *character* or *byte* (8-*bits*) is shown in Fig. 173.

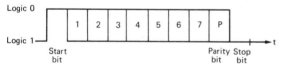

FIG. 173. RS 232-C waveform for serial transmission of one character.

The principal elements in the specification are:

(a) The *ASCII* character set is used, i.e. each character in a message uses the unique ASCII code.

(b) The transmission speed is one of the following: 110, 300, 600, 1200, 2400, 4800 and 9600 *baud* (1 baud = 1 bit per second).

(c) The signal levels are:
  logic 0 = approximately +9 V (+3 V to +25 V)
  logic 1 = approximately −9 V (−3 V to −25 V).

(d) *Parity* checking can be performed. Odd, even and transparent (parity

bit not utilised) parity can be selected.

(e) The number of data bits can be 5, 6 or 7 — 7 are shown in the diagram.

(f) The number of stop bits can be variable, e.g. 1, 1½ or 2.

(g) A 25-pin "D-type" connector should be used at each end of the link. Pin connections are as follows:

Pin 2 = Tx (transmit) ⎫
Pin 3 = Rx (receive) ⎬ Signal
Pin 7 = OV (signal   ⎭ connections
    ground)
Pin 4 = RTS (Request ⎫ "Hand-
    To Send)   ⎬ shaking"
Pin 5 = CTS (Clear   ⎭ control
    To Send)   signals

Normally a *UART integrated circuit* is used by a *microcomputer* for an RS 232-C data link. A typical message that is transmitted consists of several characters, e.g. to print a message on a printer, update a display on a VDU.

Variations of the RS 232-C standard are applied occasionally, e.g. the RS 422, in which a 4-wire link is used rather than a 3-wire link and the signal levels are expressed in milliamps rather than volts.

Run Execute a *program*.

Run-time The time during which a *program* is actually running. The term is often applied when a program is under development, and refers to the changed conditions that may exist when the program is executed in the final operational *software* system.

RWM (Read/Write Memory)

An alternative name for *RAM* (Random Access Memory). It is less commonly used, but is probably a more appropriate title.

S

Sales ledger A *software* function that is frequently offered with business *microcomputers* to maintain records of customer accounts for small commercial organisations. Printed invoices, credit notes, debit/credit adjustments and discounts are produced. Typically several hundred customer accounts can be recorded on a single *floppy disk*, and several disks can enable over 1000 accounts to be processed.

Sales order processing A *software* function that is frequently offered with business *microcomputers*. The *data base* is updated by manual entry of order details and production invoices. Invoices and credit notes can be produced and the stock file from an associated *stock control* system can be automatically updated.

Sample-and-hold circuit A circuit that stores an *analogue* signal. Effectively it performs the same function for an analogue signal that a *D-type bistable* performs for a *digital* signal.

A sample-and-hold circuit is often inserted at the input to an *A/D converter which feeds an input port* to a *microcomputer*. Its function is to remove the effects of any rapid fluctuations that may occur on the signal during the conversion process. The circuit arrangement is shown in Fig. 174.

A single-*bit* output signal (sample pulse) from the microcomputer switches the analogue signal through onto the holding capacitor. This signal is then staticised whilst the succeeding circuit, e.g. an A/D converter, processes the signal.

Satellite processor A *computer* that forms a subsidiary part of a larger computer system. Often a separate computer ("satellite processor") is employed in association with a *mainframe computer* to perform a data communication role.

Save To store a *program* or *data file* on *backing store*.

SBC See *Single board computer*.

S-100 bus The most widely used *common bus* that is applied to interconnect circuit boards in a multi-board *microcomputer*. An alternative name is the IEEE 696 bus.

The bus carries 100 signal connections via a double-row (50+50) edge connector along a *backplane* as shown in Fig. 175.

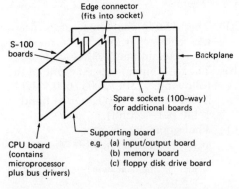

FIG. 175. S-100 bus microcomputer system construction.

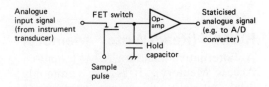

FIG. 174. Sample-and-hold circuit.

Boards can be either 5 inch or 10 inch. The *CPU* board uses an *Intel* 8080, 8085 or *Zilog* Z80 *microprocessor*, although the *Motorola* 6800 and the *MOS Technology* 6502 microprocessors can be used in adapted systems. A wide range of supporting boards is offered by several manufacturers, and can provide *input/output, memory, backing store* control, *CRT* control, and other functions.

The signal identities in the S-100 bus are listed in Table 13.

1	+8V
2	+16V
3	XRDY
4	V10
5	V11
6	V12
7	V13
8	V14
9	V15
10	V16
11	V17
12	NMI
13	PWRFAIL
14	DMA3
15	A18
16	A16
17	A17
18	SDSB
19	CDSB
20	GND
21	NDEF
22	ADSB
23	DODSB
24	φ
25	pSTVAL
26	pHLDA
27	RFU
28	RFU
29	A5
30	A4
31	A3
32	A15
33	A12
34	A9
35	DOUT1
36	DOUT0
37	A10
38	DOUT4
39	DOUT5
40	DOUT6
41	DIN2
42	DIN3
43	DIN7
44	sMI
45	sOUT
46	sINP
47	sMEMR
48	sHLTA
49	CLOCK
50	GND

51	+8V
52	−16V
53	GND
54	SLAVE CLR
55	DMA0
56	DMA1
57	DMA2
58	sXTRQ
59	A19
60	SIXTN
61	A20
62	A21
63	A22
64	A23
65	NDEF
66	NDEF
67	PHANTOM
68	MWRT
69	RFU
70	GND
71	RFU
72	RDY
73	INT
74	HOLD
75	RESET
76	pSYNC
77	pWR
78	pDBIN
79	A0
80	A1
81	A2
82	A6
83	A7
84	A8
85	A13
86	A14
87	A11
88	DOUT2
89	DOUT3
90	DOUT7
91	DIN4
92	DIN5
93	DIN6
94	DIN1
95	DIN0
96	sINTA
97	sWO
98	ERROR
99	POC
100	GND

Table 13. S-100 bus signal identities.

135

Scan To read a group of signals in sequence. A *program* is required to scan the following *computer* input signal sources:

(a) *keyboard* — normally each group, e.g. a row, of pushbuttons is read in turn by scanning *software* to determine if a key is depressed;

(b) *digital* input signals — as for keyboard, i.e. groups of contact closure (pushbuttons, relay contacts, limit switches, etc.) signals are scanned in turn; refer to *blocking diode*;

(c) *analogue* input signals — if a large number of instrumentation signals are connected to a computer, each signal is read in turn.

Notice that large numbers of input signals of these types are normally connected in a *multiplexing* arrangement.

Schmitt trigger A circuit that is applied to generate a well-defined *pulse* shape from an input voltage waveform that carries slow rise and fall times or is noisy electrically (refer to *Noise*). The circuit carries a high degree of "hysteresis", i.e. once it is triggered it requires a considerable change in input voltage to reset it. This ensures that the output does not suffer from multiple transitions caused by noise at the input. Figure 176 illustrates its action.

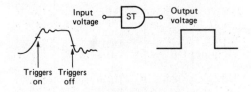

Fig. 176. Schmitt trigger.

A Schmitt trigger is offered in the *TTL* range of *integrated circuits* in the form of the SN7413, which provides two such circuits within the same *chip*. Alterna-

tively a Schmitt trigger circuit can be built using a simple *op-amp*.

Schottky TTL A variation of the familiar *TTL* range of *integrated circuits* in which the switching *transistors* are arranged never to saturate in the fully "on" and fully "off" states in order to increase the speed of operation. A Schottky barrier diode is connected between base and collector of each transistor, as shown in Fig. 177, to prevent the transistor saturating.

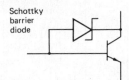

Fig. 177. Schottky TTL transistor stage.

The Schottky range of integrated circuits is the SN74S00 range, and is totally pin-compatible and function-compatible with the standard SN7400 TTL range.

A low-powered variation of Schottky TTL is available — see *Low power Schottky*.

Scratchpad An area of *memory* that is used for temporary storage of *data* values.

Screen mode A method of displaying information on a *CRT* such that when the display screen is full, a new screen "page" is selected. Contrast with *Rackup*.

Sector A block of *bytes* on a *floppy disk* or *hard disk*. Normally 1 sector = 128 bytes.

Security A system for protecting a *computer* against unauthorised access by an operator to *programs* or *data files*. Frequently this is performed by the requirement for a *password* to be entered, or by *hardware* measures, e.g. setting a *floppy disk* or *cassette* recorder to *write protect*.

Seek The action within a *floppy disk* or *hard disk* of moving the read/write *head* to the required *track*. Normally the seek action is controlled by a *stepper motor*.

Segment A section of *program* or *memory*. The term is applied to the following:

(a)   a section of program that *overlays* another section;

(b)   an area of memory with a clearly defined boundary, e.g. the Intel 8086 (see *Intel microprocessors*) can apply one 64K section of memory for program and a different 64K for *data* — each section is termed a "segment";

(c)   part of a *track* on a magnetic drum *backing store*.

Segment display A display device that constructs numbers and letters by means of an array of segments. Such displays are ideally suited to connection to a *microcomputer* because single-*bit* output signals can drive individual segments.

Segment displays which employ 7 segments are most popular, but better resolution displays, which use larger numbers of segments, are available. The connection of a single 7-segment display unit to a microcomputer *output port* is shown in Fig. 178.

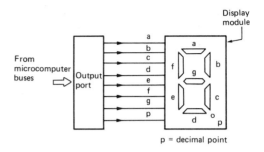

p = decimal point

FIG. 178. 7-segment display.

This display is well suited to numerical display, e.g. number 2 requires segments a, b, g, e and d, but cannot display letters adequately.

Commonly numeric displays require several digits, and the arrangement of Fig. 179 is generally applied.

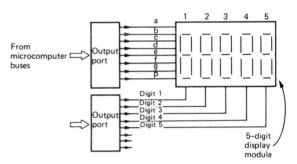

FIG. 179. Multiplexed segment display.

In this case the same segment signals are shared by each of the five digit displays. The particular display that is selected to receive the segment pattern is determined by the setting of only one of the output signals from the lower port.

Segment displays are normally either:

(a)   *LED* (Light Emitting Diode) — greater brightness;

or

(b)   *LCD* (Liquid Crystal Display) — lower power consumption.

Self-test A test that is performed by a system on itself. Examples are:

(a) *printer* that generates a test message print-out automatically on switch-on;

(b) *microcomputer* that employs *diagnostic software* to exercise parts of its own *hardware*, e.g. *RAM, input/output* circuitry, etc.

Semiconductor A material that is part-way between an electrical conductor and an electrical isolator. *Silicon* and germanium are the most common semiconductors, and the former is the base material of virtually all *integrated circuits*.

Semiconductor memory *Memory* circuits made using *silicon*, and forming either *ROM* (Read Only Memory) or *RAM* (Random Access Memory — read/write memory) devices.

Semi-graphics *CRT graphics* that construct shapes using text *characters*, or special shapes that occupy character positions, on the CRT screen. See *Character graphics*.

Sensor Another name for *transducer*.

Sequencing The control of a particular system using a set order of steps.

Sequential access Method by which *data* are retrieved in a manner that involves stepping through locations before the selected one. Therefore sequential access is slow compared with *random access*, in which any location can be immediately accessed. *Magnetic tape* devices, e.g. *audio cassette, digital cassette* and *cartridge tape*, are sequential access devices.

Sequential logic A gating (see *Gate*) and *logic* system that employs memory elements. Contrast with *Combinational logic* which does not use memory elements.

Serial The transfer of *data* items by setting one *bit* at a time on a single conductor. Serial transmission is correspondingly slower than *parallel* transmission, which involves setting all signal bits simultaneously, with one conductor for each bit. However, serial connection requires fewer cable cores, and is applied for communications between *computers* and remote devices, e.g. *VDUs, printers* and other computers. Refer to *RS 232-C*.

Series mode An electrical *noise* signal that is present on only one of two input connections to a circuit, as shown in Fig. 180.

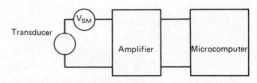

V_{SM} = series mode voltage

FIG. 180. Series mode noise signal in instrumentation system.

The unwanted noise signal that is in series with the input signal to the amplifier can be caused by electromagnetic radiation from adjacent electrical equipment that generates sparks, e.g. motor commutators, switches, welding equipment, etc., or from rf (radio frequency) equipment. Series mode noise signals are very difficult to eliminate, but can be reduced by:

(a) good cabling practice, e.g. the use of screened cables with screens well earthed, the use of twisted-pair cables, the separation of small signal cables from power cables in cable trays, etc.;

(b) filter input signal, i.e. block high-frequency noise;

(c)   reduction at source.

Servo   An electromechanical system that performs a position-control function and is often driven by a *microcomputer*. A servo is applied commonly in the following applications:

(a)   *robot* — one servo controls one of several movements, or "degrees of freedom";
(b)   pen recorder — for pen deflection;
(c)   *plotter* — for X and Y deflection;
(d)   aerial/gun/crane/etc. positioning.

The connection arrangement from a microcomputer is shown in Fig. 181.

graphics *CRT*. Typically a series of *bytes* in *RAM* is used to define a single symbol, and several groups of bytes constitute a shape table.

Shift   A movement of *data* to the left or right. Shifting a *binary* number to the left or right is equivalent to multiplying it or dividing it by 2 for each shift. *Software* shift functions are present in any *computer's instruction set*, e.g. an *8-bit microprocessor* normally possesses the shift *instructions* shown in Fig. 182.

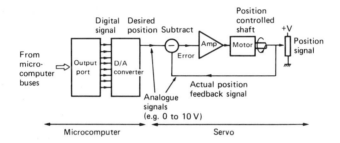

FIG. 181. Servo driven from microcomputer.

An alternative device to a servo is a *stepper motor*, which gives poorer resolution for position control but offers a simpler and cheaper system.

(a) Shift left   (b) Shift right

FIG. 182. Shift instructions.

Set   To assign a level 1 to a signal or *bit*, if *positive logic* is applied, or to assign a level 0 to a signal or bit, if *negative logic* is applied.

Set-up time   The time for which a signal must be established before it can be transferred (perhaps by a *strobe* or *clock* signal) into a circuit or device.

Shape table   A list of *data* values used by some *microcomputers* to draw predefined symbols or shapes on a

8-bit microprocessors possess only single-bit shift instructions; 16-bit devices normally offer multi-bit shift instructions.

   Shift instructions can be categorised as one of three types:

(a)   logical shift — shift 0 into a vacant bit;
(b)   arithmetic shift — retain the *sign bit*, e.g. if the sign bit is 1 for a negative number, then a 1 is shifted into the vacant sign bit in an arithmetic right shift;

(c)   shift cyclic, or *rotate* — a bit that is shifted out at one end is shifted in at the other end.

Hardware shift operations occur in a *counter* in which a count is shifted through the circuit, and a *shift register*, which is used commonly for *parallel* to *serial* and serial to parallel conversion.

Shift register
A *register* in which the stored *data* can be shifted to the left or right. A shift register is used to convert data from *parallel* to *serial* form and from serial to parallel. The most common *microcomputer* application of a shift register is in a *UART*, which contains two shift registers — one for the transmit signal to a remote device and one for the receive signal.

The action of a shift register is illustrated in Fig. 183 for a parallel to serial converter.

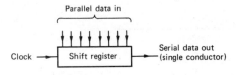

FIG. 183. Shift register.

The data directions are reversed for a serial to parallel converter.

Shotgunning
A fault-finding procedure that involves replacing each component in a system until the fault disappears. Principally this involves changing each *integrated circuit* in a *microelectronic* system in turn.

Signature
The signal activity at a circuit test point indicated by a four-digit display on a *signature analyser*.

Signature analyser
An item of test equipment that is applied to assist fault-finding in *microcomputer* circuits.

The physical appearance of a signature analyser is illustrated in Fig. 184.

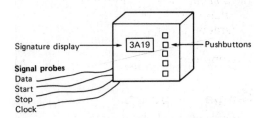

FIG. 184. Signature analyser.

The test signal probes are connected to suitable points in the circuit under test. The signal pattern occurring at the circuit node, at which the Data probe is connected, is displayed as a four-digit "signature". This is compared with a reference list of signatures for different circuit test points. A circuit fault can be traced through the circuit to highlight the faulty component.

Sign bit
The left-hand (most significant) *bit* in a *binary* number that can take positive or negative values. A sign bit is used with *two's complement* representation.

Signed binary number
See *Two's complement*.

Silicon
A *semiconductor* material that is used to fabricate virtually all *integrated circuits*. See also *Planar*.

Silo memory
Another name for *FIFO*.

Simplex
A *serial data* communication link which is unidirectional, i.e. data can only be transferred in one direction. An example is the serial connection of a *microcomputer* to a *printer*.

Simulator A *program* that runs on one *computer* and simulates execution of the *machine code* of another computer. A simulator is used to test and *debug* programs for a *microprocessor* on a *microcomputer* which employs a different microprocessor.

Single board computer (SBC) A ready-built circuit board that supports a complete *microcomputer* circuit and can be used for prototype development. It is often more cost-effective during the development procedure for a microcomputer application, e.g. an industrial control application, to utilise a fully-tested circuit board that offers a general range of *hardware* functions. Typical hardware facilities are *CPU, RAM, EPROM* and *input/output* circuitry. The designer only requires to add a tailored *program* on EPROM to the SBC to construct a prototype system. This system may require little alteration to convert it to an application system.

Single-chip microcomputer A single *integrated circuit* that offers a complete *microcomputer* circuit. An example is the *Intel 8084*, which is a 40-pin device offering an 8-*bit CPU*, 64 *bytes RAM*, 1K bytes *EPROM* and 3 *input/output ports*.

Single density (disk) A measure of the packing density of *bits* stored on a *floppy disk*. Either single or double density is used. Single density recording has the following specification:

(a) 8 inch disk — packing density = 3200 bits per inch
data transfer rate = 250K bits per second

(b) 5¼ inch diskette — packing density = 2581 bits per inch
data transfer rate = 125K bits per second

See *Double density (disk)*.

Single precision arithmetic The use of a single *word* to represent a number in a *computer*. Contrast with *Double precision arithmetic*. If a single *byte* is used to represent an *unsigned binary number*, a number range of 0 to 255 is possible.

Single-step The execution of a single *instruction* in a *program* testing procedure. A *debugger* and a *monitor* normally offer the operator the facility to single-step through a section of program. At each step the contents of *CPU registers* and *memory* locations can be displayed to assist in verification of correct program operation and in the detection of program errors.

Sink To accept current flow from the preceding circuit. In a *TTL* circuit the maximum sink current is 16 mA, as shown in Fig. 185.

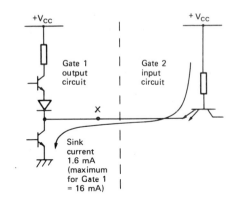

FIG. 185. Current sinking.

This diagram demonstrates the effect of connecting virtually any TTL circuit to another. The first circuit sinks current from the second circuit if *logic* 0, i.e. a voltage level of 0 V, is present at the output connection X. A TTL circuit, e.g. Gate 2, normally requires a sink current of 1.6 mA, and the maximum sink current of a TTL circuit, e.g. Gate 1, is 16 mA. Therefore, the maximum number of *gates* that can be connected to a TTL circuit (called the "*fan-out*") is 10.

See also *Source*.

Sixteen-bit microprocessor A

microprocessor that processes *data* and *program instructions* in 16-*bit* form. 16-bit devices offer several advantages over 8-bit devices, e.g. much larger number range (64K cf. 256), more *addressing modes*, more *instructions* and more *registers*.

The most popular 16-bit devices are:

(a) *Intel* 8086 and 8088;
(b) *Zilog* Z8001;
(c) *Motorola* 68000;
(d) *Texas Instruments* 9900;
(e) *National Semiconductor* 16032;
(f) *Ferranti* F100L.

Skip To ignore one or more *instructions* in a *program*.

Slave processor A *CPU*, e.g. a *microprocessor*, that performs a subsidiary role in a *computer* system. That role may be *input/output* control or *memory management*.

Small-scale integration (SSI)

A measure of the degree of integration of electronic components within a single device. An *integrated circuit* is said to be SSI if it possesses less than 10 *gates*. Several *TTL* devices are SSI. See also *Medium-scale integration*, *Large-scale integration* and *Very large-scale integration*.

SN Abbreviation of Semiconductor Network, which is used in the series name for the most common *TTL* range of *integrated circuits* — the SN7400 series.

Soft-sectored disk A *floppy disk* or *hard disk* in which the divisions between *sectors* around each *track* are marked by the storage of special control *data*. Refer to *IBM 3740* for a full description.

Software *Programs* and associated *data files*. Software in a *computer* can be *system software* (required to run the computer) or *application software* (programs to provide the facilities for the specific application of the machine).

Software house A company that offers *software*.

Software trap A *software* condition that causes entry into an *interrupt service routine*. Examples are:

(a) an *overflow* causes automatic entry to an interrupt service routine;
(b) an *instruction* effectively "calls" the interrupt service routine.

Solder bridge A blob of solder that connects two points in a circuit. Normally this is an unwanted fault condition.

Sort To arrange *data* items in a logical sequence by *software*, e.g. to rearrange a list of numbers in order of magnitude.

Source To provide current flow into a succeeding circuit. In a *TTL* circuit the maximum source current is 400 μA, as shown in Fig. 186.

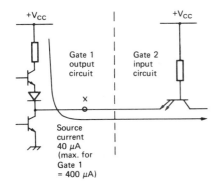

Fig. 186. Current sourcing.

This diagram demonstrates the effect of connecting virtually any TTL circuit to another. The first circuit sources current for the second circuit if *logic* 1, i.e. a voltage level of +5 V, is present at the output connection X. A TTL circuit, e.g. Gate 2, normally requires a source current of 40 µA, and the maximum source current of a TTL circuit, e.g. Gate 1, is 400 µA. Therefore, the maximum number of *gates* that can be connected to a TTL circuit (called the "*fan-out*") is 10.

See also *Sink*.

Source code See *Source program*.

Source current The current drive capability of a circuit.

Source program A *program* written in other than *machine code*, i.e. in *assembly language* or *high-level language*. Normally the term is used to describe an assembly language version of a program, and it helps to distinguish this version from the final machine code version, which is often called the "*object program*".

Speech synthesis The generation of speech by electronic means. Words and sentences can be created by a circuit that contains a special speech synthesiser

chip, which is normally supported by *EPROMs* to hold the sound signals and control circuitry. There are two basic methods of speech generation:

(a) sound generation, such that several sounds can be joined to produce a word — this allows a very large vocabulary, but unfortunately words are often of poor intelligibility;

(b) word generation — this is the more popular method because of its improved clarity, and normally several hundred words are offered for a complete speech synthesiser circuit.

A typical interconnection system to a *microcomputer*, which outputs a series of *data* items to activate the required speech pattern, is shown in Fig. 187.

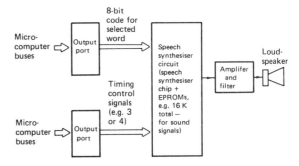

Fig. 187. Speech synthesiser circuit connected to microcomputer.

Microcomputer-driven speech synthesis is becoming increasingly used in the following applications: *personal computer*, car, industrial plant monitoring (e.g. spoken alarm message), games, disabled people.

Typical speech synthesiser chips are the General Instruments SP-0250, the Votrax SC-01A and the Texas Instruments TMS 5100 and TMS 5200.

Spreadsheet A *microcomputer-*generated financial planning aid.

Sprite A display shape that can be created and manipulated by the programmer using a *graphics CRT* if a special *CRT controller chip* is available. An example of an "intelligent" CRT controller chip that offers this facility is the Texas Instruments TMS 9918A. The use of rapidly overlapping sprites facilitates fast and complex display animation.

Sprocket holes Holes in *paper tape* which are used by the paper punch or paper reader *stepper motor* to move the paper tape past the punch or read mechanism.

S-R bistable The simplest type of *bistable multivibrator* or *flip-flop*. The circuit is described under *Bistable multivibrator*.

SSI See *Small-scale integration*.

Stack A reserved area of *memory* (*RAM*) that is used to store the return address in a *subroutine* or an *interrupt service routine*. The action of a stack is illustrated in Fig. 188.

A *CPU register*, called the "stack pointer", holds the memory address of the stack (6000 in this example). When the subroutine *CALL instruction* is implemented, the return address (the address of the instruction that follows the CALL instruction) is stored automatically on the stack. The stack pointer then alters to point to the next free location on the stack. The subroutine is entered, and when the RETURN instruction is encountered the return address is removed from the stack and placed in the *program counter*. The main program is re-entered and the stack pointer is reset to its original value.

If the subroutine calls another subroutine, i.e. "nesting" occurs, two return addresses must be stored on the stack when the second subroutine is entered. Notice also that *data* values as well as return addresses can be stored on the stack if the *push* and *pop* instructions are used.

Stack pointer A *register* within a *CPU* that points to the next free *memory* location in the *stack*. The stack pointer is automatically changed and then reset

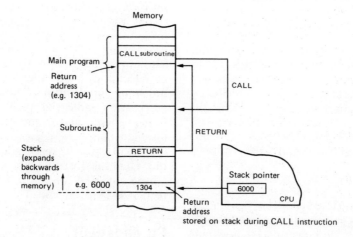

FIG. 188. Use of stack for subroutine call.

when the *call* and *return instructions* are implemented.

Notice that the initial setting of the stack pointer, which is performed by *software*, must allow sufficient free space in memory for stack expansion. Normally the stack expands backwards through memory.

Start bit A *bit* that marks the commencement of a *character* transmission over a *serial data* link using the *RS 232-C* interface. Refer to *RS 232-C* for a full description of the signal waveform.

State The condition of a signal. The term is often applied to refer to the output of a *gate*, a *flip-flop* or an *output port*, and the signal state can be either *logic* 1 or 0.

Statement A *command* in a *high-level language program*.

Static memory *Memory* devices that retain stored *bit* patterns when power is removed.

Static RAM Conventional *RAM memory*, as distinct from dynamic RAM. Refer to *RAM* for a full description.

Status The current condition of a device or circuit, e.g. "*peripheral* busy". See *Status register*.

Status register A *CPU register* that indicates the state of the *ALU*. Every *microprocessor* possesses a status register, which consists of a collection of *flag bits*. Refer to *CPU* for a description of the overall role of the status register.

Most *instructions* set one or more bits in the status register. These bits are examined occasionally in the *program*

using a *conditional jump* instruction. Typical functions of these status bits are:

(a)   zero — set if the result of an ALU operation is 0;
(b)   sign — set if the most significant bit of the result is 1;
(c)   carry — set if the result exceeds the number range that can be handled by the ALU;
(d)   *parity* — set if the result has even parity.

Stepper motor A motor that rotates one small arc of a circle (called a "step") in response to a single *pulse* input. Stepper motors are increasingly used with *microcomputers* because of the simple *digital* interface that is required. The method of connection is shown in Fig. 189.

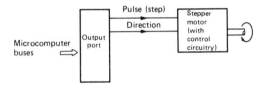

FIG. 189. Stepper motor driven by microcomputer.

Only two single-*bit* signals are required to rotate the motor shaft to a required position, e.g. for position control, or to rotate the shaft continuously. If each pulse moves the shaft by 7°30', then 48 pulses rotate the shaft by 1 revolution. A continuous stream of pulses rotates the shaft continuously. The setting of the direction bit causes clockwise or anti-clockwise movement.

The stepper motor is used in many microcomputer applications, e.g. industrial valves for process control, *robot*, *floppy disk head* drive, X-Y *plotter*, *paper tape* punch and reader, numerically controlled machine tools.

Stock control A *software* function

that is frequently offered with business *microcomputers* to maintain records of stock items. Reports from the system can be printed in user-selectable sequence by depot or part number selection. Additionally stock movements, stock usage, stock valuation and re-ordering reports can be produced. Typically several hundred items can be recorded on a single *floppy disk*, and several disks can enable several thousand stock items to be processed.

Stop bit A *bit* that marks the end of a *character* that is transmitted over a *serial data* link using the *RS 232-C* interface. Refer to *RS 232-C* for a full description of the waveform.

Store To transfer to *memory*. A *data* value currently being processed within a *CPU* can be stored to memory (*RAM*) within a *program*, or a complete program can be stored on *backing store*.

Stress testing A method of introducing mechanical or thermal variations to a component or a circuit to assist in highlighting the location of an intermittent fault.

String A group of *characters*. A string can be processed within a *high-level language*, e.g. a *printer* message can be defined as a string at one stage in a *program* and referenced several times later in the program by simply using its defined name.

Strobe A signal that is used as a reference, e.g. a timing or an enabling signal. An example of a strobe is a "write" signal line, which forms part of a *CPU's control bus,* that is set to trigger the transfer of *data* from the *data bus* to *memory* or *input/output*.

The word is also used to describe the

action of reading an external signal, or a group of signals, in to a CPU under *software* control. An example is the *program* action of scanning a *keyboard*, i.e. the settings of a group of keys are "strobed" in using a *multiplexing arrangement*.

Structured programming The technique of designing a *program* in the form of a set of constituent parts. Each part has a single entry and a single exit point. These parts can be combined so that more complex structures can be created, each possessing a single entry and a single exit point. The technique produces programs which are easier to understand, test, modify and document.

Subroutine A section of *program* that is separated from the main program and can be called several times from the main program. The action of a subroutine is illustrated in Fig. 190.

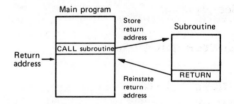

FIG. 190. Calling a subroutine.

The *call instruction* transfers program control to the subroutine. The subroutine performs its particular function, which is generally an autonomous function (e.g. perform a mathematical calculation), and it terminates with a *return* instruction. This causes program control to return to the calling program at the instruction which follows the call instruction. Although not shown in the diagram, the subroutine can be called at several points in the main program.

The advantage of using a subroutine is that an identical section of program does not have to be inserted several times into a program to perform that particular software function. If the section of program is segregated outside the main program as a subroutine, *memory* space is saved and the subroutine can be called any number of times. Additionally the overall program is more readable and easier to test.

One subroutine can call another subroutine in a "*nested*" arrangement.

The normal method of storing the return address in a *microprocessor* is to use a reserved area of memory, called the "*stack*". Refer to *Stack* and *Stack pointer* for a full description.

Subscript A value that indicates a particular item in an *array* or a *list* in a *high-level language program*. For example, in the following *BASIC* command:

230 DISCOUNT (4) = 105
           ↑
      Subscript

the fourth value in a list named DIS-COUNT is set to 105.

Subtract To generate the difference between two numbers. The subtraction of two single-*bit* numbers is described as follows:

Minuend	Subtrahend	Borrow	Difference
0	0	0	0
0	1	1	1
1	0	0	1
1	1	0	0

The subtraction of two multi-bit numbers is demonstrated as follows:

Borrow	00100010	
Minuend	01001101	77
Subtrahend	00100010	34−
	00101011	43

Microprocessors offer *instructions* that perform the subtraction process. Notice that one way of performing subtraction is to generate the *two's complement* of the subtrahend and then perform addition.

Successive approximation A/D

An *analogue to digital converter* that generates a *digital* value by a process of generating successive fractions of the input *analogue* voltage. The device is available as a single *integrated circuit*, and its operation is illustrated in Fig. 191.

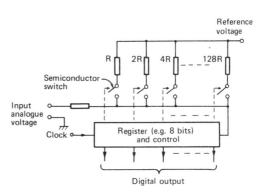

FIG. 191. Successive approximation A/D converter.

A clock signal triggers the *register* and control module to switch in one-half of the reference voltage through resistor R. If the input analogue voltage is greater than this value, the resistor R is left switched in; otherwise the resistor is switched out. One-quarter of the reference voltage is then introduced by switching in resistor 2R, and again a comparison is made between input voltage and generated voltage. The process is repeated with different value resistors contributing *binary* weighted fractions of the reference voltage until the generated voltage most closely matches the input voltage. The register contents indicate the state of each of the binary fractions and represent the digital version of the input analogue voltage. The digital output signals typically pass to a *microcomputer input port*.

8-, 10- or 12-bit converters are available, and conversion time is typically 20 μsec. The successive approximation A/D converter is the most widely used A/D converter due to its high speed and good resolution.

Switch debouncing See *Contact bounce.*

Symbol
A group of *characters* that represent a *label* or a *mnemonic* in an *assembly language program.*

Symbolic language
Another name for *assembly language.*

Symbol table
A list of all *label symbols*, and the values assigned to them, produced by some *two-pass assemblers* at the end of the first pass.

Synchronous
A circuit or a system that is synchronised by a common *clock.* In a synchronous *serial data* link between two *computers*, a clock signal generated by the master computer times the arrival of data *pulses* at the other computer — see Fig. 192.

Syntax
The rules for constructing:

(a) an *instruction* in a *low-level language* (*assembly language*);
(b) a *command* in a *high-level language*, e.g. *BASIC.*

The programmer must ensure that he applies the correct syntax in each line of his *program* otherwise the *assembler* or *interpreter/compiler* will reject that line.

System
An assembly of modules forming a whole.

The word is sometimes used as an abbreviation for *operating system.*

System analyser
Another name for a *microbus analyser.*

Systems analysis
The process of analysing a problem and designing a *software* solution to it.

System software
The essential *software* that is required to run a basic *computer* system. Special software that is required to tailor a computer to perform

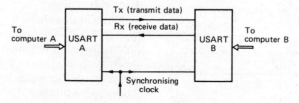

Fig. 192. Synchronous serial data link.

Typically a *USART chip* processes data transfers at each end of the link.

Synchronous transmission is not as common as *asynchronous* transmission for serial data links.

specific functions is called *application software.*

System software includes the *operating system, compilers, assemblers, debuggers* and other *utility programs* as necessary.

T

Table A collection of *data* items available for easy reference by *software*. Normally a table of values is stored in sequential *memory* locations. An individual item can be accessed in the following ways:

(a) by the use of a *subscript* if the table is used within a *high-level language program*;
(b) by *indexed addressing*, or some other additive technique, if the table is used within a *low-level language* program.

Talker A device that presents *data* to a *CPU*, e.g. a *ROM*. The word is applied with the *IEEE 488 common bus* arrangement that is used to interconnect different boards in some *microcomputer* systems, and it describes any board that supplies data to the main CPU board. A board containing *input ports* only is a "talker".

TDM See *Time division multiplexing*.

Telemetry The technique of transmitting plant measurements ("metering" signals) over long distances. The measurement signals, which may be *analogue* or *digital*, are transmitted by:

(a) firstly generating digital representations for all signals;
(b) modulating a carrier signal (sine-wave) with a series of *logic* 1s and 0s, which represent the digital signals.

The sequence in which the telemetry transmission station scans and transmits the plant signals identifies the signals. The receiver station demodulates the signals for presentation to an operator or for storage within a *computer*. The arrangement is illustrated in Fig. 193.

The telemetry signal is often passed through the telephone network, e.g. in a water distribution monitoring system which is dispersed over a wide geographical area.

There are two types of modulation applied in telemetry applications: *frequency division multiplexing* and *time division multiplexing*.

Teleprinter Another name for *printer*.

Teletext The television system that displays static pages of information. A series of pages of information on a wide range of topics, e.g. weather, news, sport, holidays, is broadcast over conventional television frequencies, and specific pages can be selected by the user. The BBC system is named Ceefax, and the ITV system is named Oracle.

Teletype Another name for *printer*.

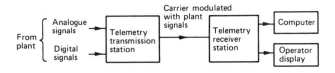

FIG. 193. Telemetry systems.

Telex The national and international text communication system that transfers text through the telephone network.

Terminal In general terms a point in a *computer* system at which *data* can enter or leave. However, the word is generally used to describe a *VDU*, or occasionally a *printer* with *keyboard*, which an operator uses to enter commands to run *programs* or to enter data.

Texas Instruments microprocessors A range of 4-*bit* and 16-bit *microprocessors*. Texas Instruments produced the most common range of 4-bit microprocessors in the TMS 1000 family. They then jumped the 8-bit market, in which they offer no devices, to the 16-bit microprocessor market. They were the first manufacturer to make widely available a 16-bit device, and although largely upstaged by *Intel, Zilog, Motorola* and others, their 9900 range of 16-bit microprocessors possesses many unusual and attractive features.

Figure 194 shows the internal organisation of the 9980A, which is one of the 9900 range of microprocessors.

The *CPU* does not possess any *work registers* on-*chip*. *The 16 work registers are contained in memory* (*RAM*), and the CPU's "workspace pointer" holds the start address of this register block. This feature means that *program* execution times are slow. However, an *interrupt service routine* automatically uses a new block of RAM for its registers, and so it is not necessary to store away the main program's registers, on *interrupt*. Notice that only 14 address lines are used; this gives the device an addressing range of only 16*K bytes*. Other microprocessors in the 9900 range offer larger numbers of address lines.

Text Groups of *characters* suitable for *computer* display to an operator on a *CRT* or recording on a *printer*.

Text editor See *Editor*.

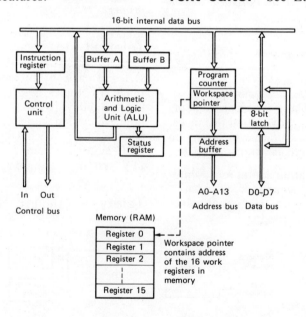

Fig. 194. Texas Instruments 9980A CPU (16-bit).

Text string See *String*.

Three-state A *digital* signal type that possesses three states. A three-state (or "tri-state") device has outputs that can take the following states:

(a) *logic* 0;
(b) logic 1;
(c) high-impedance, or *"floating"*.

A *microprocessor's data bus* is a three-state bus, and every device — *CPU, ROM, RAM, input/output chip* — that connects to it must possess three-state outputs. The signal that is used to take a ROM, RAM or input/output chip out of the floating state and connect its data output signals to the data bus is the *chip select*, as illustrated in Fig. 195.

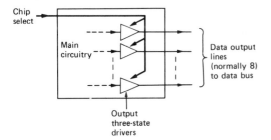

FIG. 195. Three-state device, e.g. ROM, RAM, input/output chip.

An *address decoding* circuit ensures that only one chip select signal is set for one such device within the overall *microcomputer* circuit. In this way only one chip can pass data onto the data bus at any time.

Throughput A measure of the volume of *program* processing that a *computer* can perform. Invariably a 16-*bit microcomputer* can execute more programs in a given time than an 8-bit machine.

Time division multiplexing (TDM) A method of *telemetry* transmission. Telemetry is used to transmit *data* over long distances, and TDM is a version in which voltage *pulses* of two different levels, representing a *logic* 1 or 0, are transmitted in a sequence.

See also *Frequency division multiplexing* (FDM). It is possible to TDM an FDM system.

Time domain The state of a signal with reference to time. An oscilloscope, which displays a signal against time, operates in the time domain.

Timer Another name for a *counter/ timer*.

Time-sharing The provision of a *computer's* services to several users simultaneously. Normally a time-sharing computer is a *mainframe computer* which possesses a large number of remote *terminals*.

Toggle The reversal of a *digital* signal level. The term is commonly applied to the output of a *J-K bistable* and the use of that circuit in a *counter*.

Top-down design The technique of identifying the total system function and then partitioning it into several tasks. These tasks can then be further divided. Top-down design is applied to assist in both the *hardware* design of a *computer* application, e.g. a system involving several *microcomputers*, and in the design of the overall system *software*.

Totem pole The name given to the normal output stage of a standard *TTL* circuit. Figure 196 shows the circuit arrangement.

151

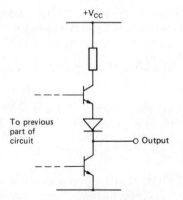

FIG. 196. Totem pole output of TTL circuit.

This output circuit gives the advantages of low output impedance in both low and high output states and also the ability to switch at high speeds into capacitive loads.

In some TTL circuits (see *Open collector driver*) this totem pole circuit is broken, and the top three components (diode, transistor and resistor) are missing. The external circuit must provide a load resistor to $+V_{CC}$ (the positive dc rail voltage).

Trace The action of indicating the results of the execution of each *instruction* in a *program* debugging operation. A *debugger* program normally allows the operator to select a "trace" operation on a nominated number of instructions in a program under test. After each instruction is implemented the contents of the *CPU work registers* are displayed as well as the contents of the *status register*, *program counter* and any other relevant information, e.g. a disassembled (see *Disassembler*) version of the instruction.

The word is also applied occasionally in place of *debugger*, i.e. it describes the whole debugger program.

Trace table A record of *data* values that should occur, and actually do occur, at various points in the execution of a

program. Incompatibility between expected and actual values can help to highlight *bugs* in the program. A trace table may consist of a list of data values in *CPU work registers* and *memory* locations.

Track A circular *data* recording area on a *floppy disk* or *hard disk*. The disk surface is divided into concentric tracks. The outer track is numbered track 0. A track is subdivided into "*sectors*".

Tracker-ball A manually-adjustable input device that is applied to generate a variable signal to a *computer*. It is a variation of the *joystick*.

Transducer A component or device that converts one form of energy to another. Transducers are applied when *computers* are used to monitor plant measurements, and typically convert heat energy or mechanical energy into electrical energy suitable for connection to *input/output* circuitry.

Common transducers are:

(a) thermocouple (junction of dissimilar metals) — to measure temperature;

(b) anemometer (rotating vane assembly) — to measure flow;

(c) conductivity gauge (two electrodes immersed in liquid) — to measure level;

(d) diaphragm (flexible disc) — to measure pressure;

(e) strain gauge (foil with variable electrical conductivity) — to measure weight.

Generally electrical signals from transducers require amplification in an *op-amp* circuit before they can be applied to an *analogue to digital converter*.

Transistor A three-terminal *semi-*

conductor component that is used in *digital* circuits, e.g. *gates*, and for amplifier circuits for *analogue* signals. There are two types of transistor:

(a) *bipolar* — this is the traditional transistor that is manufactured in discrete component form and is also the main component in *TTL* circuits;

(b) *unipolar* — this is the *FET* (field effect transistor) that initiated the advent of modern microelectronics with its application in *MOS* and *CMOS* circuits.

Transistor differential amplifier

A circuit that employs two *bipolar transistors* and amplifies the difference in voltage between the two input connections. A differential amplifier is used to amplify dc voltages, and forms the main circuit element in an *op-amp integrated circuit*.

A simplified representation of a differential amplifier is shown in Fig. 197.

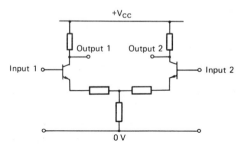

FIG. 197. Transistor differential amplifier.

Each limb of the circuit gives identical voltage gain. If the dc rail voltage or the operating temperature varies, both halves of the circuit are affected in an identical manner, e.g. the voltage gain increases by the same amount. In this way no output voltage difference occurs. The amplifier only amplifies a difference between the two input signals, and in this way *common mode noise* is rejected.

An op-amp consists of several stages of differential amplifier within the same integrated circuit.

Transistor transistor logic
See *TTL*.

Translate
To convert a *source program* into *machine code*. A translator may be a *compiler, assembler* or *cross-assembler*.

Trap
To detect a particular set of signal conditions. A *logic analyser*, which is used for hardware fault finding, can be set to trap and staticise *digital* signal levels when a selected mixture of test signals are set. Alternatively, a *debugger program* may have the ability to trap a chosen *memory* address or *data* value and allow the programmer to examine program operation around that point.

The word is also used to identify a *non-maskable interrupt* with the Intel 8085 microprocessor (see *Intel microprocessors*). Refer to *Software trap* for a description of how *interrupt service routines* can be entered for a variety of trap conditions.

Tri-state
See *Three-state*.

Troubleshoot
To seek the cause of a malfunction in a system. Troubleshooting a *computer* system can involve the use of test equipment to locate a *hardware* fault, or the use of diagnostic *software*, e.g. a *debugger*, if an erroneous *program* is suspected.

Truth table
A chart that presents all possible states of the inputs and outputs of a system. Truth tables are presented at various points in this book to summarise *Boolean logic* functions, e.g. *AND, OR, NAND* and *NOR*, and the 2 to 4 *decoder*. Consider the 3 to 8 decoder in Fig. 198.

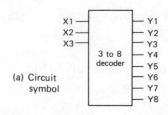

(a) Circuit
symbol

X3 X2 X1	Y8 Y7 Y6 Y5 Y4 Y3 Y2 Y1
0 0 0	0 0 0 0 0 0 0 1
0 0 1	0 0 0 0 0 0 1 0
0 1 0	0 0 0 0 0 1 0 0
0 1 1	0 0 0 0 1 0 0 0
1 0 0	0 0 0 1 0 0 0 0
1 0 1	0 0 1 0 0 0 0 0
1 1 0	0 1 0 0 0 0 0 0
1 1 1	1 0 0 0 0 0 0 0

(b) Truth table

FIG. 198. Truth table for a 3 to 8 decoder.

T state A time division in the implementation of an *instruction* with some *microprocessors*. *Intel* use the term to identify each *CPU clock* pulse in the *fetch/execute cycle* for an instruction.

TTL (Transistor Transistor Logic)
A circuit technology that is applied in the manufacture of a range of *integrated circuits*. TTL circuits dominated the *digital* electronics market through the late 1960s and 1970s, and they are still applied widely in conjunction with *MOS* and *CMOS* circuits in *microprocessor*-based circuits.

A typical TTL circuit is shown in Fig. 199.

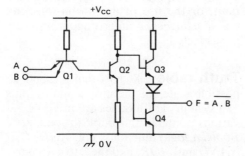

FIG. 199. TTL NAND gate.

The *NAND logic* circuit is based upon conventional *bipolar transistors*. The input transistor Q1 is a multi-emitter device. When both inputs A and B are at logic 1 (e.g. +5 V) the output is at logic 0 (0 V). If either input is at logic 0, the output changes to logic 1. The *truth table* for this circuit is presented under *NAND*.

Typical gate characteristics are: speed 10 nsec, power dissipation 10 mW/gate, *noise immunity* 1 V, fan-out 10.

Typically a TTL integrated circuit consists of four such circuits on the same chip. The SN7400 range of TTL devices offers the following circuit functions:

(a) *logic gates, e.g. NAND, NOR, AND* and *OR*;
(b) *flip-flops*;
(c) *registers*;
(d) *counters*;
(e) *decoders* and *multiplexors*.

Although packing density is much lower and power dissipation much higher than MOS and CMOS, TTL offers one big advantage over these other technologies — speed of operation.

Variations of the standard SN7400 range are:

(1) SN74L00 — low power;
(2) SN74S00 — Schottky (see *Schottky TTL*);
(3) SN74LS00 — *low power Schottky*.

Refer to *Planar* for a description of the circuit fabrication process and *Bipolar* for a description of the basic transistor.

TTL compatible
The characteristic of a circuit whereby its input and output signals can be connected to *TTL* devices. The most important feature of an interconnecting signal that is TTL compatible is its absolute voltage level, viz. high voltage must be +5 V (dc rail voltage is also +5 V) and low voltage must be 0 V, and the tolerances around these levels.

TTY An abbreviation for *teletype*, which is synonymous with *printer*.

Two-pass assembler An *assembler*, which is applied commonly with *microcomputers*, that processes the *source program* in two stages before the *machine code* version of the *program* is generated. On the first pass a *symbol table* is generated. On the second pass the full machine code is created using the numerical values for program *labels* held in the symbol table.

Two's complement A method of representing *binary* numbers which can be positive or negative. Positive numbers in two's complement form are the same as normal binary, with the restriction that the most significant (left-hand) *bit* must be zero. Negative numbers in two's complement form are the *complement* of normal binary with 1 added, and the most significant bit must be one. Therefore the left-hand bit indicates the sign of the number — 0 positive, 1 negative.
Consider the following example:

$$
\begin{array}{lll}
+18 \text{ (decimal):} & 0001\ 0010 & \\
\text{Complement:} & 1110\ 1101 & \leftarrow\text{Called "one's} \\
\text{(invert all bits)} & & \text{complement"} \\
\text{Add 1:} & 1110\ 1110 & \leftarrow\text{Two's comple-} \\
& & \text{ment}
\end{array}
$$

Therefore -18 in two's complement form is 1110 1110.

Notice that the same rules apply for conversion in the opposite direction:

$$
\begin{array}{lll}
-18 \text{ (decimal):} & 1110\ 1110 & \leftarrow\text{Two's comple-} \\
& & \text{ment} \\
\text{Complement:} & 0001\ 0001 & \\
\text{(invert all bits)} & & \\
\text{Add 1:} & 0001\ 0010 &
\end{array}
$$

Computers hold negative numbers in two's complement form, and addition and subtraction can be performed on these numbers, e.g.

$$
\begin{array}{ll}
\text{Add } +23 \text{ to } -18 & \\
+23: & 0001\ 0111 \\
-18: & 1110\ 1110 \\
\hline
1 & 0000\ 0101 \\
\uparrow & \\
\end{array}
$$

Ignore carry

Answer = binary 0000 0101
= decimal +5

U

UART (Universal Asynchronous Receiver Transmitter) An *input/output integrated circuit* that handles *serial data* transfer. A UART is used to connect a *microcomputer* by serial link to a *VDU*, *printer* or another *computer*. A typical UART is shown in Fig. 200.

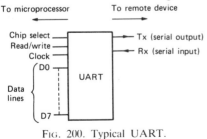

FIG. 200. Typical UART.

The *chip select* signal is generated by an *address decoder* circuit and the read/write *control bus* signal selects direction of data transfer along the *data bus* (D0 to D7). A clock signal is required to trigger the *parallel* to serial conversion process that is required to transfer the eight data *bits* to the Tx signal connection in serial form. Additionally, the clock signal triggers the serial to parallel conversion process that is required to transfer the eight serial input bits received on the Rx signal connection into parallel form for connection to the data bus. One or two *address bus* lines may be connected (not shown) if the UART occupies several input/output addresses.

155

If it is required to send a *character* from a microcomputer to a serial drive VDU, *software* outputs an 8-*bit* character in parallel form to the UART. The UART transmits the 8 bits in serial form, i.e. one bit after the other. Characters are represented by the universal *ASCII* code, and the UART applies the serial signal standard contained in the *RS 232-C* specification, e.g. it transmits bits at a predetermined speed and signal level. The UART can be programmed, or *"initialised"*, by software to operate at different bit speeds (called *"baud* rate") and signal characteristics. This is performed by sending control *bytes* to the *control register* on the UART.

If one microcomputer is connected to another by serial link, then clearly the Tx signal from one must be connected to the Rx signal on the other, and vice versa. The connection to a serial printer involves only the Tx connection (plus a 0 V reference).

Unconditional jump
A *program instruction* that causes a *jump* operation with no condition testing. Contrast with *Conditional jump*.

An unconditional jump instruction is used in a *low-level language* program to transfer program control to another part of the program. Frequently the last instruction in a program is an unconditional jump instruction, which transfers control back into the main body of the program (if this program section performs a *loop*) or to the start of another program.

Unidirectional
Signal flow can only pass in one direction. Most signals and *buses* in *digital* circuits and *microcomputer* systems are unidirectional. Contrast with *Bidirectional:*

Unipolar
Possessing a single pole, i.e. containing electric charge of only one polarity. A unipolar *transistor* is the *FET* (field effect transistor), which is the circuit building block of *MOS* and *CMOS* circuits.

Universal asynchronous receiver transmitter
See *UART*.

Universal peripheral interface
A name given by some manufacturers to a *PIO*.

Unix
An *operating system* that is used widely in *minicomputers* and *microcomputers*.

Unsigned binary number
A *binary* number that can take positive integer values only. No *sign bit* is used, and therefore all *bits* are used to represent the magnitude of the number.

USART (Universal Synchronous and Asynchronous Receiver Transmitter)
A *UART* that can also operate in *synchronous* mode. The interconnection of two systems, e.g. two *computers*, by synchronous *serial data* transmission using USARTs is described under *Synchronous*.

USASCII
An elaboration of the term *ASCII* (US = United States).

User-friendly
The feature of a *computer program* that makes operator involvement straightforward, with some form of guidance provided for operator actions. An example of a user-friendly program is a *menu*-driven program that presents a *CRT* display of different options within a program as well as a message display at each point when operator entry actions are required.

Utility program A *program* that performs a development function that is required by a programmer during the *software* development procedure. Examples of utility programs are an *editor, assembler, loader, locater* and *debugger.*

UV light Ultraviolet light that is applied to erase *EPROMs.* Typically a standard *EPROM eraser* possesses a UV lamp of 12,000 W/cm^2 power rating and 2537 Angstroms wavelength. Erasure time is 15 min.

V

Variable A quantity in a *program* that can take multiple values. A variable is given a name, i.e. a group of characters, in a *high-level language* program, and it can be set to different values in the program and used in calculations and expressions later in the program.

VDU (Visual Display Unit) An operator device, comprising *CRT* and *keyboard*, that links to a *computer*. A VDU is used to present text and *data* to an operator, and to allow entry of information. A typical VDU is shown in Fig. 201.

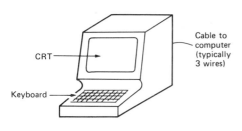

CRT

Keyboard

Cable to computer (typically 3 wires)

Fɪɢ. 201. VDU.

Connection to the computer is normally a *serial* link using an *RS 232-C* interface. Three signal connections are required — Tx (transmit), Rx (receive) and 0 V (signal ground).

Vector See *Interrupt vector.*

Vector graphics *Graphics* that are used with some *microcomputers* to produce high-quality graphics *CRT* displays,

e.g. in video arcade games. Vector graphics can draw lines directly between any two points on the CRT, and a *raster scan* technique is not used.

Verify To confirm a successful *data* transfer operation. One of the most common applications of a verify operation is when a *program* (perhaps with data) is transferred to an *EPROM* during an EPROM programming procedure. The *software* that implements the transfer normally reads back the stored *bytes* and performs a compare function to confirm successful transfer.

Very large-scale integration (VLSI) A measure of the degree of integration of electronic components within a single device. An *integrated circuit* is said to be VLSI if it possesses over 1000 *gates. Microprocessors* and most *ROM, RAM* and *programmable input/output chips* (e.g. *PIO* and *UART*) are VLSI. Indeed many *MOS* and *CMOS* devices in this category of applications are sometimes defined as "very very large-scale integration".

See also *Small-scale integration, Medium-scale integration* and *Large-scale integration.*

Video signal The signal that is applied to a *CRT* in order to generate an image on the screen. Normally a *raster scan* technique is applied to deflect the CRT scanning beam of electrons across the screen in a series of horizontal scans, and the video waveform that is applied to modulate the intensity of this beam determines the picture information that is displayed, as demonstrated in Fig. 202.

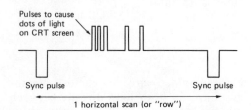

Pulses to cause dots of light on CRT screen

Sync pulse   Sync pulse

1 horizontal scan (or "row")

FIG. 202. Video waveform to CRT.

Sync pulses mark the end of each row and cause the electron beam to "fly-back" to the left-hand edge of the screen. Several hundred such rows are required to construct an entire picture, and the complete image is continually redrawn — this is called "refreshing" the screen.

A *microcomputer* that drives a CRT directly must apply a circuit which generates this waveform — see *Video generator*.

Video generator A circuit that creates a *video signal* for connection to a *CRT*. A *microcomputer* that drives a CRT directly possesses a circuit that continually extracts picture information from *main memory RAM* and generates a video signal that can be applied to the CRT, as shown in Fig. 203.

RAM under *DMA* control. One complete row is extracted at a time. The CRT controller *chip* presents each character code in turn to the character generator *ROM*, which acts in a look-up manner to generate a series of dots which form a single row in the dot matrix arrangement for that character. The video signal for one complete horizontal scan is created before the next row of dots for the same character set is generated. During the seven horizontal scans which may be necessary to construct that single row of characters on the screen, the next row of characters is extracted from main memory RAM by DMA.

This system generates a video signal to create a CRT display of text in monochrome. Colour graphics video generation for *pixel graphics* (as applied in *home computers*) similarly uses a reserved area of main memory to store picture information, but does not require a character generator ROM.

Viewdata *Data* that is transmitted remotely for viewing on a domestic television receiver. Data can be transmitted along the telephone network (see *Prestel*) or through the atmosphere in the manner of a conventional television transmission (see *Teletext*). The word is normally applied to refer to the former technique.

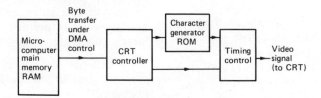

FIG. 203. Video generator circuit.

This system extracts a series of *character bytes*, e.g. 80 characters for each of 40 rows (each character forms a 5 × 7 *dot matrix* on the screen), from main memory

Virtual memory Normal *main memory* addressing in a *computer* that is expanded to include *backing store*. Refer to *Memory management unit*.

Visicalc A *software* function that is offered on many *microcomputers* that are used for scientific and business applications. Visicalc allows the operator to use the *CRT* screen as a worksheet, and to define formulae and calculations.

Voice synthesiser See *Speech synthesis*.

Volatile memory *Memory* that loses its stored *data* when power is removed. *RAM* is volatile because its stored *bit* pattern changes when power is removed, and for this reason battery back-up is occasionally applied.

VLSI See *Very large-scale integration*.

VRAM Video *RAM*, i.e. RAM that is used to hold *data* that defines an image that is displayed on a *CRT*. Refer to *Video generator*.

VVLSI A level of circuit integration that even exceeds *VLSI*. The term is applied loosely and has no consistent numerical definition. Refer to *Very large-scale integration*.

W

Wait state A state into which some *microprocessors* can be set such that normal microprocessor activity is suspended. The wait state may be entered during the normal *fetch/execute cycle* if the microprocessor is accessing slow *memory* or *input/output*.

Walking-ones A test *bit* pattern that is applied to *memory*, e.g. *RAM*. If the memory block under test contains all 0s, a single 1 bit is passed through each location in turn.

Warm boot The action of entering the main *program* ("*operating system*"). An application *program* in a *microcomputer* frequently ends with a warm boot function, i.e. *jump* to the operating system. This is unlike a *cold boot*, which initially reloads the operating system into *main memory* from *backing store* before entering it.

Watchdog A timing circuit within a *computer* that must be addressed regu-

larly to prevent automatic isolation between computer and important external equipment. The action of a watchdog circuit is illustrated in Fig. 204.

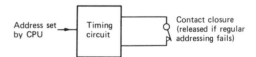

Fig. 204. Watchdog circuit.

The timing circuit is given an *input/output* address, and *software* sets this address at regular intervals, e.g. every 100 msec. A relay contact closure is latched closed by this timing circuit, and if the regular addressing function fails the contact is opened. The contact signal can be used:

(a) to trigger an audible or visual alarm;
(b) to isolate important plant equipment (perhaps with automatic changeover to manual control);
(c) to trigger changeover to a standby computer.

Causes of failure to address the watchdog

may be software, e.g. system *"crash"* due to a faulty *program*, or *hardware*, e.g. *CPU* failure or power supply failure.

Wild card   The facility for an operator to request a *computer* to provide information without the operator presenting full information to the machine. For example, an operator may ask for all *file* names which begin with CL to be displayed — the machine may reply with CLOCK, CLARA and CLEAR.

Winchester   The familiar name given to a *hard disk*.

Wire AND   A circuit arrangement that uses *TTL open-collector* devices with their outputs connected together to generate a *logic AND* function. The circuit is shown in Fig. 205.

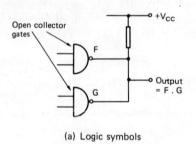

(a) Logic symbols

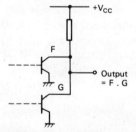

(b) Circuit (showing only output circuits of open collector gates)

FIG. 205. Wire AND.

The use of the open collector *gates* in preference to normal TTL gates allows interconnection of their outputs in this manner. This avoids the use of a subsequent AND gate.

Word   A group of *bits* that is handled by a *computer* as a single unit. An 8-bit *microprocessor* processes words which can represent the following:

(a)   *data* items, e.g. a number in *binary* form or a *character* — normally processed in the *ALU*;

(b)   *instructions*, which may be 1, 2 or 3 words long — processed in the *control unit*.

Word length   The number of *bits* in a *computer word*. *Microprocessors* use either 4-bit, 8-bit or 16-bit words. *Minicomputers* and *mainframe computers* possess word lengths of 16 or more bits.

Word processor   A *computer* that is used to assist a typist in the flexible generation, storage and modification of documents. *Microcomputers* are used widely as word processors, and typical features of a word processor *program* are:

(a)   entry of text, e.g. letter or report, via a *VDU keyboard*;

(b)   addition of named text files, e.g. a mailing address or standard paragraph, held on *backing store*;

(c)   modification, e.g. deletions and insertions as necessary; perhaps also character justification, i.e. character spacing to fill one line;

(d)   storage of complete document on backing store;

(e)   printing of document on *printer*.

Wordstar (registered trademark)   One of the most widely used *word processor programs*.

Work file A temporary *data file* that is used by a *program* only during its execution. A work file may be on *backing store* or in *main memory*.

Work registers *Registers* within a *computer*'s *CPU* that are used for temporary storage of *data* items during the execution of a *program*. Normally a *microprocessor* possesses several work registers within the *chip*, and they are referenced by letter, e.g. A, B, C, etc., or by number, e.g. register 0, 1, 2, etc. In many microprocessors one special work register receives the results of most *ALU* operations, and this register is called the "*accumulator*".

The particular register that is to be used in a program *instruction* is specified in the *mnemonic*, or *assembly language* form, for the instruction in the following manner:

MVI D,3

which moves the number 3 into the D register.

Wrap around A method of displaying information on a *CRT* such that when the display screen is full an additional line of text overwrites the top line.

Write To transfer *data* from *CPU* to *memory*.

Write enable The name given to a signal that is applied with read/write *memory* to select the *write* mode. A *microprocessor*'s *control bus* carries a write enable (or "read/write") signal that selects the read or write operation to *RAM* devices.

Write protect To prevent a storage medium being applied in the *write* mode.

Write protect notch A cut-out in a *floppy disk* cardboard envelope that is used to inhibit *write* operations by the drive circuitry. Presence of the notch is detected by an *optoelectronic device*. The notch must be covered with a paper label to prevent write operations with a 5¼-inch floppy disk (see *Diskette*), but uncovered with an 8-inch floppy disk to perform the same function.

Write time The time that *data* must be present on the data lines, together with the setting of the *write enable* signal, to ensure a successful write operation to *RAM*.

Z

Zap To change the contents of a *computer*'s *memory* location.

Zero flag A *flag* which is set in a *microprocessor*'s *status register* when the result of an *ALU* operation is zero. The zero flag is frequently checked by a *conditional jump instruction* at the bottom of a *program loop*, and indicates the result of the previous instruction, which commonly *decrements* a loop count. Additionally it can indicate if the result of

an arithmetic operation is zero. Further, it can be used to indicate if all *bits* read in from an *input port* are zero.

ZIF socket Zero Insertion Force socket. A socket into which *integrated circuits* in *DIL* form can be placed for easy insertion into and removal from circuits. Insertion is frictionless, and a locking arm grips the legs of the *chip*. Release of the locking arm facilitates removal.

A ZIF is a cumbersome and expensive module for circuit assembly, but it is particularly useful for quick and easy insertion of *EPROMs* in an *EPROM programmer*.

Zilog microprocessors A range of 8-*bit* and 16-bit *microprocessors* produced by Zilog. The most popular devices are the 8-bit Z80, which is generally regarded as the most powerful 8-bit device offered by any manufacturer, and the 16-bit Z8000.

The Z80 was designed as an update on the early *Intel* 8080, and in fact possesses improved features over the later Intel 8085. It is "upwards-compatible" with the Intel devices, i.e. its *instruction set* includes all the *instructions* which the 8080 and 8085 possess, plus several more. *Machine code programs* written for the Intel devices will run on the Z80 without modification.

A block diagram of the 40-pin Z80 is basically the same as described under *CPU*, with its *register* set as shown in Fig. 206.

A	F (flags)	A′	F′
B	C	B′	C′
D	E	D′	E′
H	L	H′	L′
	Interrupt vector I	Memory refresh R	
	Index register I X		
	Index register I Y		
	Stack pointer		

FIG. 206. Registers in Z80 microprocessor.

Refer to *Intel microprocessors* to recognise the similarities of this register set with that of the Intel 8085. Notice that the Z80 possesses a duplicate set of its A to L *work register* set (A′ to L′). This allows the programmer to select the second set of registers at any time, e.g. at the start of an *interrupt service routine* — this avoids the necessity of storing off the contents of the registers in memory. The device allows *indexing addressing* (using the IX and IY registers), as well as *direct, indirect* and *immediate addressing*. The *interrupt vector* I is used to point to the memory address that contains the start address of an interrupt service routine — it contains the least significant *byte* and the interrupting device provides the most significant byte of this memory address. The memory refresh register R is an unusual feature. It is a 7-bit *counter*, which is incremented automatically during each *fetch/execute cycle* and can be applied to refresh dynamic *RAM*.

The Z80 has achieved widespread use in *home computers* and *business computers* (refer also to *Desktop computer*).

The 48-pin 16-bit Z8001 is the leading member of the Z8000 range and offers 23-bit addressing, which gives an addressing capacity of 8M bytes. It possesses 16 general-purpose work registers, and pairs of these registers can be combined to give 32-bit processing. Derived versions of this CPU are the Z8002, 8003 and 8004.